Desmond F

The Second Burial of Bishop Shanahan

VERITAS

First published 1990 by
Veritas Publications
7-8 Lower Abbey Street
Dublin 1

ISBN 1 85390 195 4

The author and publishers are grateful to Father John Jordan, the Religious Sisters of Charity, the Holy Ghost Fathers, The Medical Missionaries of Mary and Saint Patrick's Missionary Society for permission to reproduce some of the material in this book.

Cover design by Philip Melly
Typesetting by Printset & Design Ltd, Dublin
Printed in the Republic of Ireland by The Leinster Leader

Acknowledgements

First and foremost, the author has to acknowledge the assistance of the Holy Rosary Sisters, at whose invitation this book was written. Their archives contain a great wealth of material on Bishop Shanahan, including many of his letters, and all this was put at the author's disposal by the infinitely patient and invariably helpful archivist, Sister Miriam Tracey. Acknowledgements are also due to Sisters Philomena Fox, Catherine O'Carroll, Augustine Cahill, Magdalen Brady, Madeleine Sophie Cullen, Edith Dynan and Rosaire Lawler for giving generously of their time in interviews with the author.

The Holy Ghost Fathers were equally generous with their co-operation. Father Leo Layden gave the author every welcome and facility on his many visits to their Irish archives. Father Sean Farragher provided much of the material for the first two chapters and checked them for factual errors. Father John Jordan, Shanahan's friend and first biographer, was a constant source of information on Shanahan's Nigerian years. Valuable additional material was provided by Fathers Michael O'Carroll, Ned Fitzgerald, and Michael Grogan.

Much useful information was obtained from the archives of other Irish religious orders. Special gratitude is due to Sister Anastasia Taggart of the Medical Missionaries of Mary, Father Tom Kiggins of Saint Patrick's Missionary Society, and Sister Eucharia Ryan of the Religious Sisters of Charity. Sister Mona Considine provided copies of Shanahan's correspondence with the Franciscan Missionaries of Mary.

Information about Shanahan's family and childhood was given by Mr Daniel Shanahan, his nephew, and Mr Donal Shanahan, his grandnephew. Father Nivard Kinsella OCSO, Father Roy Donovan, Father John O'Driscoll, Mr Tom O'Halloran, Mr Paddy Gilmartin and Sister Geraldine Leahy helped to fill in the background to his early days in the lovely valleys of Glankeen and Templederry.

Contents

Foreword

The title of this book, *The Second Burial of Bishop Shanahan,* is the key that unlocks our understanding as to why it needed to be written.

In these times of reconciliation it is not only those of us who have been closely associated with the life and times of Bishop Shanahan, or with the Church in Ireland or Nigeria in his day, who will find this story timely. It is timely now for young and old, men and women throughout the world.

This story of joy and pain speaks to the human heart of each of us who have been wounded; as well as to those of us who have hurt others. It is a true story leading to the glory of repentance and forgiveness on a pathway that was both rugged and consoling.

The journey which Bishop Shanahan and the Rosary Sisters travelled together began in the early 1920s. It was, as I saw it, a journey filled with light and joy, yet sometimes bleak and confusing when sisters asked themselves: Have I been called to a contemplative life or to an active missionary one? Will active mission life in a foreign land take from my spiritual life? Can I survive without the monastic-like atmosphere of my formative days? Gradually the answer came clearly: I am an active, contemplative missionary, following in the footsteps of our founder.

We could say that the pathway our founder travelled started in Glankeen and ended on Calvary or, we could say with truth that it began in Bethlehem and ended in Onitsha. Looking back over those years of joy and pain, those of us who had been involved in them must feel, I am sure, overwhelmed with love and gratitude, and with peace as well as with wonder, at the handiwork of God.

People that I knew so well have been, for me, brought to life again in this beautiful book by Desmond Forristal: Bishop Shanahan in all his greatness; the courageous and generous Dominican Sisters of Cabra; the conscientious and energetic Dr Edward Leen; the exuberant Nigerians; our own intrepid pioneer Sisters and first Superior General: these have been drawn with precision and insight. This story of reconciliation most surely needed to be written for Ireland, Nigeria and our world.

Philomena Fox, M.S.H.R.

Introduction

Among the Ibo people of Nigeria there was a custom known as second burial. The first burial took place soon after death. The body of the dead person was laid out, washed, and anointed with camwood dye. The eyes were circled with white paint and ceremonially washed with sacrificial blood. Then the corpse was wrapped in a mat and buried by the men in a grave near the dead person's home. Meanwhile the women proclaimed their sorrow in loud shrieks and wails, rushing to and fro, beating their breasts, rolling on the ground in extravagant displays of emotion, until the frenzy of grief began to abate. That was the first burial, the burial of the body.

The second burial took place some weeks later. This was the burial of the spirit. According to Ibo belief, the shades of the dead wandered about unhappily in the world of spirits until they were laid to rest by the ceremonies of second burial. This was no longer a time for grieving but a time of commemoration and thanksgiving. The atmosphere was festive and jubilant. Animals and fowl were slaughtered, sacrifices were offered and prayers recited. Processions wound their way through the village. The family provided the friends and neighbours with the most lavish feast they could afford, followed by music and dancing that went on all night. Only then was the ghost of the dead person appeased and enabled to enter fully into its new life in the world of spirits.

Bishop Shanahan's first burial took place in Nairobi in 1943, far from the Ireland he loved and the Nigeria he loved even more. After his death many tributes were paid to his achievements. In his thirty years among the Ibos and other tribes of Southern Nigeria he had built up one of the most flourishing missionary churches in the world. Through his founding of the Holy Rosary Sisters he had given a new religious family to the Church and helped to evangelise many other parts of Africa. He was acclaimed as the leader of the great Irish missionary movement that marked the first half of the twentieth century.

All this was true but only a part of the truth. No mention was made of the sadness and suffering that clouded the last years of his life. During those years he was subjected to a twofold rejection, first by the mission he had served and then by the sisterhood he had founded. An active and vigorous man of sixty, he was forced against his will to leave Nigeria and spend the rest of his days in exile and frustration. Back in Ireland, he became the subject of accusations, especially among the members of the Holy Rosary Congregation which he had himself set up. A cloud of suspicion hung over his name for the remainder of his life and continued after he had died.

Twelve years after his death his remains were brought from Nairobi and laid in Onitsha cathedral in the heart of Iboland. To the Ibo people the symbolism was obvious. It was Bishop Shanahan's second burial. For ten days the whole country rejoiced at his homecoming. Now he knew how welcome he was among them. Now he knew how much they loved him. Now at last his spirit could rest in peace.

Yet there were other ghosts that still needed to be appeased. There were accusations to be answered and wrongs to be righted. There was a story that still remained to be told. It was not the simple story of a heroic missionary who had worn himself out in the preaching of the gospel. It was a much more complex story of a much more complex man.

This book attempts to tell the story in full for the first time. It is a cautionary tale of how words can be misunderstood and actions misinterpreted, of how good people can act from the highest motives and yet inflict great suffering on one another. It is a story that has no villains but still has a hero. His light shines all the more brightly in the darkness that surrounds it.

1

Early years

Joseph Shanahan was born on 4 June 1871 in a herdsman's dwelling in the valley of Glankeen, Co Tipperary. The house where he was born was a little thatched cottage built on the side of a country road, with its back to the hill and its door and windows facing south across the lovely expanse of Glankeen. The name Glankeen means beautiful valley in Irish and the place fully deserved the name. One day when the local schoolmaster was trying to explain to his pupils the meaning of the word 'picturesque', he simply pointed at the surrounding scenery and said 'Look!'[1]

The view over Glankeen is as beautiful now as it was then, but the house where Joseph was born has disappeared. The site is marked by a monument in the form of a small archway, which is believed to show the position and size of the original doorway. The men of the Shanahan family were tall and broad-shouldered and the baby's father must have been used to bowing his head and stooping his body every time he passed through the little opening.

Three days later, on 7 June, young Joe was brought down the hill to the nearby village of Borrisoleigh to be baptised in the parish church. The baptismal register names his parents as Daniel Shanahan and Margaret Walsh and the townland where they lived as Currafrusha. The godmother was Bridget Ryan, thought to have been the midwife who assisted at the birth. No godfather is listed. According to local tradition, this was a sign of the family's poverty. They could not invite relatives or friends to act as godparents, because they were unable to offer even the modest hospitality such an occasion demanded.[2]

Towards the end of his life, Bishop Shanahan wrote a list of the favours for which he wished to give thanks. It has become known as Bishop Shanahan's Magnificat. It begins appropriately with his birth and baptism.

> In bringing me into the world and into the Catholic Church —
> my dear Catholic parents and the parish priest.

The remains of the old church are still to be seen in Borrisoleigh, hidden behind the small houses and shops of the village square. It was built about the year 1813, when the laws against the old religion were beginning to relax but it was still considered provocative to build a Catholic church in a place where it could easily be seen. The building fell into disuse in the 1890s when a handsome new church was built on the opposite side of the square. The old church is a substantial T-shaped building, part of it now used as a barn, the rest of it roofless and filled with briars. A holy water font near the door and a few fragments of carved marble are the only signs that it was once the parish church.

According to the church records, young Joe was the third child in the Shanahan family. His parents had been married in the neighbouring parish of Templederry on 17 June 1864. The story goes that after their marriage they lived on for a short while in Templederry in a place called Glenmore, where Dan worked either as a herdsman or as a farm labourer. Before the birth of their first child, the young couple found themselves evicted from their home by the local landlord, an all too common occurrence in those days.[3] They then moved to Glankeen, where their first child Michael was born in 1866, followed by John in 1869.

Shortly after Joseph's birth in 1871, the family fortunes took a turn for the better. There was a wealthy landowner in Templederry called John Dwyer O'Ryan, who was one of the few Catholic landlords in the area and who was to prove himself a good friend to the Shanahans in the years that followed. He offered Daniel a position as herdsman on his land and the offer was accepted.

Every parish in Ireland is a mosaic of tiny townlands, sometimes no more than a few fields in extent. Each townland has its own Irish name, sweet-sounding and descriptive of the locality. Glenmore is the big valley, Currafrusha is the flowing weir. Now the Shanahans found themselves back in Templederry parish in the townland of Gortnalaura, the field of the ancient ruins.

Life in Gortnalaura was far from easy but Dan Shanahan was a hard worker and a good provider for his growing family. A new baby was added on average every second year and brought to the parish church in Templederry for baptisms. Richard was born in 1873, Louis Patrick in 1875, Jeremiah in 1877, Mary in 1878, Bridget in 1880, Margaret in 1882, and finally Daniel junior in

1885.[4] In addition, Patrick Walsh, a younger brother of Mrs Shanahan, lived with the family until 1875. He was to play a crucial role in his nephew Joseph's life.

In those days, a herdsman's wages were small. His main duty was to look after his master's cattle. In return, he received a house to live in, along with 'the grass of a donkey and a small bit of a garden plus a shilling a day'.[5] Herdsmen's families lived mainly on potatoes and milk, a monotonous diet which provided however most of the nourishment needed by a growing child. The Shanahans probably kept a few hens and a couple of pigs as well, to make an occasional variation in their daily fare.

Dan Shanahan is remembered as a tall, well-built man, loyal to his faith and his country, commanding in appearance and not easily frightened. These traits were to be inherited by his son Joe. On the political side, Dan was a supporter of the movement for Irish independence but he refused to be drawn into the agitation organised by Michael Davitt's Land League, then in its heyday. He favoured more peaceful means of achieving political ends and he had a particular belief in the power of education. He knew that education was the only way his children could escape from the poverty of Gortnalaura. His esteem for education was also to be inherited by Joe.

Every morning the Shanahan children set off from Gortnalaura for Templederry school. The school was in fact more than a mile from Templederry village, in a little valley called Gortnagoona, the field of the calf. For the Shanahans, it was a short walk across the fields and over a small hill to the modest one-storeyed building which was the only school in the parish. A long lifetime later, Joe's younger brother Louis Patrick was to look back nostalgically on those early morning expeditions and remember the roads and streams they crossed and the flock of partridges that suddenly rose up before them as they climbed the little hill.[6]

The school still stands somewhat forlornly by the side of the road, now turned into a cowshed. All that remains of its former glory is the old stone tablet set into one of the walls, bearing the finely carved inscription 'Templederry National School'. It was here that young Joe learned to read and write and was introduced to the mysterious world of addition and subtraction. It was here too that he received the first formal instruction in his religion, for the National Schools, though in theory non-denominational, were in practice Catholic in most parts of the country. The

Templederry teacher's faith and devotion earned a place in the Shanahan Magnificat.

> In teaching me in school —
> the school teacher.

In the evening time, back in the cottage in Gortnalaura, their father would oversee them as they did their homework and remind them yet again of the importance of education. In later life, the bishop liked to tell younger priests about those evenings and what they taught him.

> You people study education problems in books and at universities. I learnt its value from my father. When the neighbours used to sit around the fire at night discussing the social questions of the time, I often heard him say: 'Davitt says, "Agitate, agitate." But I say, "Educate, educate."' He believed in education as the most potent of all means to the improvement of a people. As we sat around the table in the evenings doing our homework, he would pass around studying our efforts, encouraging, correcting, and at the end of the week there would be an examination with a prize for the best.[7]

Before they went to bed, there was the nightly and unalterable ritual of the family rosary. Parents and children knelt on the rough floor and said together the five mysteries of the Rosary, the joyful mysteries on Mondays and Thursdays, the sorrowful mysteries on Tuesdays and Fridays, the glorious mysteries on Sundays, Wednesdays and Saturdays. These were followed by the 'trimmings', a selection of prayers, litanies and devotions which were often as long as the Rosary itself and extended the time of prayer to a full half-hour.

Then for a few minutes the children were allowed to sit around the turf fire, while their mother told them stories from the gospels or from the lives of the saints. She would finish by saying, 'Now children, talk to God.' Hands would be joined and eyes closed and the firelight would flicker on small earnest faces, as they made their own secret petitions in the silence of their hearts. If the strength of Bishop Shanahan's faith came from his father, then its tenderness must surely have come from his mother. Many years later he was to write, 'What a book a mother's heart is for each of us to read and ponder over and meditate on and imitate and live in our own lives. God's life is revealed to us in the hearts and lives of our mothers — aye, of our sisters too.'[8] With such good and loving parents, the Shanahan children could not but love one another. He gave thanks for that love to the end of his life.

> In making my home-life happy —
> my brothers and sisters.

* * *

The new church in Templederry was built in the early 1870s, just around the time the Shanahan family returned to the parish. It replaced an earlier church which dated, like the old Borrisoleigh church, from the beginning of the century. In this new church the family attended Mass each Sunday, their babies were christened, their children made their first confession and received their first Holy Communion. It still serves the people of Templederry as their parish church, solidly built of local stone with apse, transept, rose window and belfry, the most impressive building in the little village.

It was a period when the Catholic Church in Ireland was slowly emerging from the shadow of the penal laws and trying to enter the mainstream of European Catholic life. In 1850 a synod of all the Irish bishops was held in Thurles, a town some fifteen miles from Templederry, the first such synod to be held in the country for seven centuries. One of the effects of the synod was to restore the central importance of the parish church in the life of the people. During the centuries of persecution, Mass was usually said and the sacraments administered in private houses. Now it was decreed that the church was the proper place for the celebration of Mass and the sacraments of baptism, penance and matrimony.

The prime mover behind the synod of Thurles was Archbishop Paul Cullen of Armagh, later to become Archbishop of Dublin and Ireland's first Cardinal. Cullen had spent almost thirty years in Rome as student and professor and was a devoted supporter of Pope Pius IX. He returned to Ireland with the ambition of ending the Irish Church's isolation and he sought to do this by strengthening ties with the papacy and bringing in many of the customs and devotions he had known in Italy.

Under his influence, the parish church became the normal place for Mass and the sacraments. Devotion to the Blessed Eucharist was cultivated, Benediction of the Blessed Sacrament and the Forty Hours' Prayer were introduced. The cult of the Sacred Heart of Jesus was encouraged and the practice of observing the nine First Fridays became widespread. Even the decoration of the churches was affected. Italian-style images of the Sacred Heart, the Blessed Virgin and the saints were featured in statues and pictures and stained-glass windows. The Stations of the Cross were hung on the walls, the crib was set up at Christmas time.

In the new church at Templederry all these influences were brought to bear on young Joe at his most impressionable age. The Blessed Sacrament, which had normally been kept in the priest's house, was now in the tabernacle on the altar, with the red light of the little sanctuary lamp to remind him of the Real Presence.[9] On one side of the caen-stone altar was a statue of the Madonna and Child, on the other a statue of his own patron, Saint Joseph. The church itself was dedicated not to one of the traditional Irish saints but to the Immaculate Conception of Our Lady, a dogma which had been proclaimed by Pius IX in 1854. Joe grew up in a religious atmosphere which was subtly different from that of his parents, where Irish customs and devotions were giving way to those of Italy and where unquestioning loyalty to the Pope was becoming the hallmark of the sincere Catholic.

At the same time, he did not altogether lose touch with his Irish roots. The memory of the old Celtic saints was too well preserved in the district to let that happen. Early in the sixth century Saint Odran or Otteran founded the monastery of Latteragh within the boundaries of the present parish of Templederry, and it was to become renowned as a centre of piety and learning. It had a rival in the nearby monastery founded by Saint Cúilán in Glankeen, not far from the Shanahans' previous home. Little or nothing remained of these Celtic monasteries in the nineteenth century but the names of their founders were still remembered and the places where they laboured were held in reverence. Saint Odran's pattern or festival was an important annual event in Latteragh and Saint Cúilán's holy well in Glankeen was visited by people in search of cures and other favours. The respect that Bishop Shanahan would show towards African traditions and holy places may have owed something to the memory of the patterns and pilgrimages of his youth.

* * *

In the year 1875, when Joe was just four years of age, his uncle Patrick Walsh left the home in Gortnalaura to join the Congregation of the Holy Ghost. The Congregation, known in Latin as the Congregatio Sancti Spiritus, or CSSp for short, was an old French religious order which had recently been given a new lease of life by the dynamic Francis Libermann, a convert from Judaism.

Libermann's special ambition was to bring Christianity to the peoples of black Africa, an area which was being opened up by European colonists in the first half of the nineteenth century. The mission was a particularly difficult one. The west coast of Africa had become known as the white man's grave because of the high death rate among Europeans who attempted to live there. It was quite common for white men to die within weeks or even days of their landing on the disease-infected coast.

The Congregation's first missionary expedition to West Africa was a catastrophe. Libermann sent a group of seven priests and three brothers from France to start a mission in Liberia. Hardly had they landed when one after another they began to fall ill. Within a few months nine of the ten were dead. It was a shattering setback but it did not put an end to Libermann's plans for Africa. The courage of these pioneers inspired other young Frenchmen to join the Congregation and gradually the Holy Ghost missionaries began to establish themselves in West Africa as well as in the more healthy climate of Southern and Eastern Africa.

It soon became clear that France could not supply all the missionaries that were needed for these new mission territories. The Congregation began to look elsewhere for vocations and it was natural that they should turn their attention to Ireland, one of the most devoutly Catholic countries in Europe. Up to this the Irish Church had been too preoccupied with its own survival to consider involvement in foreign missions but now it was beginning to become more confident and outward-looking. There was the further consideration that the Irish were English-speakers and citizens of the United Kingdom, which gave them a great advantage in those large areas of Africa which were coming under British influence.

The move to Ireland was not made during Libermann's lifetime. His few contacts with the Irish had left him with a low opinion of their character. In one of his letters he spoke of the difficulty of recruiting Irishmen for the African mission and added the unkind comment: 'The Irish are not generous enough to renounce everything to the extent that is necessary for our vocation.'[10]

In 1859, seven years after Libermann's death, four members of the Holy Ghost Congregation came to Dublin with the intention of opening a house of the order and looking for vocations. Their leader was a priest from the north of France, Father Jules Leman. He soon decided that the best strategy was to start a school and in 1860 he obtained permission from Archbishop Cullen to open a college in Blackrock, a suburb of Dublin. The college became known as the French College and it catered for lay students as well as for those who intended to enter the Congregation. It was an immediate and lasting success. In 1864 they took over another college in Rockwell, Co Tipperary, about thirty miles from the Shanahan home, and it was to prove equally successful.

It may have been through Rockwell College that Patrick Walsh came into contact with the Holy Ghost Fathers, or it may have been through meeting some of the divinity students from Blackrock. The young men studying for the priesthood in Blackrock were encouraged to look for vocations in their home areas during their holidays. One of them, Joseph Gleeson, came from Silvermines, which is only a short distance from Templederry, and in August 1874 he was in his home parish visiting priests and schools in search of volunteers for the missions.[11] It is quite possible that he met Patrick Walsh at this time, which would explain why Patrick applied for admission to Blackrock rather than the much more convenient Rockwell.

Patrick was accepted by the Blackrock authorities and an entry in the old Juniorate register dated 20 September 1875 lists him as 'Patrick Walsh, c/o Mrs D. Shanahan, Templederry, Co. Tipperary'. He was now twenty-two years of age and had been working on the land since he left primary school. His ambition was to be a priest but he must have found the studies a great burden after so many years away from his books. Two months in the Blackrock juniorate was enough to convince him that he was more fitted for the brotherhood than for the priesthood. He was transferred to the Brothers' novitiate, which was then in Rockwell College, and in 1878 he was professed, taking Adelm as his name in religion. He was then appointed to Blackrock as one of the team of brothers who looked after the various services in the community and college. He remained there until 1881.[12]

During his years in Rockwell, it was easy for Brother Adelm to keep in contact with his sister's family in Templederry. No doubt he visited them from time to time, and they visited him. He came to know the children as they grew and developed, and he formed a special bond with young Joe, who was beginning to show signs of a vocation to the priesthood. Physically, the two were very unalike. A photograph taken of them many years later shows Joseph as a typical Shanahan, a tall, broad-shouldered, commanding figure. Adelm is small and slight of build, a rather worried-looking little man, completely overshadowed by his nephew. But the two were of one mind in their commitment to the missionary vocation, an unusual one in the Ireland of those days.

Brother Adelm's desire to go to Africa was not to be granted for a while yet. In 1881, when Joe was ten years of age, Adelm was appointed to the mother house of the Congregation in Paris. The following year he was transferred to a college in Normandy, where he remained four years. In 1886 he was moved again, this time to a college run by the Holy Ghost Fathers in Beauvais, some fifty miles north of Paris.[13]

At this time Saint Joseph's College in Beauvais was under the direction of Father Amet Limbour, a man who had great qualities of dynamism and leadership, though he had an unfortunate habit of letting his ambitions outrun his resources. The college was the headquarters of an organisation called the Archconfraternity of Saint Joseph, which had as its main object the spread of devotion to that saint. Limbour started a magazine called *The Messenger of Saint Joseph* and he used it to raise funds for the education of students for the priesthood in the college. With the help of these funds, he was able to take interested boys until they were ready to enter a seminary or religious order. Naturally enough, most of these boys were from France, though there were also a few from other French-speaking countries.

When Brother Adelm arrived in Beauvais, his nephew Joseph was just fifteen years of age. He had learnt as much as there was to learn in the school in Gortnagoona and the question of his further education was causing his parents some concern. Joseph himself was more firm than ever in his desire to be a missionary, but to become a missionary he would have to attend a secondary school and the family were too poor to pay the fees. Adelm was aware of the problems and he approached Father Limbour and asked him to take Joseph into the college at Beauvais. Limbour agreed, the Shanahans were told the news, the parents gave their consent, and on 16 August 1886 young Joseph left the little home in Templederry on the long road that led to Beauvais and the priesthood.

> In making it possible for me to be a religious —
> poor old Uncle Adelm.

* * *

Joseph probably thought he could complete his secondary education in three or four years and then return to Ireland to serve his time as prefect or junior master in one of the Irish colleges. Events turned out otherwise. It was to be eleven years before he saw his family or his home again.

The college was situated in the town of Beauvais in the shadow of the magnificent gothic cathedral, one of the glories of French architecture. Its builders had dreamed of creating the greatest cathedral in France but their dreams were doomed to disappointment. Time and time again, the soaring arches collapsed in rubble, and the great tower finally fell in 1573, never to be raised again. But even in its present truncated form, it is a sight to take the breath away. For the fifteen-year-old youth from Templederry, the first view of it must have been an overwhelming experience.

In the college itself the regime was simple and austere. The students rose at five in the morning, washed in icy water, ate the plain fare that was set before them, mingled their studies with manual work. None of this would have caused any problem for Joseph, whose lifestyle in Templederry had been equally simple. A much greater difficulty was the cultural gap between him and his fellow students, all of whom were French-speakers. Until he began to master the language, he found himself almost completely cut off from human contact. Had it not been for the presence of his uncle, Brother Adelm, those first few months in Beauvais would have been a time of great loneliness and isolation.

In a comparatively short time, Joseph was able to make himself understood in French. Eventually he became so fluent that he was sometimes mistaken for a native of France. The other boys got on well with him and if they teased him from time to time there was little malice in it. He was liked for his easygoing good nature, and perhaps a little feared as well. He was tall for his age, strong and well-built, and there was a streak of determination about him that could turn to stubbornness. He was emphatically not someone to be trifled with.

There was one small incident of those days that Joseph was never to forget. Like most Irish lads of his time, he grew up under the impression that the French lived on a staple diet of frogs and snails. He was not aware that the snails eaten in France were a special variety and were carefully prepared and cooked before being offered at table. One day his fellow-pupils took advantage of his ignorance and challenged him to eat a live garden snail. It was a dare and Joseph felt that the honour of Ireland was at stake. If the French could do it, so could he.

He loved to tell the story in later years, vividly describing the sliminess and ugliness of the snail and the special repulsiveness of its two waving horns. It took a supreme effort to swallow the noisome creature but he did it. From then on, nobody dared to question his courage or his patriotism again. The memory of that feat was to stand him in good stead when he was offered unfamiliar delicacies at native feasts in Nigeria. 'If I managed a snail for the honour of Ireland,' he used to say to himself, 'I can surely manage these things for the souls of Nigeria.'[14]

The year 1888 was a year of change in the college. Brother Adelm was moved again, this time to help with the setting up of a secondary school in Ballarat in Australia. His nephew naturally felt the loss, but by now he was well acclimatised to life in Saint Joseph's. The same year saw the departure of Father Limbour as a result of a disagreement with the Bishop of Beauvais. As so often happened, Limbour's plans for future expansion seemed over-grandiose to others. He was appointed superior of Rockwell College in Ireland, where the same melancholy cycle of ambition and frustration was to take place once more. Shanahan always remembered him with gratitude for having received a penniless Irish boy and given him an education.[15]

> In taking me, a poor boy, for nothing into a secondary school —
> Father Limbour, CSSp, at Beauvais.

In 1889 it was time for Shanahan himself to move. Now that Father Limbour had gone, the Bishop was anxious to reclaim the college for diocesan use. The students who came from other parts of France or from foreign countries had to start looking for alternative accommodation. Shanahan was now eighteen but he had not yet completed his secondary education. As he was still as determined as ever to enter the Holy Ghost Congregation, he decided to try the juniorate in Blackrock. A juniorate was a college or section of a college where students intending to enter the Congregation could complete their secondary studies. He applied for admission to the French College, as it was still known. His application was turned down.

On 12 September 1889 he wrote a second application, this time to Father Victor Bertsch, superior of the Holy Ghost juniorate at Cellule in central France. The letter is preserved in the Paris Archives, the earliest of his letters to survive. It was written in French and says in part:

> I am asking then, Father, if you are willing to accept me, an Irishman. I had opted for Blackrock. I renounced this idea when Father Huvétys remarked that my age (I am eighteen) and our system of studies rendered me unsuitable for the French College; it is unnecessary for me to say that I am attracted by the life led in the Congregation. I dare to hope that you will receive my request favourably.[16]

The letter was backed up by a recommendation from the Superior General of the Congregation, which was the next best thing to a command. Shanahan was accepted by Father Bertsch and he moved to Cellule in the autumn of 1889. The following summer he formally requested in writing to be admitted to the Congregation of the Holy Ghost and his request was granted. In a ceremony on 29 June 1890 he and five other students were officially received by Father Bertsch and clothed in the black soutane and sash, the habit of the Congregation. It was enough to earn the superior a verse in Shanahan's Magnificat, the last person mentioned there by name.

> In receiving me into the Congregation —
> Father Bertsch at Cellule.

Grateful though he was for being admitted to Cellule, Shanahan must have been disappointed that he was not allowed to return to Ireland. It seems strange that his application for Blackrock was refused. The reasons given — his age and his course of studies — had some validity, in view of the differences between the French and Irish systems. But they were hardly an insuperable obstacle and one wonders whether there might have been another reason for the refusal.

Was it meant as a test of the firmness of his purpose and the solidity of his vocation? If so, he passed the test convincingly by accepting the fact that he would not see his country or his family for many more years. Or was it felt that he had the potential to make an outstanding contribution to the work of the Congregation and that it was only in France that he could receive the necessary formation? This is a distinct possibility. The French distrust of the Irish was very real at the time, though later events showed how baseless it was. In any event, there is no doubt that Shanahan's long years in France were an important element in his later success in Africa. He was able to relate to the French missionaries in Nigeria in a way that would not otherwise have been possible.

His stay in Cellule was to be much longer than he expected. As year followed year he found it increasingly difficult to conceal his impatience. As early as 1890 a report from one of his superiors complained that he was *entêté* and *gamin* — headstrong and impertinent. The reasons for this judgement are not known, but one of his French fellow-students later related how Shanahan had prompted him during an oral English examination by coughing whenever he made a mistake. Behaviour of this nature could reasonably be considered as insubordinate.[17]

No letters survive for the years 1891 to 1893 but a number of group photographs of the students at this period were discovered in Cellule by Father Seán Farragher seventy years later. They are the earliest known photographs of Shanahan, who had now entered his twenties. It is easy to pick him out, even in a large group. The strong build, the jutting brows, the firm lips, the determined set of the jaw, the reserved and almost sullen glance of the eyes, all bespeak a young man who was, if not actually headstrong, certainly not somebody who could be easily pushed around.

A new superior came to Cellule, Father Spielmann. He was anxious to attract more fee-paying lay students to the college by securing good results in the public examinations. At his bidding

Shanahan sat reluctantly but successfully for the first and second parts of the Baccalaureate, the latter in the summer of 1894. He felt by now that he had as much secular education as he needed and was looking forward to beginning his priestly studies in the autumn of that year. Then to his dismay Spielmann told him that he was to stay on in Cellule and prepare for the Baccalaureate of Science. This was too much. On 5 August 1894 Shanahan wrote a respectful but firm letter to the Assistant General, in the course of which he said:

> I am already in my twenty-fourth year. This means that if I delay another year, I shall not have the happiness of being a priest or a professed member of the Congregation until the very advanced age of thirty years! Now, Very Reverend Father, it is unnecessary for me, I believe, to tell you with what ardour I desire that thrice happy day when I may join that holy phalanx which combats and dies over there in Africa for the holiest and most sacred of all causes. I have now been studying for eight years and have come to find life in the Junior Scholasticate trying — not that the life there leaves anything to be desired — quite the contrary; but because I find myself among men who for the most part are much younger that I am. Also I have not had a holiday in my country of Ireland for eight years. I shall be very glad, Father, if you can allow me to go immediately to the Senior Scholasticate, as I feel somewhat tired as a result of the last two years of preparation for the first and second parts of the Baccalaureate. Studying in a language which is not my own and at such an advanced age, I can tell you I am experiencing serious difficulties and at times anxieties.[18]

He ended the letter by emphasising that he was willing to accept his superiors' decision, whatever that might be. 'In doing their will, I shall be sure of doing the will of God.' This time his appeal did not fail. He was granted permission to transfer at once to the senior scholasticate. Without too many regrets, he packed his bags and left Cellule for ever.

2

Student and priest

Joseph Shanahan spent the first year of his priestly studies in the Abbey of Langonnet, situated in a beautiful but remote part of Brittany. Founded as a Cistercian abbey in the twelfth century, it was turned into a cavalry stud during the French Revolution and horses were stabled in the old monastery church.

In 1857 the abbey was bought from the state by the Holy Ghost Congregation and in course of time it was used to house a training centre for Brothers, an orphanage, and a juniorate. In addition, when the senior scholasticate at Chevilly became overcrowded, Langonnet was used to house the first year students.[1] Here Shanahan found himself one of a class of some seventy young men, most of them around his own age and a number of them from Ireland. It was a welcome change from the isolation and frustration of Cellule.

No letters of his survive from his time in Langonnet and our only source of information is the *Bulletin Générale* of the Holy Ghost Congregation, a monthly printed record of events. There was a number of Irishmen among the students, the first time since he came to France that Shanahan had fellow-countrymen among his classmates. The superior at the time was Father Francis Xavier Libermann, a nephew of the founder, and he preached the eight-day retreat for the students as they started their academic year. The teaching staff included an Irish priest, Father John Joseph O'Gorman, who was to become a good friend of Shanahan's. Another friend of his paid a flying visit to Langonnet during the year and gave a talk to the students. This was Father Limbour of Beauvais, who had finished his term as superior of Rockwell under something of a cloud but was as full as ever of splendid plans for his next assignment, a college in Haiti.

The year passed uneventfully in a daily round of prayer, study and recreation. The study concentrated on scholastic philosophy as a preparation for the theology which was to form the major part of the students' training. They ended their year on 15 August 1895 with a solemn thanksgiving ceremony. The following morning at dawn they gathered in front of the statue of the Blessed Virgin in the inner quadrangle and sang the hymn *Ave Maris Stella* with gusto. Then they set off in a procession of horse-drawn carriages for the railway station and the two-day journey to Paris.[2]

Their destination was the senior scholasticate, a large and imposing building in Chevilly, one of the northern suburbs of Paris. It needed to be large, as the arrival of the contingent from Langonnet swelled the student population to 150. Some of the Langonnet priests were also transferred to Paris. The superior, Father Libermann, was promoted to the post of superior at Chevilly. Father O'Gorman was made professor of theology for the senior students.

As a junior student of theology, Shanahan had little contact with either of these men. The principal influence on him at this time was the director of the scholasticate, Father van Haecke. Van Haecke came from the north of France and had previously been on the staff of two of the Congregation's secondary colleges, one at Merville near his birthplace, the other in the West Indian island of Martinique. He came to know Shanahan well and to respect him highly, and these feelings were returned.

Shanahan had been only a short time in Chevilly when Van Haecke came to him with an unexpected proposition. The death had just occurred of Father Lutz, a returned Nigerian missionary who had been teaching English in the college at Merville. Shanahan had the necessary fluency in both French and English to make a suitable replacement. Was he willing to take on the job?

The proposition can hardly have been an attractive one. He was just beginning his longed-for study of theology. The goal of priesthood and life on the missions was at last within view. Now he was being asked to go to yet another French secondary school and do work which seemed to have no relevance to his missionary vocation.

In this dilemma, van Haecke proved helpful and understanding. He arranged that Shanahan would start his English teaching after Christmas but would at the same time continue studying theology under the direction of Father Thierry, one of the priests in the Merville community. The period spent there would be counted as part of his theology course and would not cause any postponement of his ordination. Under these conditions, he set off after Christmas for the college in Merville, which was near the Belgian border, about 150 miles north of Paris.

The six months he spent there had one important side-effect. All during the period he corresponded regularly with van Haecke, giving him an account of his daily life and especially of his prayer-life, and receiving advice and spiritual direction in return. These letters have been preserved and they give us our first insight into his mind and soul.[3] After a fortnight in his new post he wrote:

> I have eight hours of English in the week and an hour and a half of history and geography with the Third Years, not to mention the one hour's grind I give to Father Lithby, who is to replace me next year. As you see, Father, I have sufficient time for my theology.
>
> With regard to spiritual exercises, I am regular in attending those of the Community. For the past two days I have done my hour of spiritual reading. Here in front of me is a huge volume of Rodriguez which will suffice until the end of the year (at least for ascetical reading). My meditations? They are not going too badly. In the beginning it was always the same story. It would not be easy to say what road I followed in the three quarters of an hour!
>
> We do not fail in charity at recreation. In that respect there is nothing to fear, Reverend Father Thierry being always with us. However, Saint Thomas and Aristotle are not always the subject of conversation. We amuse ourselves as best we can; each one contributes his share so that everything goes excellently.

In his next letter, written about six weeks later, he was still reading Rodriguez, a sixteenth-century Spanish Jesuit whose *Practice of Christian and Religious Perfection* had been written for the instruction of Jesuit novices. He was going to confession once a week and receiving Communion three times a week, in accordance with van Haecke's direction: it was to be another ten years before Pius X recommended the practice of daily Communion. Each day he said the Rosary and made his meditation, the name generally given to mental prayer at that time. He was supposed to prepare the subject of the meditation the previous day from a meditation book.

> This latter point is not observed very faithfully. I do not like the author. It is a real mortification for me to read him for ten minutes. I do not find a single meditation appropriate

> to the season in this book. But I continue to read it, if only as a mortification — and I promise to be more faithful to it in future.

Later letters describe his struggle with some of his faults of character, particularly lack of charity towards others, which he describes as his old defect. His work in the school was not causing him any problems and he felt that the English classes were going well. But he was still finding difficulty with meditation. 'At the beginning of meditation I tell Him I have no taste for it, that I am as dry as a piece of wood, full of faults, yet I beg Him not to forget me all the same.'

The last letter was written in June 1896 after news had come that van Haecke was being moved to the post of assistant to the new Superior General. In it Shanahan laments both the loss of his trusted director and his own lack of progress in the spiritual life.

> I had promised you that I would be an exemplary student. In fact, Rodriguez has been abandoned for a fortnight. As for meditation, I have to sweat blood and tears not to sleep. Even my work itself leaves much to be desired. In spite of vigorous resolutions in regard to charity, so recommended in your last letter, I have failed pretty much in it again, though less often, all the same. All this shows you that I have not much reason to be proud. But thank God I am launched again. Perhaps it is only the Sacred Heart who has rendered me this service. Constancy in following your counsels which are the voice of God for me, a little good will and a great confidence in the Blessed Virgin should be enough to carry me safe and sound to the end of the year.

Shanahan's self-criticism need not be taken too literally. Difficulties with mental prayer are nothing unusual with men of his age or indeed of any age. The typical nineteenth-century meditation manual, which tended to turn prayer into a purely intellectual exercise, was unlikely to be of much help. Even Rodriguez' classic work, running to three large volumes of 500 pages each, demanded considerable stamina in the reader. Shanahan was intelligent rather than intellectual. He had no great gift for abstract thought but he had remarkable intuition. In theology and spirituality he worked more by feeling than by reasoning. Many years were to pass before he came to trust the soundness of his instincts, which could reach so quickly to the heart of the matter. In the meantime, he felt inadequate in comparison with his more conventional confrères.

His often repeated confession of lack of charity is a different matter. How seriously are we to take it? Was he over-sensitive in regard to minor failings or did he experience genuine problems in his relations with his pupils and colleagues? There was always a touch of steel in his character and it is likely that he could still appear headstrong and stubborn. Many Irishmen take refuge in dogged obstinacy when attempts are made to pressure them. They can be led but not driven. There was always something of this in Shanahan and it cost him a long and hard-fought struggle to bring it under control.

Another memento of these months is a small black notebook, inscribed on the flyleaf 'Joseph I. Shanahan, Merville 1896'. In it he copied out poems and other writings which had appealed to him for one reason or another. He may have been studying Italian at this period as the first pages are given up to poems in Italian. Then there is a long treatise on aesthetics entitled *Le Beau,* The Beautiful. A number of poems in English, French and Italian follow with a few pages on graphology, the art of reading character from handwriting. The last section includes hints on etiquette for the clergy and warns against such solecisms as pouring one's coffee into one's saucer in order to cool it.[4]

As the school's summer holidays approached Shanahan wrote to Van Haecke's successor, Father Clement Hubert, to ensure that his stay in Merville would not be prolonged any further. Artfully greeting him as 'an old missionary', he went on to express his desire to follow in the footsteps of those who had carried the banner of the faith to Africa.

> Ah! Father, at the thought of Africa one does not count the cost any more! What a sacrifice for those who have been there not to be able to return there any more! As for me, I have three more years to wait. I have only done one year's theology. I have been teaching English at Merville since January. I have not yet received the tonsure. I have written regularly to Father Van Haecke. Since May, pressure of work has prevented him from replying. At the moment all goes

> well. I have but one desire: to return to the Senior Scholasticate the day after the prize-giving here. It is the one request that I dare ask of you for the moment.[5]

So touching an appeal proved irresistible and he was relieved of his teaching duties. An entry in the notebook reads, 'Departure from Merville, 29 July 1896'. He returned to Chevilly, where he expected to complete the remaining three years of theology and receive ordination to the priesthood in 1899. But once again, the event was to turn out very different from the anticipation.

* * *

The first disruption was caused by Rome. Hitherto it had been the custom in the Holy Ghost Congregation to have the novitiate or spiritual year immediately after ordination. This provided an opportunity to give pastoral training when the candidates were mature enough to profit by it. The Vatican now issued instructions that they were to have their novitiate at the traditional time, that is, at the beginning of their religious life.

The Superior General decided that the theology students were to interrupt their studies for a year and do their novitiate. So Shanahan and his classmates, sixty-three in number, had to lay aside their theology books in the autumn of 1896 and begin a year of spiritual exercises. This meant that ordination would be postponed for a year, which was a further disappointment. But the novitiate year itself was no disappointment for Shanahan, due in large part to the Master of Novices, Father Grizard.

The two main elements of the novitiate were prayer and manual work. Long hours were spent in the garden at simple repetitive work which left the mind free to contemplate eternal truths. As a special project they designed and built an outdoor Calvary with life-size figures of Christ on the cross and the Blessed Virgin and Saint John standing on either side. At the base of the cross they set a large globe on which the various missions were marked.

Their prayer life was under the direction of Father Grizard, a man of deep and genuine spirituality. He was born near Ars and as a youth he asked advice about his career from the famous Curé of Ars, Saint John Vianney. The Curé told him, 'You will be a priest, you will have a long career, and you will do a lot of good.' All of it came true.[6]

It may have been at his suggestion that Shanahan started a spiritual journal on 2 April 1897. It was written in a notebook even smaller than the Merville one and has happily been preserved. It covers the period from the first Friday of April to the first Friday of August in sixty-nine pages of incredibly tiny handwriting. The language is French and it is so fluent and idiomatic that its writer must by now have given up even thinking in English. It is a remarkably candid and revealing document, the unvarnished story of four months in the life of a soul.[7]

The flyleaf has an inscription that must give pause to the reader and even more to the biographer: 'I consider everything contained in this notebook to be like ''secrets of confession''.' This was evidently written to discourage the prying eyes of his fellow-students. Does it also apply to the modern reader? The answer must be No. A man has a right to privacy during life but after death he is part of history. Every scrap of information about a person of Shanahan's stature must be preserved and treasured. Moreover, though the journal openly notes faults and failures, it does not reveal everything. The secrets of confession are still unviolated, as shall shortly be seen.

The first page begins with the words: 'This notebook, begun on the first Friday of the month of April, will accompany me wherever I go. In moments of difficulty, I will re-read it. The memory of the lovely days of the novitiate, a time of peace, of happiness, of prayer, will give me new life.' This was no idle promise. He was to keep the notebook all his life, re-read it often, and add comments from time to time in the unused pages.

The first eight pages are devoted to a somewhat academic study of the virtue of obedience. There is little that is personal about it and it was obviously drawn from books or from the talks given by the Novice Master. The subject itself, however, was of more than academic interest to a young and independently minded religious expected to give unquestioning obedience to the commands of his superiors. Already he had experienced the conflict between his own wishes and the tasks to which he was assigned. He concludes that it is the duty of religious 'to follow the commands of the superior with the same zeal as if Jesus Christ himself were giving us the command in person. One may submit one's own opinions to the superior, but one must accept his when he has decided the question.' It was the course he had already followed more than once.

Passion Sunday, the fifth Sunday of Lent, fell on 4 April that year. From then until the end of May, he wrote each day a page or so of reflections of a more personal kind. During Passion Week he took up the subject of his dominant fault.

> Dominant fault: often tempted, almost every time I succeeded in overcoming the temptation through the grace of God. I have carried out with two or three exceptions the little mortifications, or rather avoiding of unmortification, that I made a resolution to do. During free recreation time I will do my best to be in the company of those confrères whom I like least. Resolution: To keep a special watch over myself during Springtime.

These are two themes to which he will constantly return in later entries. One is his relations with his confrères. The other is his dominant fault. Spiritual writers of the time held that most people had a dominant fault or ruling passion which was the underlying cause of their sinful actions; it was important to identify this fault and take steps to overcome it. Though he never states outright what the dominant fault is, it gradually becomes evident that it lies in the area of sexuality. A healthy young man of twenty-five could be expected to feel the urgings of nature, not least during springtime. The dominant fault may have been the general strain of living a celibate life or it may have been some particular habit of sexual sin. Which it was is never made clear.

Each day during Holy Week he enters a reflection on the liturgy of the day and adds a suitable resolution. He refers more than once to the subject of temptation. On Good Friday his resolution is: 'I will think of the Passion of my God, Jesus Christ, during difficult temptations.' In Easter week, the reflections are more joyful in tone and a holiday atmosphere creeps in. He mentions making a pilgrimage to the basilica in Montmartre. 'I am so happy to have been able to pray in that magnificent church built in honour of the Sacred Heart.' On the Saturday, he returns to a familiar theme. 'O my God, I beg you to give me the grace to triumph over my dominant fault, the source of all my failings.'

On the following Monday, 26 April, he examines again his relations with his fellow students and does not like what he sees. He paints a savage portrait of the artist as a young pup.

> This morning I reflected a little on my failures in regard to community life. Well, in my relations with my confrères my self-esteem shows itself in the arrogant tone I take in conversation, as if my opinions and my viewpoint were the only right ones. That's why even if I know nothing about a subject I stick to my ideas so doggedly. Some of the time, or rather all of the time, I go too far. I'm not polite in my way of carrying on a discussion. I may even put on an air of contempt for some of my confrères. For some time past I've been trying to display my wit. Instead of doing that, I'm hurting my confrères and making myself unbearable. Another thing — I try to be first with the news, whether it's true or false. This is bad. Now it has come to the point where I am being called a liar. O Mary, I implore you to help me get rid of these faults. Let me have more respect for the most dear members of Jesus Christ, those whom he loves the most.

It would be a damning indictment if made by anyone other than himself. As it is, one wonders whether he may not have overstated the case. If his behaviour was so insensitive, how could his description of it show such startling sensitivity? There are those who judge themselves harshly because the standards they set themselves are so high. It is certain that those who knew Shanahan in later years and experienced his gentleness and kindness would have been unable to recognise him in his own self-portrait.

The first day of May marked the beginning of the month traditionally dedicated to Mary. 'Looking back at the past, it seems to me that the month of Mary has always been a happy and blessed time for me. But my passions have grown with the years. Now it is warfare. And so it will be until the grave.' His resolution is, 'To be vigilant about purity during this month.'

On the evening of the following day, Saturday, he began his eight-day retreat. It was to prove one of the high points of his novitiate and indeed of his whole life. The director of the retreat was the Novice Master, Father Grizard. On the first evening he gave the novices the opening conference, the name given to a spiritual talk. On each of the following eight days he gave two, one in the morning and one in the evening, a total of fifteen in all.

The eight days were days of total silence. No-one spoke to

anyone else. There was nothing to distract them from the words of the Novice Master, measured, weighty, uncompromising words, echoing in the hearers' minds all during their waking hours. He brought them back to the fundamentals of their relationship with God, the fact that they were created by him, owed everything to him, could find fulfilment nowhere but in doing his will. The intensity of his conviction was matched by the clarity of his exposition. Shanahan filled page after page of his notebook with detailed accounts of the conferences and of the reflections and resolutions to which they gave rise. 'From now on the glory of God shall be my happiness. This calls for war. ''Man's life on earth is a battle.'' I shall fight.'

Tuesday was the Feast of Saint Monica, whose tears and prayers brought about the conversion of her son Augustine from a life of sin. Shanahan too had a kind of conversion experience that day.

> After reading the penitential psalms, I went out with the intention of making a good confession. Then, for what reason I don't know, I made a promise to the Blessed Virgin to go and tell the Father Director all about a matter which was causing me great anxiety. Oh the pain of that moment! But I did it. O Mary, thank you, thank you. I am so happy! I kept my promise. I know you will keep yours. I will make a good general confession. The rest of my novitiate will be happy. May the memory of that grace never leave my heart.

Impossible to know what the cause of the anxiety was, unprofitable to speculate. The wound, whatever it was, was lanced. The poison was at last released. The short staccato sentences convey the emotion and the relief.

The conferences during the second half of the week concentrated on the exalted nature of the vocation to which the young men were being called, the triple vocation of religious, missionary and priest. 'I must be a saint because of the triple vocation,' Shanahan noted, 'but above all because of the priesthood.' He ended with the resolution, 'Because of my vocation, work to become a saint. Do it perseveringly, seriously, but with trust and without anxiety.'

The final conference dealt with the subject of temptations. If the choice of subject was surprising, the message was consoling. 'Father Grizard said that the saddest religious and priests were those who arrived at their goal without having ever had temptations. On the other hand, someone who has gone through the mill is someone you can rely on.'

As the retreat drew to its close, he tried to sort out his feelings and impressions after what had proved to be an overwhelming experience.

> And so the retreat has come to an end. Eight wonderful days, perhaps the most wonderful of my life. Not one moment of boredom. What a joy to hear God speaking! He has given me so many graces. But I think that it is because of Mary that he gave me the grace of making a good general confession of my whole life. Thank you, Mary, my most kind and gentle mother, you have really kept your promise. Yesterday, Saturday, at half past nine I made my confession to the Father Master. Never have I been so happy. Today I will receive communion as an act of thanksgiving. What I must do above all is to prepare my prayers properly and make them properly. The same for the other exercises of piety — charity towards God, towards my neighbour whom I must love as myself. Fervour in the service of God, sacrifice of all my pleasures and generous acceptance of difficulties, pains, temptations.

The journal continues after the retreat with entries for almost every day until the end of May. He is concerned about the quality of his prayer. He is distracted, his mind wanders, he is failing to prepare the subject for prayer the night before. The battle against the dominant fault goes on. 'I must not listen to the loud cries of the flesh but endure them. Generous courage befits a good soldier of Christ.' He stresses the need for self-control. 'I must watch my sensuality, especially with drinking and eating. All the more so since drink especially goes straight to my head.'

On 25 May he makes the first mention of his sermon. 'Resolution: to give my sermon with no concern for myself but only for the glory of God, not caring what people may say about it.' By 31 May it has become his principal concern. 'My sermon is taking up all my time, but it will be over next Saturday. I place it under your protection, Mary. My first sermon will be given on the eve of the day I was baptised 26 years ago.'[8]

The first sermon of a student priest was always an ordeal.

Normally it was not given to an ordinary congregation in church, but to professors and fellow students in the college chapel. This did nothing to lessen the ordeal, since these listeners were far more likely to be critical than the average church-goer. Over-preparation, inexperience and sheer nerves usually combined to reduce the preacher's chances of success. Shanahan's post-mortem was gloomy.

> My first sermon was a total failure. Blessed be the holy name of God! It has done me a great service. From now on I will be better able to undergo humiliations. It's good to have gone through it because nothing will take me by surprise any more. For a week or two all my exercises have suffered. But at any rate I am now convinced about the truth which I was trying to expound for my listeners.

He does not mention the sermon's subject, of whose truth he feels he has managed to convince only himself. Once again one suspects that he may be exaggerating his failure, over-reacting understandably to a nerve-wracking experience. In later years, he was to become a spell-binding preacher and public speaker. His first sermon can scarcely have been the complete fiasco he describes.

During June and July the entries become shorter and less frequent. He continues to judge himself severely in his relations with his fellow students. He associates only with those he likes. He talks too much. As soon as a thought enters his mind, he has to say it. He takes offence too easily. He is less than frank. He laughs at everything. He judges and blames others, never himself. As for the Assistant Novice Master, 'I will have to make sure that I don't even mention his name and that I keep a strict silence whenever anyone else talks about him.'

During the month of July he spent much of the time working in the graveyard and this gave rise to some predictable reflections. 'Yesterday Father Leclerc was brought to the cemetery. Today it was Father Brunetti's turn. One day I will be brought there the same way. Where will that be and when?'

The final entry was made on Friday, 6 August 1897. The one-day retreat that day was the last retreat of his novitiate. 'I sincerely regret not having done my novitiate better, not having tamed my passions and acquired the virtues necessary for one called to so sublime a vocation.' His last resolution: 'To have a good and happy vacation by carrying out my duty.'

The journal ends there. If he ever kept another such journal, it has not survived. It is unlikely that he did. He never again had the time for such leisurely introspection.

* * *

Shanahan was not allowed to resume his studies in Chevilly after the vacation. Instead he was appointed to Rockwell College in Ireland.

The appointment seems to have come as a complete surprise. There is nothing to suggest that he asked for it or that he ever even imagined it could happen. The news must have been a cause of great joy. To be back in his native country after eleven years' absence was happiness enough. To be back in his home county of Tipperary, only a short distance from his parents and family, was sheer bliss.

His parents were alive and well, his brothers and sisters grown almost beyond recognition. The youngest, Daniel junior, barely a year old when Joseph left for France, was now twelve. The fortunes of the father, Daniel senior, continued to improve. His employer and benefactor, John Dwyer O'Ryan, had never married and he seems to have practically adopted the Shanahans as his own family. He left them a valuable property in a will dated June 1893: 'to my faithful servant, Daniel Shanahan, my farm at Clohinch.'[9] The house and land at Clohinch, a short distance from the village of Templederry, are still the home of Dan Shanahan's descendants.

There was now a strong Shanahan presence in Rockwell itself. Joseph's uncle, Brother Adelm, after spending some years in Australia and West Africa, was back in the College, looking after the housekeeping and bookshop and giving lessons in French. Joseph's twenty-four-year-old brother, Dick, also joined the staff around this time as a lay teacher. Later he was to become a doctor and it is said that John Dwyer O'Ryan paid his university fees.

Rockwell College, after a rather lean period, was now enjoying considerable success in the examination hall and on the playing field. During his period as superior, Father Limbour raised academic and sporting standards and more than doubled the number of pupils as a result. He then embarked on an over-ambitious expansion scheme which was once again to prove his downfall. He had his architect in Beauvais prepare plans for an imposing college church in the French style but the building never got beyond the crypt. Despite his many gifts, he had never really understood the Irish temperament and it was felt that an Irish superior was needed. In 1895 he departed for Haiti and was replaced by Father Nicholas Brennan.

Father Brennan got an Irish architect to draw up more modest plans for the chapel and it was opened in 1897, the year of Shanahan's arrival. That same year, the college came first among all the schools of Ireland in the published results of the summer examination. The total number of students had now reached two hundred and there was a staff of ten priests, thirteen brothers, ten prefects and four lay teachers. Shanahan found the college riding the crest of a wave.[10]

His fellow prefects were young men like himself, studying for the priesthood in the Holy Ghost Congregation. Among them was the poet Thomas McDonagh, who eventually decided he had no vocation and left the Congregation; he was executed in 1916 for his part in the Easter Rising. The duties of prefects were to help in the college as teachers and as game-masters. Shanahan's subjects were mathematics, Greek, Latin and of course French, which he now spoke more fluently than English. He also had to take part in the training of the rugby teams. Rugby was completely new to him but he quickly mastered the essentials of the game and became as enthusiastic as any of his pupils. His height and strength and broad shoulders served him well as player and as trainer.

One of the many bones of contention between Father Limbour and his Irish confrères had been the prefects' custom of donning football gear and playing with the boys. As a good French churchman, Limbour disapproved of clerics being seen in public without their soutanes. Now that he was gone, the prefects became an essential element in the success of the Rockwell teams. The only surviving photograph of Shanahan during his Rockwell years is a group shot of the senior team of 1898/99. At one end of the back row is Joseph, at the other his brother Dick, both resplendent in the striped college jerseys and knee-length shorts.

Shanahan's prowess on the rugby pitch won him the hero-worship of the younger boys. One of them was a twelve-year-old from Co. Limerick named Edward Leen, who was later to become one of his closest friends. Lying in bed in the ground floor dormitory, he would peep over the edge of the bedclothes and watch Shanahan emerging from the prefect's cubicle on his way out to an early morning training session. Leen remembered him as 'a fine build of a man; he walked with a characteristic stride, and he had a look of determination but also of reserve and intentness.'[11] On the playing field he was 'a splendid footballer, famous for his tackle; he played with set jaw, without speaking a word.'[12]

Near the lake in the college grounds was an old house, known appropriately as the Lake House. This was renamed Saint Joseph's and in 1898 was designated as the centre where the theology students were to receive their training. There were two professors, both French. Father Meistermann, the director, taught dogmatic theology, canon law and Church history; Father Desnier taught moral theology, scripture and liturgy.

It was not easy to combine the duties of a prefect with those of a theology student. As at Merville, Shanahan had to fit in his studies in the time left over from his teaching. He did his best but to the end of his life he felt that his priestly training had been skimped and he suffered from a certain sense of inadequacy when dealing with questions of theology. The mother house of the Congregation in Paris was also unhappy with the situation but the Rockwell authorities insisted that the college could not survive without the help of the theology students. Paris yielded with a bad grace on condition that the students should not teach for more than one hour a day.[13]

Because of the move to Rockwell, Shanahan had not made his first vows. In accordance with the usual practice, he made a written application to the Superior General and he used the occasion to repeat his wish to become a missionary. 'I beg of you, My Lord, not to forget how great is my desire to go to Africa and die beside my brothers. You do not believe, I hope, that a few months spent in the company of the heroes of Homer and the theories of Euclid have made a professor of me. You know, My Lord, that I am here not by choice but by duty. However, it will be as the good God wills.'[14] The profession ceremony took place in the college church in Rockwell at Easter 1898.

Shanahan and five of his fellow students were due to finish their four-year course in theology in the summer of 1900. Father

Meistermann recommended that all six of them should be ordained priests that year. The Paris authorities agreed and Bishop Emile Allgeyer, a Holy Ghost missionary from East Africa, came to Ireland to perform the ordinations. As he had spent some of his student years in Blackrock College, he was considered an appropriate choice for the occasion. The first three ordinations took place in the college church at Rockwell. The fourth, Shanahan's, was scheduled for Blackrock.

The ceremony took place on the first Sunday after Easter, 22 April 1900. It was a memorable occasion in the history of the French College. It was the first ordination to take place in the college chapel and it was performed by the first past pupil to have reached the rank of bishop. Shanahan himself had no particular connection with the college, apart from the rather unhappy one of having been refused permission to go there in 1889, but he did not allow this to lessen the joy of the occasion. In a letter of thanks to the priest who organised the ceremony, Father Ebenrecht, he wrote, 'Blackrock will ever in my fondest recollections be linked with the happiest day of my life.'

Father Ebenrecht was himself the architect of the church, which had been built in Gothic style in the years 1867-69. Plain on the outside, it was richly decorated inside with carved choir stalls and an ornate altar topped with gilded spires. In a niche over the altar, artfully lit from above, was a statue of the Virgin and Child, surrounded by clouds and cherub heads. It provided a dignified and festive setting for the always emotional ceremony of priestly ordination.

The Shanahan family were there in force, including a proud and happy Brother Adelm, and the boarders of the college were in the congregation that filled the nave. Among those on the roll at the time were a future Irish president, Eamonn De Valera, and a future Cardinal Primate, John D'Alton. They joined in the litany of the saints while the white-robed candidate lay prostrate before the altar. Then he knelt and Bishop Allgeyer laid his hands on his head, followed by all the priests present. The bishop clothed him in priest's vestments, anointed his hands with oil, and presented him with the chalice and paten. As a newly ordained priest, he joined the bishop in concelebrating the remainder of the Mass and in distributing Holy Communion to his family and friends. When the ceremony was over, he gave his priestly blessing to all those present, and no doubt he followed the old

Irish custom of giving his first blessing to his mother.

The following morning, Monday, Father Shanahan said his first Mass in the college church. Later that week he returned to his home village of Templederry to say Mass for all his neighbours and friends and to receive the traditional welcome given to a new priest in rural Ireland. But there was to be no prolonged holiday for him. He was expected back in Rockwell as soon as possible to finish the last few weeks of his theology and to resume his teaching duties.[15]

The summer holidays came and he waited impatiently for his first priestly appointment. His desire to go to Africa was as strong as ever, and now that he had finished his studies there seemed no further reason for delay. His superiors thought otherwise. In August 1900 the Superior General, Bishop Le Roy, visited Ireland and came to Rockwell. He brought bad news for Shanahan. Over the previous years, he had proved himself a solid and dependable member of the teaching team and the college could not afford to part with his services. He was to remain in Rockwell, resume his full work-load of languages and maths, and in addition take on the responsible post of Dean of Discipline for the 215 boys in the college. The prospect of Africa receded into the far distance, perhaps for ever.

There was nothing he could do except set the famous Shanahan jaw and get on with the job. He had become a religious in order to be a missionary, but in becoming a religious he had promised total obedience to his superiors. If they decided that he was to stay in Ireland as a teacher, that must be God's will for him. He could respectfully make his preferences known, but if they were set aside all he could do was swallow his disappointment and offer it up.

The keen-eyed Edward Leen was still at Rockwell, now in one of the senior classes. He watched Shanahan on the football field, in the classroom, on the rostrum in the study-hall. He noticed how everything he did was touched by his deep but unobtrusive spirituality. 'Instead of doing Aeschylus or Xenophon in Greek class, he insisted on translating Saint Luke's Gospel. He scorned the prevalent attitude that all non-classical Greek was barbarous. He explained to us that he wanted to Christianise as well as to teach.' Young Leen found himself set on fire by his enthusiasm and by the way he appealed to the idealism of his pupils rather than to their self-interest. But many of those who heard him were less responsive. 'I felt the shock it must be to one of his fine sensibility to be dealing with our earthiness.'[16]

Matters continued in this way for two years. In the summer of 1901 Shanahan attended the annual retreat in Blackrock and made his final vows in the college church, before the altar where he had been ordained a year before. Then he returned to Rockwell for another year's work, like a lion returning to his cage. It was to be the last year of his captivity.

Two incidents were to happen in that year which had a bearing on his future. One was the visit to Rockwell of Father Xavier Lichtenberger, a missionary from Southern Nigeria, who gave a lecture illustrated by lantern slides which made a deep impression on all who heard it. It must have reinforced Shanahan's commitment to the African mission and focused his attention on the place which was to be the scene of his future work. It is likely that it was this that led him to renew his appeals to his superiors and to volunteer specifically for Southern Nigeria.

The other incident was the affair of the Cork rugby match, which was to make him famous or infamous throughout the Congregation, according to one's point of view. Leen believed that it was this incident that brought his career in Rockwell to an end and opened the door to Africa for him at long last. Leen's own eye-witness description is the best account we have of what happened.

> The college rugby team, of which the dean of discipline had charge, had a fixture in February 1902 with a Cork team. The venue was in Cork itself. At that time the college team, in order to reach the south, had to make a long journey of fourteen miles by car to Limerick Junction. On this particular day the arrangements miscarried, and when the players arrived at Limerick Junction they found to their dismay that the train for Cork had left.
>
> There were no motor cars in those days and the situation seemed desperate. The match was an important one. The followers of the game in Cork looked forward to it with eagerness and large crowds were expected. A telegram announcing the impasse evoked a reply that was a cry of consternation. The station master on being consulted said the only possible course was to charter a special from Dublin, but of course that would involve considerable

> expense. With characteristic generosity of spirit, Father Shanahan said that honour was involved in fulfilling an important engagement and expense could not be allowed to weigh against that.
>
> The decision was taken. The wires were set going. The line was cleared. The driver, having nothing to handle but the engine, the tender, and a saloon carriage for the football team, made a record run from Dublin to the Junction and from the Junction to Cork. Prompt to time, the dean led his players on to the Mardyke field amidst roars of applause, for news of his splendid sportsmanship had reached the grounds.
>
> The Rockwell team won the match and Father Shanahan was overwhelmed with congratulations on the victory and the generous decision that prepared the way for it. The home authorities however did not share the enthusiasm of the sporting world. They were not to be blamed. The dean's fund, which had to meet the expenses of a special train, had received a set-back from which it did not recover for years.[17]

The incident was a pointer to the kind of man Shanahan had become. It showed a man who was ready to make a decision and take a lead, a man who kept his word and honoured his commitments. Above all, it showed a man who was not to be deterred by financial considerations. If a thing was worth doing, it should be done, whatever the expense. One need not be surprised at the suggestion that the college authorities did not altogether share this view. They may not have actually asked to have him transferred but they are not likely to have put up any great resistance if the idea was proposed. He was a luxury they could no longer afford.

In the summer of 1902, Shanahan received the news from the mother-house in Paris. It was the news he had been hoping and praying for. His period of schoolmastering was at an end. He was to go as a missionary to Southern Nigeria.

The months of August and September sped past in a flurry of preparations. There were travel arrangements to be made, clothes to be bought, farewells to be said. The last meeting with his parents must have been particularly emotional, as there was no certainty that he would ever see them again. But any natural sorrow was swallowed up in the great joy of being at last on the way to Africa.

On 9 October 1902 he and his travelling companions, Father McDermott and Brother Eusebius, were entertained to dinner in Clareville House beside Blackrock College, recently purchased as the headquarters of the Irish Province. Father Ebenrecht, the College chronicler, had been responsible for the financial expenses of the journey. He accompanied them to the North Wall in Dublin and saw them off on the 8.00 p.m. boat for Liverpool. It was a very rough crossing. Ebenrecht noted in the college journal: 'Next day the gale was awful in the extreme — the boys could not go outside for one minute.'[18]

3

Father Gaboon

On 13 November 1902 Shanahan reached his destination, a small settlement on the east bank of the river Niger. It was called Onitsha, a name that would be forever linked with his own.

The journey had been entirely by water. First the crossing from Dublin to Liverpool. Then the long voyage from England down the west coast of Africa to the mouth of the Niger. Finally the two hundred miles upstream in a local river steamer. In 1902 Southern Nigeria was without roads or railways. There were only two ways of getting about. One was by foot along the narrow paths that wound through the bush, the name given to the dense tropical trees and undergrowth that covered the country. The other was by boat along the Niger and its sister rivers.

The Niger is one of the great rivers of the world, more than 2,500 miles in length. In its last three hundred miles, after it has been joined by the river Benue, it expands to a mile and more in width. Then, as it approaches the sea, it fans out into dozens of smaller rivers and enters the Gulf of Guinea through a delta even larger than that of the Nile. The Niger was the highway which opened up a vast area to British explorers in the nineteenth century and led to the formation of the Royal Niger Company, a trading organisation which gradually took on more and more of the character of a colonial government.

As he made his way up river, Shanahan was retracing the journey of the first Catholic missionaries some seventeen years earlier. They were four Frenchmen, members of the Holy Ghost Congregation, two priests and two brothers. Their leader was a thirty-two-year-old Alsatian, Father Joseph Lutz. In the year 1885 they journeyed up the Niger and stopped at Onitsha because no-one was prepared to bring them any further. They were not the first missionaries to land there. The Church Missionary Society, affiliated to the Church of England, was already established in Onitsha under the leadership of Bishop Samuel Crowther. Despite his English name, Crowther was a Yoruba tribesman from the west bank of the Niger.

The King of Onitsha, sitting on a throne and wearing a golden crown, received Lutz graciously in audience. He would be happy to grant him a site on the river bank but for the fact that the area had already been given to Bishop Crowther. He suggested that since Crowther was not using the land he might be willing to let Lutz have it. Lutz went to see Crowther, who readily agreed. 'I received this land for the cause of God', he said magnanimously. 'Take it.'

Lutz took the land and on it he and his companions started to build the rough hut which was to be their first mission house. By this time all four of them were showing signs of sickness. One of the brothers was suffering from a particularly severe attack of malaria which refused to respond to treatment. Less than two months after his arrival in Nigeria he was dead.

It was a pattern that was to repeat itself with sad regularity during the years that followed. New missionaries continued to come from France and were carried off by malaria, dysentery, sleeping sickness, yellow fever or some other ailment within months of their arrival. A convent of French sisters belonging to the order of Saint Joseph of Cluny was founded in Onitsha in 1889 and they too suffered tragic losses. Lutz himself had to return to France through ill-health and died there in 1895 at the age of forty-two. His last job was teaching English in Merville, where he was replaced by Shanahan himself. His two successors as head of the mission lasted only four years between them.[1]

Then in 1900 the the redoubtable Father Léon Alexandre Lejeune was appointed superior of the mission and Prefect Apostolic of Southern Nigeria. He was a man of tremendous vigour and energy, a flamboyant and often controversial character who could be loved or hated but never ignored. This was the man who met Shanahan as he stepped on the wharf at Onitsha and who made such an instant and indelible impression upon him.

> I shall never forget my first meeting with him there on the banks of the lordly Niger. A massive, red-headed giant, with a flaming red beard covering half his chest, he was built on herculean lines. By birth he was a Norman, the blood of the Vikings ran in his veins, and certainly one needed no imagination to picture him at the head of a band of savage Norsemen. He welcomed me to Africa in a voice that thundered in my ears like the roar of a mighty cataract. 'Ho, ho! Just the man I want. Young and fresh and strong. Well, there's plenty to do here for a strong man, mon ami.'[2]

Shanahan at this stage had only the vaguest idea of what a missionary in Southern Nigeria was expected to do. He knew next to nothing about the country or its people, could not speak a word of their language. Unlike modern missionaries, he had received no specialised training to prepare him for the realities of life in his adopted country. He looked forward to beginning the work of preaching the word and administering the sacraments but that was not the work that Lejeune had in mind for him just then. What Lejeune needed was someone to help him make bricks for a new mission house, and that took priority over everything else for the moment. Shanahan was wise enough not to argue. 'That was Father Lejeune's way of looking at things,' he said, 'and he was not the man to argue with.'

Everyone was agreed that Lejeune was not a man to argue with. He was definite in his views and direct in his methods. He knew what he wanted and was determined to have his way. Those who were prepared to share his vision and work as hard as he did, found him an inspiring and charismatic leader. Those who differed from him complained that he was dictatorial in his manner and unwilling to listen to any opinion other than his own.

From the start, Lejeune was favourably impressed with Shanahan. The young newcomer was as strong and tall and broad as he was himself. He was willing to learn and willing to work. He spoke fluent French and English, which meant he could communicate equally well with the French missionaries and the English colonial officers. He took part in the back-breaking work of brick-making without complaint. He even showed signs of beginning to grow a beard. All in all, he seemed surprisingly normal for an Irishman. In the evenings, when darkness put an end to the building, the two men would talk, or rather one would talk and the other would listen. Gradually Shanahan began to get a grasp of the Nigerian mission situation and to see its strengths and weaknesses through Lejeune's eyes.

Lejeune had come to Nigeria at a turning point in its history, in the year when the territory was incorporated into the British Empire. He was already an experienced missionary, having spent fifteen successful years in the Equatorial African territory of Gaboon (now known as Gabon). By comparison, the Nigerian mission seemed to him a failure. There were only about thirteen hundred Catholics in the whole of Southern Nigeria after fifteen years of hard work and tragic sacrifice.

The first thing he questioned was their strategy of founding Christian villages. This was a traditional method used by French missionaries in Africa. These villages were intended to be settlements where new converts could live a full Christian life without interference from their pagan neighbours and build up a Christian presence in the country. In Nigeria, these villages had become places where the outcasts of society were taking refuge. There were former slaves, some of them runaways, others bought by the mission with funds collected in Europe, there were abandoned children and orphans, there were cripples and lepers and homeless old people, there were criminals and murderers, there were all those others who for one reason or another did not fit into the traditional tribal pattern. To look after such people and bring them the faith was undoubtedly a work of charity. But they were draining the small resources of the mission and they were hardly the kind of foundation on which a flourishing Church could ever be built. The rest of the people were beginning to look on their religion with contempt as something fit only for slaves and outcasts.

Another matter that gave Lejeune cause for concern was the living conditions of the missionaries. On arriving at Onitsha, he was shocked at the miserable huts in which they were housed, built with mud walls and red clay floors and thatched roofs which kept out neither rain nor sun. He saw the graveyard where so many of them lay buried under little wooden crosses after so short a time in the country. That same day he visited the convent and found that one of the sisters was seriously ill. Two days later she died. She was twenty-four years of age and had been two weeks in Nigeria.

Within weeks of his arrival, Lejeune called a meeting of the priests who were working as missionaries in his prefecture, Fathers Vogler, Bubendorff, Ritter and the two Lichtenberger brothers. All were Frenchmen, the German-sounding names due to the fact that they were natives of Alsace. In language which was forceful rather than diplomatic he told them that their methods were mistaken and their efforts misdirected. Changes would have to be made at once. The mission villages were no longer to be a refuge for the work-shy and the unwanted. No more motherless babies were to be accepted. No-one would be allowed to stay unless they were prepared to work. Lepers, cripples, old women, children, would all have to give whatever help they could to support themselves and the mission. More emphasis must be given to the work of education, the founding of schools, the training of teachers. The missionaries themselves must live in properly built houses, like those in Gaboon. It was the only way they could protect their health and put a stop to the tragic haemorrhage of young lives.

The reaction of the Fathers to this new approach was described by the Superior-General, Bishop Le Roy.

> It was a rude awakening. There on the placid banks of the Niger, people were not used to such activity, such toil, such sudden decisions, such flurry, such commotion. The nickname Gaboon was given to the new prefect, who so often invoked the scene of his first apostolate, and it was soon on everyone's lips but not in everyone's hearts. This opposition was a source of pain to Father Lejeune but it did not stop him from carrying out his reforms, which perhaps needed to be done, but with more method, more calm and more forethought.[3]

Father Gaboon, as they were now beginning to call him, lost no time in translating his plans into action. He investigated the building situation and found that there was little stone available in the locality. The only materials to be had were wood and corrugated iron. There was, however, an abundance of red clay which could be turned into bricks and so the building programme was started, with Lejeune himself doing the lion's share of the work. The inhabitants of the mission village and the pupils in the school were pressed into service, the women carrying water from the river and the children collecting firewood for the ovens. Four Holy Ghost brothers from France trained the men in the skills of brick-making, brick-laying and carpentry. The foundations were laid and the walls of the first permanent mission buildings began to rise above ground level. By the beginning of 1902 Lejeune had completed a substantial convent for the nuns in Onitsha. Then he started on a house for the priests and brothers. He was working on this when Shanahan arrived and he immediately initiated him into the mysteries of the craft.

> If anyone wants to know how, let him visit a brick-making factory. It is hot work in Ireland. But Ireland is an ice-cream

> shop compared to Africa. We had plenty of red clay, of course. Nor was there much trouble constructing the huge galvanised ovens for burning the bricks when they were moulded by hand and dried. But stoking those immense fires under a roasting African sun and shovelling for hours and hours on end, while the perspiration fell in cupfuls, was an experience I shall always remember. Father Lejeune slaved like a Trojan — and expected me to keep pace with him. When we got dead beat, he would just plunge into the Niger, emerging a minute later apparently quite refreshed. Mosquitoes could come down upon us in thousands (and they did, there beside the river), blisters arise on face and arms and legs, the skin peels, the fingernails crack, but a Mission had to be opened up. That was what we had come to Africa for.[4]

The priests' house was finished early in 1903. It was a two-storey brick building, a hundred feet in length and thirty in width, with five rooms on each floor. There were wide doors and windows and spacious corridors to let air circulate freely through the building. Coincidence or not, the number of early deaths among the missionaries fell after the completion of the new houses in Onitsha and the other principal missions.

Shanahan was not left to enjoy the comforts of the new house for very long. Soon after its completion he received a change of appointment from the prefect. It was made with characteristic abruptness. 'There's a village called Ogboli two miles away. Go up and evangelise it! And listen. Don't waste time coming down here for dinner — I'll send it along to you. Your job is to evangelise. Nothing else. You can look after your teaching quarters yourself. Au revoir.' Shanahan went without a word.[5]

* * *

Shanahan spent a year-and-a-half in Ogboli. It was a formative period in his life, his first experience of missionary work. The people living in the area belonged to the Ibo tribe and the village was a typical Ibo village, unlike anything he had known in Ireland. There was no main street, indeed no streets at all. The houses were built of mud with roofs of thatch or matting and were scattered higgledy-piggledy among the trees and bushes. Some of them were in compounds surrounded by mud walls, others stood unprotected in the forest. Goats, sheep, pigs and chickens foraged everywhere among the vegetation. The houses seemed to be used only for sleeping and for shelter from the rain. Cooking, eating and all social events took place in the open air.

Ogboli was part of the conglomeration of villages called Onitsha Town, as distinct from the settlement on the river's edge which was called Onitsha Wharf or Onitsha Waterside. The people of the area were familiar with the sight of white men but, since they spoke no English and Shanahan spoke no Ibo, communication was difficult. He could not even ask for lodging. He poked around for a while and managed to find some material for a shelter, a few sheets of corrugated iron and half a dozen wooden stakes. From these he fashioned a primitive hut and retired there for the night with his few belongings. Something of the flavour of that first night in the bush is captured in Father John Jordan's description of night sounds in Nigeria.

> Punctually at about 8.00 p.m. the frogs began their raucous croaking, and after that every living thing felt a compulsive urge towards noise. Mosquitoes whirred and droned; huge beetles, big as bantam eggs, buzzed through the darkness at full throttle; tiny crickets squealed piercingly at high doh; monkeys barked from tree-tops; bats squeaked and chattered; lizards chased each other along the tops of the rest-house walls and down them, tumbled headlong into pot or pan or basin on the floor and thrashed about energetically before smashing a way out to begin all over again. Even humans, the lords of creation, sensed that night was not intended for deep and slumberous rest; the incessant throbbing of their drums kept time to the stamping of feet the whole night through, being varied at set intervals by the loud explosion of gun-powder and the piercing wail of the hunter's horn.[6]

The following day, he began to learn the language. He found the children easier to talk to than the adults. They were curious about this white man living among them in such primitive conditions and they soon got over their fear when they found he was as interested in them as they were in him. Bit by bit he learnt simple Ibo words and phrases and in return he taught them a smattering of English. It was time to start a school.

He got some slates and pencils from Lejeune and the youngsters helped him to rig up a mud hut as a schoolhouse. Fifteen boys between the ages of six and twelve turned up for the first day's lessons. All of them were naked so he cut up some old sheets from the mission in Onitsha to provide them with trousers. Gradually the numbers increased until there was a sizeable group coming to the school and receiving religious instruction in preparation for baptism.

The adults were still a little wary of the newcomer. Then something happened which helped to break down the barriers. An outbreak of some disease of the spleen struck the village and infected many of the villagers, especially the children. Shanahan found himself giving spiritual and physical aid to the victims. He nursed them and fed them, he brought medicines and antidotes from the mission. He prayed with the sick and instructed them in the Catholic faith. He baptised many of them before they died. 'Ah, what a joy it was,' he wrote later, 'to give the highest of all lives, the Divine Life, to those poor outcasts!'

The crisis passed but the bonds that it had forged between Shanahan and the people remained. He had become part of their lives and their homes, someone who had shared their sorrows and brought light into their darkness. It was as if a door had suddenly opened. Increasingly fluent in Ibo, he spoke to them about God, the father of all the human race. He shared his faith with them and they shared theirs with him. Both he and they were surprised to find how much they had in common.

The Ibos, he discovered, were a deeply religious people. Like most casual observers, he had tended to dismiss their religion as a mass of superstitions, dominated by idols and maintained by witch-doctors. It was true that there was much that was cruel and evil in their beliefs. There were shrines to malevolent spirits in Iboland where human sacrifices were offered and children sold into slavery. There were strange taboos affecting many aspects of life, especially birth. Twins and breech birth babies were considered to be accursed and were abandoned in the forest to die of exposure or be eaten by wild beasts. All this was the repellent surface of Ibo belief. Beneath it lay something very different.

The Ibos saw the world as filled with the spirit. Each individual had his own chi, a personal guardian spirit who attended him from the cradle to the grave. This chi was represented by an Abosi stem planted in front of the house and consecrated by a *dibia* or priest. Villages and local communities also had their own guardian spirits and there were special spirits or gods of the rivers and streams. Above all these lesser gods and spirits was one supreme *chi* who was addressed by his attributes: *Chukwu,* the Great God, or *Chineke,* God the Creator, or *Obasi bi na igwe,* the God who lives in the heavens. Unlike the minor deities, Chukwu had no shrines or cult houses built in his honour.

There was a strict moral code among the Ibos and those who offended against it were required to repent and offer sacrifice. For lesser offences, a simple sacrifice could be offered by the offender. For graver offences, a more elaborate sacrifice was required and this could only be offered in a suitably ceremonious manner by the dibia. Sacrifices could also be offered for the souls of the dead to release them from their sins and give them peace. Otherwise their spirits would continue to roam around the world as restless and unhappy ghosts.[7]

Shanahan was struck by the similarities between their faith and his own. Their Chukwu was the same God whom he worshipped and preached. The other spirits were not unlike the angels and saints whose intercession he invoked, especially the guardian angel to whom he had a particular devotion. The sacrifices they offered through their priest for their own sins and the sins of the dead were a foreshadowing of the sacrifice of the Mass. The Ibo seemed to have an *anima naturaliter Christiana,* a naturally Christian soul.

He began to see his black neighbours in a new way, different from the way his fellow missionaries saw them. The French missionaries loved the people they preached to, they sacrificed themselves gladly for their sakes, but they could not get rid of a certain patronising attitude towards them. They spoke of them as the *chers noirs,* the dear blacks, lovable children who had to be guided with a firm hand for their own good. The French, like the British, saw themselves as a great colonial power whose God-given duty it was to rule the African and teach him the ways and the wisdom of the white man. It never even occurred to them that there could be anything of value in African culture or religion.

Shanahan's Irishness may have helped to give him a different perspective. He could see the other side of the colonial coin. The Irish were not the colonisers but the colonised. They knew what it was to have their language and traditions uprooted and their faith persecuted by well-meaning foreigners. It seemed to him that the religion of the Ibos was not something evil to be destroyed but something good to be purified and refined. As he came to know the people of Ogboli, to share their joys and sorrows, to learn about their faith and to teach them his, he found himself deeply touched by their humanity and their goodness. Many years later he described what his time in Ogboli taught him.

> It was a lesson for me for the rest of my days, and it showed me what I thank God everlastingly for having let me know, the innate goodness and attractiveness of the African soul. That soul aspires to God, to All Goodness, by some inborn tendency, and the missionary has but to foster the tendency. The African, once you understand and love him in Christ, is a treasury of goodness and lovableness. Only those who have lived with him, and spoken to him of God from the depths of their own souls, know that.[8]

While Shanahan was working away quietly in Ogboli, a short distance away in Onitsha the prefect apostolic was planning a major expansion of the mission. He had been bombarding Rome and Paris with requests for missionaries and money and had met with some success. He had been sent additional funds and a few more priests, brothers and sisters, including a third Irish priest, Father Ward.

Up to this, the Catholic missionaries had confined their activities to a small area around Onitsha. The main mission was in Onitsha itself, there was a second mission and Christian village at Aguleri, and a third rather struggling mission at Nsugbe. Lejeune now took the bold decision to found two new missions, one in the extreme south-east and the other in the extreme north-west of his prefecture. The southern town of Calabar was a cosmopolitan port with a mixture of races and tribes, and the mission there got off to a good start. Father McDermott, who had travelled from Ireland with Shanahan, was appointed its first superior and it soon had a church, a school and a convent.

Dekina in the north was a far bleaker prospect. It was populated mainly by Hausa tribesmen, most of whom were Muslim and hostile to Christianity. The elderly priest who was sent there, Father Joseph Lichtenberger, was unable to make any progress and Lejeune was advised to close the mission. He refused to listen to such defeatist talk. 'I will never surrender to Satan a single foot of land we have gained for Christ', was his response.

At the same time, he continued to develop the educational side of the mission. One of his priests wrote a catechism in the Ibo language, another produced an Ibo dictionary. He expanded the schools in Onitsha and employed a number of Ibo converts as teachers and catechists. Not all of these catechists were willing to work as hard as he expected and when he threatened to dismiss them a bitter dispute broke out. They organised protest marches in Onitsha carrying banners which said 'Lejeune must go' and 'Remove that whip'. They sent a letter to the Superior General in Paris asking for his removal: 'He is not a Father but a man who never has mercy even unto his dog and who always thinks he is right in everything he does.' The revolt was finally quelled but bad feeling remained even after peace had been restored.[9]

A bare two miles away, Shanahan was well aware of all that happened in Onitsha and was in frequent contact with the mission there. His relations with the volcanic Lejeune and with the other priests seem to have been smooth enough on the whole, though a certain tension between the French and Irish viewpoints was inevitable. Brother Kevin Healy, who came to Nigeria in 1907, claimed that the French missionaries were jealous of the Irishman and deliberately kept him in the bush to minimise his influence, but the evidence for this is not conclusive.[10] It is certain that he and Lejeune never lost their high regard for one another, despite the occasional clash of temperament.

Lejeune's visits to Ogboli were enjoyed by both men, and were looked forward to by the schoolchildren, who called him Grandpa. He always brought them gifts, sometimes yams or fish or oil, sometimes colourful materials, shirts or caps. One such visit occurred on the Feast of the Immaculate Conception, 8 December 1903, and was described with great gusto by Lejeune in a letter to Paris.

The little chapel was newly painted for the occasion and the walls were covered with flowers and banners. Lejeune was celebrant of the High Mass which he sang in what he called his 'big feastday voice'. Shanahan preached the sermon, with an interpreter translating it into Ibo. Among the congregation were

266 of his schoolchildren, all on their best behaviour, listening intently to the sermon, singing very sweetly the hymns to Our Lady.

Prominent in the front row was King Sami, the King of Onitsha, who had become a Catholic some ten years earlier. He displayed his authority during the sermon by stopping the interpreter whenever he made a wrong translation, which happened rather often. When the Mass was over, the King invited the children to his compound and spoke to them about the value of their souls and the need to convert their pagan town. He then provided refreshments in the form of palm wine for the Fathers, Sisters and older children. The 266 children sang *God Save the King* to honour not the far-off King of England but their own King of Onitsha.

The best was yet to come. On the way home, the missionaries ran into a rival pagan festival. Five or six men wearing grotesque masks were at the centre and around them a crowd of two or three thousand men and women, painted from head to foot, were gyrating in a frenzied and abandoned dance. This was the kind of challenge Lejeune could not resist.

> Resolutely I pushed my way through the crowd until I reached the masked men, who fled before me. Then I shouted, 'Those who want to serve God and renounce the Devil, follow me!' I was followed by about seventy children and we made our way home, Father Shanahan and myself, delighted with the way we had celebrated the feast of the Blessed Virgin Mary and put the Devil to flight. The Sisters, who were slightly nervous, went home by a short cut.[11]

A more serious incident occurred one Saint Patrick's Day. Shanahan came to Onitsha Wharf to celebrate a feast that meant much to him and little to anybody else. He was wearing his best white soutane and pinned to his chest he had a sprig of genuine shamrock sent by his mother all the way from Templederry. The lack of interest shown by his confrères, combined perhaps with other incidents in the past, seems to have nettled him. By the time they came together for their evening meal his Irish temper was rising. During the meal the conversation turned to the shamrock. One of the Frenchmen made a slighting remark about the way Saint Patrick had used it to explain the doctrine of the

Trinity and it was this remark that finally caused him to lose control. He jumped to his feet and for a moment looked as if he was about to overturn the table. Then he turned abruptly and left the room, trembling with rage.

Lejeune followed him into the night and tried to pacify him, but in vain. 'Insult me? Yes, by all means! Insult my country? Perhaps! But insult Saint Patrick? Never! Never, mon père, never!' Then he strode off into the bush, after telling Lejeune that he would never set foot in the mission house again and that he intended to return to Ireland on the next boat.

Back in Ogboli that night he found it hard to sleep. Thoughts of Saint Patrick kept running through his mind. He remembered how Patrick had spent six years herding pigs as a captive in Ireland before escaping home. He remembered how the saint had returned again after he heard the Irish people in a dream begging him to come and walk once more among them. Eventually he fell into an uneasy sleep and began to dream himself. He dreamt that he was back in Ireland and that his father and mother were lamenting the fact that their son had turned his back on the people of Africa who were crying out for the faith.

Suddenly he was jolted out of his sleep by an ear-splitting mixture of crashes and squeals that filled the little house. A wild pig had broken in and was now trying to break out again. He rose and got rid of the visitor and then went down on his knees and began to pray. He felt that the pig had been sent to remind him of Patrick returning to the land where he had once herded pigs in slavery. He thanked God for saving him from the shame of becoming a deserter and he promised that he would never let anything come between him and Africa again.

Next morning he appeared at the Onitsha mission house in chastened and repentant mood. He found an understanding Lejeune waiting for him. 'I prayed for you, mon enfant, that your faith would not fail. After all, what would have happened to your country if the glorious Saint Patrick had gone out waving the white flag of surrender instead of explaining the beautiful shamrock?'[12]

The reconciliation was complete and it left their relationship stronger rather than weaker. The two men had more in common than either of them realised. There was the same combination of strength and sensitivity, the same vulnerability, the same steely purpose, the same total dedication to the cause, the same ardent temperament so hard to control. There was a greatness of soul in each that the other could respond to. Thirty years later Shanahan could still say, 'I cannot talk of him without tears.'

* * *

By the summer of 1904 the mission at Ogboli boasted three permanent buildings, a combined chapel and school, a priest's house and a catechist's house. In a report prepared for the mother-house, Shanahan expressed the hope that a second priest might be sent there. 'It is so good to live in community, especially in Africa!' He was making good progress with the children but had not as yet succeeded in converting any of their parents. 'They want to live the same way as their ancestors in this world so that they can join them in the next.' He saw the school as the principal work of the mission. 'On it is based the hope for the future.'[13]

It was at this point that Lejeune made one of his characteristically unexpected visits to Shanahan. 'You've got to get out of here,' he told him, 'and strike out for Dekina. Follow the river for the first 160 miles. Then there's a well-defined bush path which will bring you to Dekina. It's only forty miles from your landing place. Poor Father Joseph is up there by himself and he's nearly done in. You must help him.'[14]

In the past year things had gone from bad to worse at Dekina. The people of the area were resisting attempts by Britain to subdue them and to put an end to their profitable slave trade. In December 1903 a troop led by an Irishman, Captain O'Riordan, was attacked and massacred. Father Joseph Lichtenberger said the prayers at the burial of what was left of the Captain after his body had been cooked and eaten by his killers. Then in January 1904 the bush surrounding Dekina was set on fire and the whole town, mission and all, was burnt to the ground. Lichtenberger lost everything he had, including his shoes, and arrived at Onitsha in his slippers. But by mid-March he was back again in Dekina trying to rebuild the mission and was joined in April by a young French priest, Paul Herry.[15]

It was clear to Lejeune that Lichtenberger was in urgent need of a rest and so he decided to replace him with Shanahan. It was beyond doubt the least desirable appointment in the prefecture and there were those who regarded it as yet another sign of anti-

Irish feeling. On the other hand, it could equally well have been interpreted as a vote of confidence. Rightly or wrongly — and many people thought wrongly — Lejeune was determined to maintain the mission at Dekina. He may have seen in Shanahan the one man who could save what seemed to be a hopeless situation.

In Onitsha Shanahan prepared what he called his trousseau. The principal item was a Mass kit, a case containing chalice, paten, missal, vestments and other requirements for saying Mass. He had a hammock which cost half-a-crown, some articles of clothing and a few personal belongings, including his novitiate notebook from Chevilly. A canoe manned by native paddlers was waiting at the wharf. He loaded his luggage into the canoe, took his seat and set off on the long journey upstream to his new post.

It was a week later when he arrived at Dekina, cramped from the boat, burnt from the sun, stiff and footsore from the final slog overland, and ravenously hungry. From the very beginning, the place lived up to its unhappy reputation. He described Father Lichtenberger as 'a physical wreck' and the temporary mission house as 'a lean-to structure of the most primitive type'. Even Father Herry, aged twenty-eight, was far from well. The overall impression could hardly have been worse. 'Ogboli had looked a pretty barbarous place when I first visited it. But it was heaven compared with Dekina.'

He arrived hungry in Dekina and remained hungry during all his time there. The mission had a double-barrelled shotgun and sometimes he had the good fortune to shoot a guinea-hen or a partridge. If he shot two, one was hung on a nail in an old cotton tree for future use. If he shot none, he fasted. He was not surprised when Lichtenberger returned to Onitsha. His only surprise was that the brave old man had held out so long.

The two young men managed to rebuild the mission with the help of the local king, a Muslim who was probably acting under pressure from the British authorities. It was far from elaborate, consisting basically of two circular mud huts. They had no servants and had to wash, cook, sweep and fetch water for themselves. They spent each morning with spade and machete, trying to clear the bush around the mission. After the midday meal, cooked by themselves, they studied the local languages, Hausa and Okpoto. Around three o'clock, when the heat of the day was subsiding, they returned to the work of clearing the bush until darkness forced them to stop.[16]

It was not the physical hardships, however, that Shanahan found most trying but the attitude of the local people. He had come to love the Ibos for their friendliness, their openness, their good humour. The Hausas by contrast were cold and distant. They were followers of Mohammed who looked upon the missionaries as infidels and refused them even the simplest courtesies. They had the same contempt for the Ibos and other southern tribes, whom they saw as inferior breeds fitted only for a life of slavery. In the Dekina market, Shanahan often saw slaves being sold for as little as a bowl of corn.

The High Commissioner of Northern Nigeria, Sir Frederick Lugard, wanted to use the mission in Dekina as part of his plan to pacify the north and stamp out the slave trade. He promised to send young slaves whom he had liberated to the mission to be educated and brought up as Christians. In the event only fifteen arrived and from these Shanahan formed a small community, the only island of Christianity in this vast sea of Islam. These slaves were to follow him to the south and some of them proved very faithful. He names three of them, Peter, Paul and Tom, as having taken part in the building of Onitsha cathedral thirty years later.

One day early in 1905 a visitor arrived unexpectedly at the lonely mission. He was in the last stages of exhaustion, his feet bleeding from the rough travel, his clothes soiled and torn. It was Lejeune. He had come to say goodbye.

His story was soon told. He had been unwell for some time and it had now been discovered that he was suffering from cancer of the throat. He had little hope of recovery. The only slim chance was an operation for which he would have to return to France. He believed he would never see Africa again.

They tried to console him as men do by talking of the wonders of modern medicine and the likelihood of a complete recovery, but he refused to be consoled. 'No, no, I shall never come back. I am going to die. Would to heaven the Superior General had left me here to die in Africa. However, it is God's holy will. I do not complain.'

After their evening meal, the three men sat outside their hut in the moonlight and talked late into the night. The imminence of death is often a constraint on conversation. This time it was a liberation. They talked about their hopes and dreams for the faith in Africa, the one looking back in pride and regret, the others looking forward in hope. Finally Lejeune stood up and said, 'And now, my friends, before I say goodbye to you I shall say goodbye to Africa.' He threw back his head and in his great voice sang the *Salve Regina,* Hail, Holy Queen, the old hymn in honour of Mary, Queen of Heaven. It was a typically flamboyant, even theatrical gesture, but so much part of the man that it was almost unbearably moving. Then he turned to his companions. 'Goodbye, my dear friends. Au revoir au ciel. We shall meet in heaven.'

The following morning he left Dekina on the long trek back to Onitsha. It seemed almost incredible to Shanahan that a dying man should have undertaken that long and arduous journey merely to say goodbye to two fellow priests. 'To me he has always been the picture of the perfectly dauntless soldier of Christ, the ideal missionary — big and gruff of voice, but with a heart of gold and the straightforwardness of a child, utterly fearless, a giant in soul as in body.'[17]

Thoughts of death were still in Shanahan's mind when he made an entry in his notebook on 18 May 1905.

> By chance this little notebook has come into my hands for the third time during this my third year in Africa. Now I am in Dekina, Northern Nigeria. God grant me courage, patience, unlimited confidence in Divine Providence, the true spirit of prayer and charity, to be able to do my work and never forget asking from Heaven the necessary help to perform my duties. Grant me also, O my God, a spirit of true repentance for my sins; may I never forget that I have offended and have consequently to do penance. There's no day so long that has not a night. Death and eternity are the nights which any day may come to blot out for ever the sun of life.

A letter came from Lejeune to say that he had arrived back safely in Europe. He was as full as ever of missionary zeal and more hopeful than before about recovering from his illness. But the letter had passed through the hands of the Superior General, who wrote at the foot: 'Poor Father Lejeune is dying, though he does not think so. Pray hard for him. There is no hope.' The operation had been unsuccessful and the cancer was spreading through his giant frame.

Some time during those last months he changed his mind about Dekina and decided to close the mission, after discussion with the Superior General. When the news reached the beleaguered missionaries, their feelings were mixed. In spite of all the frustration, there was a sense of sadness at leaving the scene of so much labour. At the top of the hill outside Dekina, they turned back for a last look and a last goodbye. During the long hours of walking that followed, neither of them spoke a word.[18]

Shanahan's new appointment was to Nsugbe. It was the least successful of the Ibo missions. The villagers were very attached to their local ju-ju or idol, which was credited with great powers and was visited by people from all the surrounding countryside. In trying to build a school, Shanahan got the children to clear an area of bush. He did not realise that it was 'bad bush', part of the spirit-haunted bush that surrounded the ju-ju's shrine and was not supposed to be touched. As a result, the villagers boycotted the school and refused to allow their children to go there.[19]

While he was struggling with this problem, the news arrived of Lejeune's death. In his last days he suffered greatly but his courage never left him. To those by his bedside he said, 'I'm only getting what I deserve. I was hard on others. I didn't want to see how they were suffering. It's only fair I should have to suffer in my turn.' Then he managed a smile and added, 'All the same, I wasn't wrong all the time.' He died in Chevilly on 5 September 1905, aged forty-five.[20]

On 4 October a solemn requiem Mass was celebrated in Onitsha for the repose of his soul. The celebrant was Father McDermott, Father Shanahan was the deacon, Father Douvry the subdeacon. After the ceremony there was much talk among the priests about the late prefect, his achievements, his failures. Human nature being what it is, there was also much talk and speculation about who would be appointed as his successor. A priest or even a bishop might be brought in from outside, as Lejeune himself had been brought in. Or a priest from Nigeria might be selected, someone familiar with local needs and problems. Father Vogler, who had been placed in temporary charge of the prefecture after Lejeune left for Europe, was an obvious candidate.

Unknown to them, the appointment had already been made.

It was the duty of the Superior General, Bishop Le Roy, to send the names of three suitable candidates to the Congregation for the Propagation of the Faith in Rome. The three men he recommended were all priests working in Southern Nigeria, Joseph Shanahan, Louis-Joseph Léna and Charles Vogler. All three, he wrote, were excellent missionaries but the one he believed most fitted for the position was Shanahan. It is thought that the reason for the unexpected choice of Shanahan was that he had been strongly recommended by the dying Lejeune. Cardinal Gotti of Propaganda accepted the nomination and on 26 September 1905 the decree was issued formally appointing Joseph Shanahan to be Prefect Apostolic of Southern Nigeria.[21]

It is at this point that history must for a moment give way to legend. The source once again is Brother Kevin Healy. According to his account, Shanahan was in Dekina when the official letter of appointment reached him. Nobody else in Nigeria knew that the appointment had been made. As soon as he received the letter, he closed down the mission in Dekina and left for Onitsha. On the way, he passed through the struggling mission at Nsugbe. He closed that down too and took the priest with him. Arriving at Onitsha, he was met by the acting prefect, Father Vogler, who asked him who had given him permission to leave his station. He answered that he now needed only his own permission, and that he had not only left Dekina but had closed it down and Nsugbe as well. The news was greeted with consternation and astonishment. Even the two Irish priests, Fathers McDermott and Ward, demanded to see his credentials before they would believe he was really their new prefect.[22]

It is a splendid story but unfortunately it does not square with the historical facts. Brother Kevin did not come to Nigeria until two years later and when he finally recorded the tale it was forty years after the event. It is of interest not as history but as a witness to a tradition. He was not telling what happened but what in the view of himself and the other Irish missionaries ought to have happened. It is a fairy story told by an oppressed race who suddenly see the light of liberation. The true Irish king returns from banishment and enters into his rightful inheritance. The wicked French are confounded and put to shame. It is not true but it is still a splendid story.

4

Schools, schools

The new Prefect Apostolic of Southern Nigeria was responsible for an area more than twice the size of Ireland. The prefecture was bounded on the west by the Niger river, on the north by its tributary the Benue, on the east by the mountains of the Cameroons, on the south by the sea. No census of its population had ever been attempted but it was estimated to be anything between eight and ten million.

As prefect apostolic he was entitled to be called Monsignor Shanahan but the title was rarely used. To the Europeans he remained Father Shanahan. To the Ibos he was Father Onyisi, Father Chief, the Great Priest. The title was a tribute not only to his ecclesiastical standing. It was a mark of their respect for his personal stature, physical and moral, which they came to recognise more and more with the passing of the years.

In mission territories, where the Church was only in its infancy, it was customary to appoint a prefect apostolic rather than a bishop as superior. The prefect apostolic had the same authority as a bishop in regard to appointment of priests, setting up of parishes, administration of property and so forth. He was also empowered to administer the sacrament of confirmation, normally the function of a bishop. He did not however receive episcopal orders and therefore could not ordain priests. When the Church had developed stronger roots, the next step was to appoint a vicar apostolic, who was ordained a bishop, but the territory was called a vicariate rather than a diocese. The third and final stage, when the Church was firmly established, was the setting up of a local hierarchy with bishops and dioceses. Shortly before his death, Lejeune recommended that Southern Nigeria should be raised from a prefecture to a vicariate, with a bishop in charge. His recommendation was not adopted until 1920.

One of Shanahan's first acts on arriving in Onitsha was to write a letter acknowledging his appointment to the Superior General. It was dated 13 November 1905.

> Never did such unexpected news reach the Lower Niger as that of the nomination of the present Prefect Apostolic. We all expected a Bishop, one endowed with the vigorous

> qualities necessary to continue and complete the work so well begun by poor Father Lejeune, so deeply regretted. This seemed all the more necessary since our ranks have been so cruelly decimated this year by sickness and death. Someone to replace the heroes would be necessary! In choosing me, the good God has wished to remind us that He alone is All; man, the instrument he uses, nothing.
>
> Nevertheless, as always may your Will be done, my God, mine never! Thank you, My Lord, for your words, so encouraging and so affectionate. Thank you for the trust you have shown me, in appointing me to this post, the most difficult, the most dangerous, in this terrible field of battle on the banks of the Niger. I think you can count on all of us here to continue courageously the work of God in these regions.[1]

His reference to difficulties and dangers was no exaggeration. With the closing of Dekina and Nsugbe, there were just two centres of Catholic missionary activity in all that huge area. Onitsha and Aguleri, with their out-stations, formed one centre on the banks of the Niger. Calabar, two hundred miles away at the mouth of the Cross River, was the other. The vast interior of Iboland, with its uncounted millions living in the dense and unexplored forest, was quite untouched. To evangelise these teeming multitudes Shanahan had twelve priests, including himself, nine brothers, and ten sisters.

As he thought and prayed about the situation, he came to a conclusion very similar to Lejeune's. The traditional missionary method of grouping the converts into Christian villages was not acceptable to the Ibos. They were a closely-knit people who did not want to leave their own communities and live under the rather regimented conditions of a mission village. But they were also an industrious and enterprising people, intellectually curious, anxious to better themselves. The offer of education was one that could make a powerful appeal to them. His own experience of the school in Ogboli had shown him how quick they were to avail of a school when it was offered. The more he considered the matter, the more convinced he was that the school was the key to the conversion of the Ibos.

Ogboli had taught him something else, that the Ibos were unusually open to the Christian message. His resources were few and it was essential to deploy them where they could do the most good. There would be no more experiments like Dekina, no more gallant outposts flying the flag just for the sake of flying the flag. Unlike Lejeune, he tempered idealism with realism. He was prepared to retreat on one front in order to advance on another. The new front was to be the uncharted bush of Iboland.

Speaking later about his decision, he compared it to the missionary technique used by Patrick in the conversion of Ireland.

> Suddenly the vision of my native land came before me, and I saw how akin Patrick's problem was to mine. He had a country peopled by a wild pagan tribe. So had I. He had one great river and a few smaller ones for communications. So had I. But he did not content himself with trying to convert a few towns along the Shannon as I was doing on the Niger. He struck boldly into the heart of the country to bring home the mystery of the Holy Trinity to all and sundry. He prepared the land for the coming of Catholic schools. I resolved to do the same.[2]

He called a meeting of the priests in Onitsha and unveiled his plans. Again, the contrast with Lejeune was noticeable. He had the same determination and drive, but he tried to work by persuasion rather than by command. He was beginning to master those faults of character which had so worried him earlier. He was more willing to listen to others and respect their views. He was less sensitive to slights and criticism, perhaps a sign of growing self-confidence. His temper could still blaze out but not as often as before and he knew how to prevent a passing difference from becoming a permanent rift.

His very appearance had changed. Photographs taken at this time show a different Shanahan, a man of gentle authority rather than a rebellious youth. The most obvious change was the addition of a beard. French missionaries of the time always wore beards and they had come to regard it as a sign of the missionary vocation. Shanahan wisely followed the French rather than the Irish tradition and grew a full beard, which he kept carefully trimmed and tended for the rest of his life. It masked the formidable Shanahan jaw and softened his whole appearance. Combined with his broad shoulders and his tall erect bearing, it made him an undeniably impressive figure. At the age of only thirty-four, he was already beginning to take on the aspect of a benevolent patriarch.

It was not a simple matter to convince the missionaries that a change of approach was needed. In the past, schools had played a very minor role in the work of evangelisation, as a small part of the services provided in the Christian village. Now the tail was to wag the dog. The Christian village concept was to be phased out and the whole thrust of missionary effort was to be put into the building and running of schools. The French priests were especially hard to persuade, with their attachment to tradition and their unhappy memories of the way the schools of France had been used to undermine religious belief and practice.

Shanahan was content to make his point without unduly pressing the issue. He concentrated on the challenge and the opportunity that awaited them in the unexplored forests of the Ibo heartland. He told them that they were only touching the tattered fringes by preaching to the mixed tribes along the waterways. A whole world was waiting to be conquered, a whole people to be won for Christ. He touched their French hearts by invoking the name of Joan of Arc, who had pressed on into enemy territory and won victory after victory in the face of overwhelming odds. His enthusiasm was real and it set fire to theirs, many of them as young if not younger than himself. 'Vers la brousse!' he urged them. 'To the bush!'[3]

He would have been happy to lead the first expedition into the interior but he had received notice to attend the General Chapter of the Holy Ghost Congregation in Europe. The honour of being the pioneer fell to an ardent young French priest, Father Victor Duhazé, not long arrived in Nigeria and now stationed in Onitsha. He was appointed to make the first foray into the Ibo hinterland and bring back reports of the situation. His journey was to be filled with incidents, many of them described in his diary.

Duhazé set off in early March 1906 and went south down the Niger for about forty miles. Then he branched off eastwards along a tributary which brought him to the large town of Oguta. The chief received him kindly and expressed interest in having a school built for his people. Next he headed north on foot for Uli, whose people were at war with the people of Oguta. From Uli he continued on to the borders of Ihiala, which was also at war with Uli.

> Just as we were nearing a tie-tie bridge over a river, we were ambushed by a crowd of Ihiala warriors, armed with guns and knives. They jumped up from the grass on the opposite side, shouting their war-cries. My unarmed carriers dropped their loads and fled. Fortunately I was able to get on to the bridge first and halt the Ihialas, who were shouting for battle and pointing their guns at some of the carriers that had been slightly in advance of the main party, and were down in the river washing. They were all set for battle when my appearance on the bridge disconcerted them. I took advantage of that and raised my hand for silence. I demanded the leaders. They came. It took time to persuade them to give up their bloodthirsty intentions but they ultimately agreed. Afterwards they became quite pleasant, took charge of my loads, and promised to put two schools in their town.
>
> On my way out of Ihiala a terrific tornado broke overhead and I had to fly for shelter to the nearest roof. It happened to be that of the town ju-ju, an old carved figure blackened by smoke and age. The roof was good, though, and as torrential rain continued to pour down until darkness fell, I lay down beside the ju-ju and slept there for the night.[4]

He arrived back in Onitsha on Holy Thursday, 4 April, exhausted but elated. In spite of the dangers and difficulties, he was satisfied that there was a real desire for mission schools among the people he had met and that this offered the missionaries an ideal opportunity. 'We must put three or four schools into that area right away,' was his recommendation.

* * *

By this time Shanahan had already left Onitsha on his way to Europe. According to their constitutions, the Congregation of the Holy Ghost held a General Chapter every ten years. Superiors of all the provinces and missions throughout the world were summoned to Chevilly to elect a new Superior General and to review the affairs of the congregation. The opening was set for 22 July 1906.

Shanahan brought with him Father Paul Herry, his young companion from Dekina, whose health was giving serious cause for concern. The hope that a spell in Europe would restore him proved vain; he died in France the following year at the age of thirty. The ship stopped at Freetown, the port of Sierra Leone, and here Shanahan was joined by John O'Gorman, his old friend from the years in Langonnet and Chevilly. O'Gorman, who was now Vicar Apostolic of Sierra Leone, was also heading for the Chapter. The voyage was not a pleasant one. The ship was barely seaworthy and Shanahan suffered a good deal from seasickness. He was relieved when they finally docked at Liverpool on the morning of 16 May.

He crossed to Dublin the same day and stayed the night at Clareville, the provincial headquarters beside Blackrock College. He had two reasons for visiting Ireland. One was naturally to see his family and particularly his parents in Templederry, both of whom were still alive though growing old. The other was to recruit more missionaries for the prefecture of Southern Nigeria. He found plenty of priests and brothers in the Holy Ghost Congregation who were as anxious to go to Africa as he himself had been four years earlier, but their superiors were not prepared to release them. Not for the first time, he questioned why a Congregation founded for the African missions should keep so many of its best men schoolmastering in Europe. He had hoped to bring back reinforcements with him to Onitsha but it now began to look as if he must return empty-handed. It left him with a feeling of deep frustration, which was to be repeated many times in the years to come.

He decided to go to Rome with O'Gorman and see if he could break the impasse by getting a letter of recommendation from Cardinal Gotti or some other member of the Curia.[5] Before leaving Ireland, he had the pleasure of meeting the man who had ordained him, Bishop Allgeyer, who was revisiting his old school before going to the Chapter. Old Father Ebenrecht, who had organised the ordination ceremony six years earlier, was still in Blackrock College and he arranged a celebration dinner to mark the reunion. Some instinct told him that this was a historic moment so he got a professional photographer to take a photograph of the three men, Allgeyer, O'Gorman and Shanahan, in the college grounds.[6]

On 8 June Shanahan and O'Gorman left for Rome. A week later he was staying in the Holy Ghost College in Susa in the Italian Alps, renewing old memories. At this time many of the Catholic colleges in France had been closed down by the anti-clerical government and had relocated themselves across the border. The college in Susa was the descendant of the college in Beauvais where he had spent his first years in France. The large statue of Saint Joseph, patron saint of the college and his own patron, had accompanied the college to its new home. He sent postcards showing the statue and the college to his father and mother and to his brother Dick. The one to his father read:

> It was at the foot of this statue of Saint Joseph that I said my first prayers in France 21 years ago, prayers in which your name and Mother's were surely mentioned. The French persecution has driven Saint Joseph from France. Fancy my delight to see the good Saint once again here in the very heart of the Italian Alps. Needless to say, your name with Mother's, not forgetting Bridgie, Dan and all the absent ones, were once more mentioned in prayer before the Venerable Saint. May his blessing and protection ever be with you all.
>
> On Monday I am going to Rome. Don't forget me in the Rosary. I want to obtain very special assistance, that humanly speaking I won't get — but if you pray hard to Saint Joseph I am sure all my wishes will be realised, but more so as they are for all those I love at home and for those other ones equally dear, away in distant Africa.[7]

His visit to Rome did not prove very fruitful. He was welcomed by the Holy Ghost community in the city and made the pilgrim's round of the basilicas, churches and other monuments. He visited the officials of the Congregation of the Propagation of the Faith, which dealt with mission territories. He was received in private audience by Pope Pius X. Everywhere he was given support and encouragement but no men. No-one had any to give.

By mid-July he was in Chevilly for the retreat in preparation for the General Chapter. The Chapter itself opened on Sunday 22 July with a High Mass and an address by the outgoing Superior

General, Bishop Alexandre Le Roy. There were forty-nine delegates in attendance from many different parts of Europe, Africa and America. The first business was the election of a Superior General and Council, which resulted in Le Roy's re-election for a second ten-year term. Then four commissions were set up to examine the affairs of the congregation under four headings: Constitutions, Houses of Formation, Missions, Finances. Delegates were free to attend whichever commission they chose.

The Chapter ended on 9 August after two-and-a-half weeks of work. The decisions were approved for publication and circulation among the members of the Congregation. No record was published of the discussions but it can be safely assumed that Shanahan's main interest was in the life and work of the missionary. The Chapter's resolutions in this area spoke of the need for self-control and discipline in the missionary's life. The importance of spiritual direction and of visits from the mission superior were stressed. There were warnings against the dangers of alcohol and tobacco and it was ruled that no member of the Congregation should keep alcohol in his house. It is clear from the context, however, that these mainly French-speaking delegates did not consider wine to come under the heading of alcohol.

Some of the observations on the training of missionaries seem to bear Shanahan's hallmark. Many young missionaries were arriving with scarcely any knowledge of the art of teaching and religious instruction; they should be given training in this as part of their theology course. It was emphasised that a young missionary's first years on the mission were a kind of 'practical novitiate'. His first appointment should be in a place where he could learn missionary methods under competent guidance. It should also be a place where he could learn the local language. Experience showed that a missionary either learned the language when he first arrived or not at all.

The relationship that missionaries built up with the local people was important and for that reason they should be moved around as little as possible. In spite of past failures and disappointments, vocations among the native population were to be fostered. Missionaries should show catechists and other likely candidates encouragement and respect.

The sentence that probably gave him the most satisfaction

occurred towards the beginning of the document. 'The missions, and the mission to abandoned souls, are the goal to which all our efforts are directed; this is what gives our Congregation its seal of unity.'[8] This was something of which he was totally convinced. He was not so sure if all the others gave the same primacy to the missions.

Back in Ireland, he made preparations for his return to Nigeria. His old friend Father Ebenrecht was hard at work collecting vestments and other useful articles for him, some of them new, some of them begged from local convents. Despite all his hopes and efforts, only one new missionary, Brother Osmund Healy, was to accompany him from Ireland. It seemed a pathetically meagre harvest. On the evening of 17 October 1906 he and Brother Osmund left the North Wall for Liverpool, where the boat to Africa awaited them. Father Ebenrecht was among the group waving farewell on the quayside.[9]

* * *

Shanahan landed in Calabar about 12 November. He was not familiar with the town or the mission so he thought it worth his while to spend a couple of weeks there. The seat of government was being moved to the new capital, Lagos, in Western Nigeria, but Calabar was still an important administrative and commercial centre.

He found that education was the topic on everyone's mind. 'It's all the rage', he wrote. 'You hear them talking about nothing but schools, schools, everywhere you go.'[10] The colonial administration was investing substantial sums of money in education and this posed a problem as well as an opportunity. The government was supporting mission schools by paying a subsidy for each pupil who passed the state examinations. But at the same time it was planning to set up twenty-five 'neutral' schools which would not be affiliated to any church. There was also a growth in the number of schools being started by Protestant bodies such as the Church Missionary Society, the Methodists, the Wesleyans, the Presbyterians, the Anabaptists, the Native Pastorate, and others. The Catholic Church could find itself left behind if it did not act quickly and decisively.

The Catholic school in the town of Calabar was flourishing but little was being done in the surrounding areas. One school had been started on the other side of the estuary, which could be reached only after seven hours in a canoe. Many other requests for schools from chiefs and parents had to be turned down for lack of teachers.[11]

He was back at Onitsha in early December. He always liked to be in Ogboli, his first mission, on 8 December, since the mission was dedicated to the Immaculate Conception. The warmth of the welcome that met him there was almost overwhelming. Large arches of flowers and palms spanned his approach to the mission and the school entrance was topped with bundles of wild flowers arranged to form his initials, J.S. The grandly named Saint Gregory's Choral Society, which he had founded to counter the Protestant choirs, came up from the Waterside and serenaded him with a concert of no fewer than twenty-six numbers. Among the songs were 'The Exile of Erin', 'The Minstrel Boy', and even 'Poor Old Joe'. His appointment as Prefect Apostolic a year earlier had been greeted with a slightly ungracious astonishment. Now was a chance for everyone, missionaries as well as people, to show their affection and esteem.

In the nine months he had been away, Onitsha Waterside and Town had changed and by no means for the better. In his report to the Mother-house in Paris, his first as Prefect Apostolic, he put the blame on the influx of Muslim traders from the north and Europeanised blacks from Lagos and Freetown.

> The Wharf, because of the government stores and workshops, is becoming more and more cosmopolitan. The Sons of the Prophet, previously excluded, are now invading the place. They are leather-workers, butchers, dyers, etc.; their little stalls have taken over the whole market. If all they were doing was selling their leather slippers and straw hats and baggy trousers, there would be no need to worry about them; but in addition to their clandestine traffic in human flesh, they are engaged in the most shameless depravities. This is something which cannot be tolerated.
>
> The other newcomers, the black gentlemen from the coast, are hardly any better. Whatever education they have received has puffed them up with pride. You would need to see the way they pass you by, with their shiny shoes and their fashionable suits and their insolent heads sticking up

> out of their enormous collars. Though nominally Protestant, they display the most mindless contempt for anything that has to do with religion.[12]

Shanahan was to return again to the subject of these gentlemen, referring to them always by the English word 'gentlemen' even though writing in French. His main quarrel was not with their aping of the latest European styles but with their godless attitude and their advocacy of the government's neutral schools.

The new year, 1907, was to see him begin the task that would occupy him for the next ten years, the exploration of the interior of Southern Nigeria. By the end of 1917 there was hardly a track he had not walked or hill he had not climbed or stream he had not crossed in all that vast territory. He did not go as an explorer, mapping mountains and tracing rivers to their sources. He did not go as an anthropologist, studying the life and customs of a strange and exotic people. He did not even go as an educationist, though the founding of schools and the teaching of knowledge was to be at the centre of his achievement. He went as a missionary, a man on fire with love for God and thirst for souls. Millions were living and dying in ignorance of the message of salvation. How could he stand idly by? How could anyone with any faith stand idly by? In that same report he wrote:

> Within a day's march of Onitsha, there are towns of from 10 to 20,000 inhabitants which are calling to us with loud cries. And to show how much they want us, these good people do not come looking for the missionary until they have built the school and dwelling-house. Then, when the priest comes, the children are always there waiting for him in their hundreds. The school is built, it is filled with children. What is the missionary to do? What we want is to make the countries of Europe understand that through their charitable help to the missionaries they will save thousands of these souls who are only waiting for the priest so that they can receive from his lips the words of truth, of salvation in Jesus Christ, and of everlasting life.
>
> The future of the mission depends on the number of missionaries who will come and dedicate themselves to it, and on the resources which Christian charity will send for their support and for the maintenance and development of

> their work. If no-one comes to the help of the Ibos, they will be the prey of heretics, of atheists, of Muslims. May the good God spare us the sadness of such a spectacle![13]

His words suggested that there was nothing to choose between Protestants, Muslims and atheists. Here he was only reflecting the opinions of his time. In his theology classes in France he had been taught that Protestants were simply heretics, and there was nothing in his Irish experience and background to soften that opinion. His unfavourable attitude towards them was normal for the period and was paralleled by their attitude towards Catholics. It was to be some time before he came to admire the zeal and commitment of missionaries of other churches.

The strategy he proposed was basically simple, though it had to be modified in different ways to suit different circumstances. It was founded on his considered belief that it was next to impossible to achieve large-scale conversions among the adults. Their minds were formed, their opinions were set. They were entangled in a web of family and tribal relationships that hindered any sudden change in their lifestyle. To take one instance, the chiefs and other men of influence usually had several wives. Conversion to Christianity meant sending away all but one of these wives.

There was no such problem among the children. Even the adults recognised this. They would say, 'We are too old to change but you may teach these things to our children.' Here at last was a foundation on which to build. If they would decide in favour of a school, if they would put up a suitable building, if they would provide a house for a teacher, if they would contribute towards his upkeep, if they would send their children faithfully and regularly, then the Church would begin to take root in that village. The teacher would impart the truths of the faith during the daily lessons. The priest would visit from time to time and use the schoolhouse as a church in which to say Mass. The children would be enrolled as catechumens, that is, candidates for baptism, if they so chose. At the end of their period of instruction, they would be examined in their knowledge of their faith and their commitment to it. Those who passed the examination would be baptised and the village would have its first Christians. Before long, they would marry and start their own families and form their own Christian community, their own parish around their own church and school and priest. It was so simple, so straightforward. But there were so many 'ifs'.

To put the strategy into effect, two separate campaigns had to be waged. One was the organisational campaign, to find young men willing to act as catechist-teachers, to give them the necessary training, and to support them when they took up their teaching positions. The other was the sales campaign, to tramp through the hundreds of towns and villages of the prefecture, selling the idea of the school. They were two different jobs that would seem to require two different people, an administrator and an explorer. But one man, Shanahan, was to do them both. He had the clear, organised mind of the administrator, but he could not be happy for long behind a desk. He could not close his ears to the call of the bush.

Perhaps it was a mistake. Perhaps he should have recognised that his role was to be the commander who sends his soldiers out on their assignments while remaining in headquarters himself. Had he done so, had he delegated more of the legwork to others, he might have conserved his energy and lengthened his active life. But it was not in his nature to be anywhere except the front line. For ten years he carried the double burden and, if he finally stumbled beneath the weight, he had accomplished more than he or anyone else had any right to expect.

At the beginning of 1907 the prefecture had four mission-stations with resident priests, Onitsha Waterside, Onitsha Town (Ogboli), Aguleri and Calabar. Dekina had been written off permanently, Nsugbe rather less permanently as it lay in Ibo territory. In and around the four main stations were a number of out-stations, visited from time to time by the missionaries. Between them, the stations and out-stations had a total of twenty-four schools catering for three thousand pupils. Some of the teaching was done by the missionaries, but the brunt of the work fell on the teacher-catechists, of whom there were thirty-three.

It was not easy to find these teachers or to train them or to pay them. Shanahan planned some day to found a teacher training college but at this stage he simply did not have the resources. Among his many problems was lack of money. The mission had an annual subvention from Rome, derived from collections for the foreign missions made in Europe and America. There was the additional income from fund-raising efforts made by the Holy Ghost Congregation and by the missionaries' families and friends in Ireland and France. A third source of income was the grant given by the colonial government for pupils who were successful in their exams; the grant for Shanahan's schools came to £500 in 1906. As against this, he spent £400 on teachers' salaries the same year, which represents a wage of about £1 per month per teacher.

At first, the teachers were little more than senior pupils. They were drawn mainly from the schools in Onitsha, the oldest and most successful in the prefecture. Senior boys who had learnt to speak, read and write English, who had some knowledge of mathematics, who had finished their religion course as catechumens, and who had received the sacraments of baptism, penance and Holy Communion, found themselves being offered posts as catechists and teachers. Their qualifications were poor by European standards but they were able to give elementary instruction in small village schools which would otherwise be unable to function.

The quality of these teachers was variable. With the increase in government and commercial activity in Onitsha and on the coast, there were opportunities in the civil service, in the telegraph company, in factories and offices. Those who became teachers were often those who had applied for better-paid jobs and failed. There were also problems about the depth of their religious convictions. It was possible for a pupil in a mission school to drift into Christianity without ever having made a real commitment. For these reasons Shanahan tried to ensure that village schools were near enough to a mission station for the priest to be able to keep an eye on them. 'We know from experience,' he wrote, 'that if a catechist is not under active supervision he is less than useless, indeed he is harmful.'[14]

These problems were to lessen as the years went on and there was a growing number of devout Catholic men to draw from. Even from the beginning, there were many catechist-teachers who saw their work not as a job but as a vocation and whose zeal made them missionaries in their own right. They taught in their mud-walled straw-roofed schools from 8.00 a.m. until 2.00 p.m. The rest of their day was given over to pastoral work, visiting houses, drumming up support for the school, recruiting new pupils, attending the sick, organising classes for adult catechumens. On Sundays, if the priest was not coming, the catechist conducted a prayer service in the school. If the priest came to say Mass, it was the catechist's duty to see that everything was prepared, the school turned into a church, the Christians and catechumens assembled, the music learnt, the altar-servers trained. He himself would normally be expected to read the scriptures and to interpret the priest's sermon. Even priests who were reasonably fluent in the language found that their sermons had far more impact if they were delivered in English and then translated into Ibo with all the passion and humour and dramatic gestures of a native speaker.

Shanahan himself contributed to the raising of standards among the catechists by the care and respect he always showed for them, even when they were still schoolboys. Their first reaction to him was often one of fear. With his huge height, his great bushy beard, and his voice that sounded like thunder in their ears, he inspired awe and even horror in youngsters who were still barely used to the sight of white men. As they came to know him better, feelings of fear turned to real affection. From his first days in Ogboli, he had found it easy to relate to the Ibo mind. The better he came to know them, the more he felt at home with them and they with him.

The difficulties he had experienced with human relations in Chevilly were gone for ever. This could have been due to a growth in spiritual maturity. A more likely explanation is that his earlier problems came from differences between the French and Irish temperaments. The reasonable, logical minds of his fellow-students found it difficult to understand his own more imaginative and intuitive approach to reality. To their eyes the Irish habit of making jokes about serious things seemed like flippancy, and the Irish tendency to embellish fact with humorous fantasy looked suspiciously like lying.

None of these difficulties existed with the Ibos. Later writers have described the Ibos as the Irish of Africa. Shanahan found in them the same humorous, easygoing approach to life that he had known in Templederry. They sang, they danced, they laughed a lot. They liked talking for the sake of talking and were rarely in any particular hurry to get to the point. Their attitude to the literal truth was inclined to be flexible, especially when dealing with the white man, but this he had no trouble understanding. It was one of the normal defences of a subject people. The exasperation felt by a colonial officer faced with the deviousness of an Ibo tribesman was identical with the exasperation of a landlord trying to get a direct answer from an Irish tenant farmer.

This rapport with the Ibo was one reason for the success of his forays into the interior. As he tramped from village to village, he came to enjoy meeting kings and chiefs and headmen, arguing the merits of the schools, haggling over pieces of land, setting his wits against theirs. The elaborate rituals, the exchanges of courtesies, the endless circlings around the point, were part of a game which he would play as happily and as patiently and as expertly as they did. He knew what they were thinking and they knew that he knew what they were thinking. It added immeasurably to the pleasure. Meeting him was not like meeting a French missionary or a district officer. Meeting him was fun.

5

The Great Trek

All through the years 1907 and 1908 Shanahan trekked through the forests and swamps of the Ibo homeland. The travels of those two years are a web of exotic names, as colourful and as evocative as the townlands of his native Tipperary. The diary kept by Father Duhazé mentions some of these expeditions. 'Father Shanahan has left for Awaba, Iboro, Isungwu, Ukpo, Okidja ... The Prefect has departed for Newi ... He has just come back from his visitation of Aguleri, Nteje and Nsude ... Father Vogler went with the Prefect to Nri and Abagana ... Father Shanahan and Father Bisch spent nine days touring the interior south of Aguleri ... Ozubulu is demanding a teacher. This town is well placed for future developments. The Prefect has gone on tour there, with the object of replacing Nsugbe with a new foundation.'[1]

It would be impossible to describe these travels in detail, even if all the details were available. Let the account of one of these treks stand in for all the others, the one which he made towards the end of 1908 and which was to live on in legend as the Great Trek. Towards the end of his life he recalled many of the details of this trek for John Jordan, who took notes of his conversations and incorporated them later in his biography.[2]

The Great Trek was the climax of almost two years of intensive exploration of the towns and villages of western Iboland. Most of these lay within a day's march of the Niger River. Further east was a vast region where no white person had ever set foot, populated mainly by Ibos, though with an admixture of Efiks, Ibibios and some smaller tribes. With his present resources, Shanahan could not hope to found schools throughout this immense area but he felt it was important that the missionaries should be the first ones to make contact with the local people. When further resources became available, the missionaries could come back again and hopefully they would still be remembered. He was right in this. None of those whom he met in the course of the trek ever forgot him.

On this occasion, Shanahan brought no missionary companion with him. It would be several weeks before he came back and the others could not be spared. Indeed, it was by no means certain that he would come back at all. There were many dangers lying in wait for the traveller. Disease was an ever-present risk, and the risk increased as the traveller moved further from his base and had to rely on local food. Wild animals were another threat. Elephants still roamed the area, the forests harboured leopards and bush-cows, poisonous snakes abounded. Even the rivers had their perils. A passing hippopotamus could easily upset a canoe and leave the passengers floundering in the water, at the mercy of the crocodiles.

The greatest danger was from people. The missionaries came in peace and to underline the fact they carried no guns. But there was no way of knowing how a town would react to its first sight of a white man. They might regard him as an enemy, come to take away their land and possessions, or as an evil witch-doctor, bringing a curse on their homes and families. They might look on him as an acceptable offering to their gods and sacrifice him in front of some grotesque ju-ju. They might decide he was a mighty warrior, whose power they could transfer to themselves by killing him and eating his flesh. In one village, the first white visitors escaped death only when the villagers saw that they had no toes and concluded that they must be spirits. The men had, of course, the usual number of toes but they were wearing shoes, which the villagers had never seen before.[3]

For his great trek, Shanahan had the company of half a dozen Ibos who would act as carriers, guides, interpreters and escort. He stocked up well with provisions before leaving Onitsha, small bush-lamps, bottles of kerosene, boxes of matches, tins of lard and sauerkraut, packets of quinine tablets, and all the other odds and ends that could be obtained only in the river trading posts. On the morning of their departure, he went into the little chapel to ask a blessing on the journey. Then his Ibo carriers lined up outside the mission house, hoisted their loads, and set off on their trek.

As they made their way along the narrow bush paths, they were watched by hundreds of eyes: farmers in their vegetable patches, palm-tappers clinging to the tree-tops, women bringing fruit to market, boys hiding in the tall grass, girls peeping from the doorways of little huts, children playing in the dust outside their compounds. The news flew from mouth to mouth, from tree to tree, from village to village. A white man was coming, a tall white man with a great beard. Who was he? Why was he coming? What did he want?

The carriers walked in single file, each one bearing a box on his head. They had no need of their hands to steady the loads; they walked easily and steadily with the skill of long practice. They carried food and cooking utensils, an empty four-gallon kerosene tin as an oven, a Mass-box with chalice and vestments, a change of clothing and a camp-bed for the Father. At the end of the line was the Prefect himself, occupying the position of honour but also the position of danger, since the last man was most vulnerable to an ambush or a wild beast. He was dressed in khaki shirt and trousers and stout walking boots and he carried a strong stick in his hand. On his head he had a pith helmet, worn by all Europeans in the tropics and considered at that time to be the one sure protection against sunstroke.

As the day wore on, the heat became ever more intense and the Prefect's clothes were soaked with perspiration. The going underfoot was rough and they raised a cloud of dust as they walked, but it was better than the mud of the rainy season. Sometimes they met a patch of sand, which reflected the heat like an oven and caused their feet to sink and slither. Every now and then there was a short pause for rest and refreshment. It was not safe for a white person to drink the water unless it had been boiled and filtered, but it was usually possible to find an orange or mango or paw-paw or pineapple. The Prefect was particularly fond of coconuts, whose milk was safe and refreshing to drink. Then the signal was given, the carriers took up their loads again and the procession continued on its way.

Shortly after 5.00 p.m. they reached a village and decided to stop for the night. In the tropics there is little variation in the length of the day from one season to another. The norm is twelve hours light from 6.00 a.m. to 6.00 p.m. and twelve hours darkness from 6.00 p.m. to 6.00 a.m. They had less than an hour of daylight in which to set up camp and, more important, give the villagers a chance to see them and satisfy themselves that the strangers came in peace. As they set down their loads in the deserted market-place, the carriers talked and laughed loudly, to show that they felt they were among friends; but inside they were as full of fear as any Ibos must be who had moved outside the borders of their own home place.

The cook began to supervise preparation for the 'meal-that-fills-belly', the main meal of the day. This was his moment of power. When the fire was lit, he dragged a protesting cock from the kerosene tin and deftly wrung its neck, all the while shooting orders at his minions. 'Hey you, bring water!' 'Yes, sah.' 'Hey, you, damn fool, bring wood!' 'Yes, sah.' The strategic use of the phrase 'damn fool', overheard from some European trader in Onitsha, gave a special ring of authority to his words. The palm oil was boiled and the fowl was added along with the yams, the favourite vegetable of the Ibos.

Soon the savoury smell of palm oil chop began to fill the market-place. Local people emerged from their huts and compounds, their curiosity overcoming their suspicion. The Prefect walked up and down, reading his breviary, nodding amiably, exchanging an occasional word of greeting. His interpreter moved among them, answering their unspoken questions. This was a proper big man, a very important person. He had come to their village to meet their chief and speak about important things. He intended to call on the chief next morning. The chief himself did not appear but everything that was said and done was faithfully relayed to him.

After they had finished chop (the universal Nigerian word for food), they gathered together for their night prayers, reciting the rosary and finishing with a hymn in honour of the Blessed Virgin. Then the Prefect's camp-bed, designed and built by himself, was set up in the open air. 'The main ingredient of my bed was a strip of thick green canvas, eight feet by four, bought in the Niger Company for half a crown. I nailed a pair of scouting poles at the extremities, with grips on them to catch the six pieces of iroko which took the weight. Four vertical bamboos at the corners for the mosquito-net, and there I was, as happy as any king in his royal couch.' While the Prefect slept in this royal and curtained splendour, the rest made themselves comfortable on the ground. The cook, as befitted his high office, slept on a red, green and yellow straw mat, which he had bought from a Muslim trader in Onitsha for sixpence.

When dawn broke the following morning, the Prefect clapped his hands and the cook awoke and once more started shouting orders. The Mass-box was opened and the altar was prepared, still in the open air. Vested in white and gold, the priest kissed the altar and began to offer the first Mass in the village, while the carriers knelt around on the red earth. The cook acted as server, answering the ancient invocations in Latin, while the interpreter read the principal parts in Ibo for the rest of the tiny congregation. A safe distance away, the villagers watched this man who was talking to Chukwu as to a friend, marvelling at his gestures and his clothing and his face that seemed all alight, wondering what holy thoughts were passing through his mind.

> As I stood there in the shadow of the palms, it came home to me that the ground around had suddenly become holy. I saw the truth of the words, 'That place is holy in which the priest prays for the sins and failings of the people. It is none other than the gate of Heaven.'
>
> Yes, the gate of Heaven! How I longed at the Gloria that heaven would open and the angels of the Nativity come down for Christ's first appearance in this African town, as they had at Bethlehem. I offered the Mass in union with those very angels and invited them to give to Our Lord the welcome the poor Africans had never been taught to give. I prayed later that the precious blood in the chalice before me would wash away their sins and one day unite them to a priest at Mass, as fully-fledged members of the Mystical Body of Christ.

After Mass, he unvested, said his prayers of thanksgiving and sat down to breakfast. The cook had prepared a slice of boiled yam and a cup of black coffee, made from beans grown at the mission. One of the villagers made bold to approach the great man while he was eating. He had been sent to greet the Prefect and to invite him to come and visit the chief in his compound.

Shanahan put on his religious habit, a white soutane and black cincture, and followed his guide through the village. The compound was impressive, with eight-foot-high walls of red mud and a massive door carved from iroko wood. Inside it were a number of small huts for the various wives and a two-storeyed wooden house in European style for the chief himself. The village was near enough to Onitsha to have felt the influence of the white man's architecture. An open area on the ground floor served as the chief's reception room and was decorated with the heads of horses, cows and bush-cows. In one corner were several bundles of brass rods, which could be used as money.

The chief himself was an old but powerfully-built man and was sitting on a carved stool with a goatskin cover. In his right hand he gripped a huge elephant tusk. His decorated iron spear and the red camwood cords around his ankle showed that he possessed the rare Ozo title, a high dignity in Iboland.

After an exchange of courtesies, a boy brought some cola nuts on a wooden plate. To break cola with one's guest was the traditional sign of Ibo hospitality. The chief divided the nuts into segments and both men ate a small portion. The nut is a powerful drug and has to be treated with respect. Then, after more courtesies had been exchanged, Shanahan got down to the purpose of his visit.

'I come not as a soldier or a trader, but as a white man who serves the mighty Chukwu. You know, of course, that he made all things?'

'I know.'

'It is good that we do his will, is it not?'

'It is good.'

'Well, I know what his will is for men. It is to teach it that I came to this country. I am the friend of Chukwu. The people of this town must become his friends too. They are a good people and are well-ruled. If they were not good, I would not have slept unarmed in your market-place last night. There was no danger for me, because yourself and your head men are both powerful and intelligent and keep good order. Is it not so?'

'Yes, we are intelligent and powerful.'

'Of course you are. And you will do wonderful work, yes, wonderful work yet for your town. Next time I come, perhaps after some six or seven moons, a black teacher trained at Onitsha will be with me and he will stay in your town; together we shall show you how to build a house where Chukwu will be worshipped properly. The children of your town will come to that house every day to learn about Chukwu. They will also learn book there and will know more than the children of other towns. After some years in that house-for-book, they will be fit for government work and will make much money. When they become men, they will say, ''Ha, the chief in our town who first met the white man was very clever. He got the white man to put a school in our town.'' '

The chief listened intently and nodded his head several times. He promised to summon the headmen and discuss the whole matter. Next time the white man came, they would give him their answer. Meanwhile, he was very pleased that the white man had chosen his town to visit. It was very good.

He clapped his hands and a small boy appeared leading a sheep on a string. 'The man of God must eat in our town', said the chief.

* * *

As the trek continued deeper into the interior, Shanahan got into the habit of choosing one village as a base for several days while he visited the neighbouring villages and towns. It took time to get to know the geography of an area and to unravel the complicated human relationships. Some villages were allied to one another by ties of blood and friendship, others were at daggers drawn. All these factors had to be taken into account when choosing the most strategic location for a future school.

On some of these visits he met chiefs and headmen to win their support and secure a site for the school. On others he spoke to groups of people in the market place about the God both he and they believed in under different names. Following Saint Patrick's example, he did not shirk the challenge of expounding the deepest mysteries, even the doctrine of the Trinity.

'Chukwu tells us that in him there are three persons, Chukwu Father, Chukwu Son and Chukwu Holy Ghost. I believe this is so because Chukwu says it and he knows all about himself. If I were not to believe, I should be like a small child who says about a big chief, I do not believe that the chief eats chop because I have never seen him eat it.'

This was greeted with a roar of laughter. The chief never ate in public, but everyone knew that he ate.

'The child understands child-palaver, the chief understands chief-palaver, God understands God-palaver. Is it not so?'

'It is so.'

He enjoyed these encounters with the village people. Sometimes it became a battle of wits, the sort of contest which the Ibo mind delighted in. A man who could hold his own in a debate of this kind, who could come up with a quick rejoinder or a telling analogy, was admired and respected. Shanahan rarely lost an argument and even when he did his good humour never failed and there was plenty of laughter and repartee.

The Ibos had an equally great respect for physical prowess. One of their favourite sports was wrestling and it became a favourite with Shanahan too. The wrestling took place in a ring formed by a circle of spectators. The two contestants began by approaching each other and touching hands in ceremonial greeting. They moved back and came forward again, this time bent low with their arms almost touching the ground and their quick eyes searching for an opening. They circled around one another, with sudden feints and grabs and slaps on the face to arouse the opponent's temper and cause him to lose control. The contest was decided when one of the wrestlers succeeded in making a lightning dive for his opponent's knee, followed by a sudden jerk which knocked him off balance and laid him flat on the ground.

These contests must have brought back memories to the Prefect of his time in Rockwell and the many weary, happy hours he had spent on the rugby pitch. There may have been times when he wished he could forget his dignity and step into the ring himself. The Shanahan tackle which laid waste the playing fields of Munster would have been no less devastating in Southern Nigeria. He had only one opportunity of using it, when a half-crazed tribesman broke out of a crowd one day and made to attack him. The next thing the man knew, he was lying on the ground without any clear recollection of how he had got there.

A more striking incident happened during the Great Trek which proved beyond all doubt that the Prefect was a man of matchless might and courage. He was striding along a forest track behind his line of bearers when a group of terrified villagers came rushing towards them in the opposite direction. As they shot past, they shouted out a warning. A huge bush-cow had appeared out of the high grass beside their village and was rampaging around in frenzy. It was every man for himself. They disappeared into the trees, followed by Shanahan's carriers.

The great man himself was not so easily intimidated. The bush-cow was a heavy and powerful animal, built on the lines of a buffalo and capable of a surprising turn of speed. Still, it was only a cow, or a bull, as the case might be. Shanahan had spent fifteen years of his childhood herding cattle or watching them being herded. He knew exactly how to deal with a raging bull. He armed himself with a hippo rod and went to meet the beast.

They met on a narrow stretch of the path. Shanahan stood his ground as the bush-cow thundered towards him, then stepped to one side at the very last moment. As the animal passed, he brought down the rod with a swish on the tip of its nose, its tenderest spot. The beast skidded to a halt in a cloud of dust, surprised, hurt, angry and deeply insulted. It turned and saw that its tormentor was still standing on the narrow track. Once again it charged, once again Shanahan stepped to one side, once again the rod descended with stinging effect on the same tender spot. This time the beast did not stop. It careered on its way down the path until it disappeared from view and the sound of its hooves died away in the far distance.

There was a short moment of silence and then the Prefect was engulfed in a flood of humanity. People came from everywhere, emerging from grass and undergrowth, climbing down from trees, chattering and laughing in excitement, describing the epic encounter, pantomiming the discomfiture of the monster, rehearsing the story they would tell to their children and to their children's children. Nothing like it had ever been seen before. The fame of that day spread all through the Ibo country, improving in the telling, until the Father Onyisi began to assume a semi-divine status. This man was indeed a friend of Chukwu.

* * *

The little group continued steadily on its journey towards the east. They came to Nimo, where Shanahan was impressed by a young boy and sent him to Onitsha for education. The boy was baptised with the name of Michael and returned years later to become chief of Nimo. They went on to Adazi, where Shanahan made friends with chief Oji, who promised to send all his family to church and school, a promise he faithfully kept.

In the Ajalli area he found a mixture of tribes, with a considerable number of non-Ibo people. There was heavy traffic in slaves in the locality. He came across some orphan children and sent them to Onitsha, probably saving them from a life of slavery. From here he went on to Uberu and from Uberu he made the dangerous journey to Amagunze through country infested with leopards, bush-cows and hordes of apes.

He continued to meet chiefs and elders and speak to them about the message of Chukwu and the benefits of education. The further he got from the Niger, the harder it was for his listeners to understand his enthusiasm for book. 'What good is book?' they would ask. 'Can a man eat book? Better for our children to work, to dig, to plant yams, to grow corn for chop.' But they always received him courteously and promised to think very carefully about all he had told them before his next visit.

He continued to preach in the market-places whenever the opportunity offered but he rarely baptised anyone. This would have to wait until the person concerned had studied the faith and proved his or her commitment over a period of years. The only exceptions he made were for those in imminent danger of death. He found that parents of dying children were very happy that they should be baptised and so secure their 'title-to-Heaven'. Once, when passing through a disease-stricken area, he met an old woman carrying a dying baby. He helped her to bring the child home where he found a heart-breaking scene. There were five adults in the house, all close to death. He prayed with them and told them about Chukwu and the home he had prepared for them. They asked him to baptise them and the baby before they died. 'If I had prepared all during my life for just that one hour of fruitful ministry in Africa,' he said later, 'I would have regarded it as well spent and every effort as well repaid.'

Many years later a priest came to one of the little villages around Amagunze to see about founding a church-school. The elders told him, 'When you were only a small child, the first white man came to our country. He was a very fine man and came to do good for us when others were afraid to come. We all believed he was sent by God, and we swore we would never allow any church in our place except his. We have not forgotten our oath.'

They said the white man had stayed for two or three days in the chief's house and agreed on a site for a school. Afterwards he sent them a teacher and the school was started but it collapsed when the teacher had to be withdrawn. What was the white man's name? They could not remember. 'White names do not sound sweet for our ear.' But a middle-aged man wearing a medal came forward to show the priest his book. The book turned out to be a worn and yellowed baptism certificate, dated December 1908 and signed Joseph Shanahan, CSSp.

The trek continued on to Abakaliki on the very furthest edge of the Ibo homeland. The number in the party varied from time to time. Many of the places where he stopped gave him gifts of food on his departure and courtesy demanded that a carrier be sent with the gift. The procession would be enlarged by a man carrying a pair of live chickens or a basket of yams or cassavas or leading a goat by a halter.

Now that they were so far from Onitsha, the cook had to be particularly careful to observe the rules of hygiene. An attack of dysentery in this remote spot could prove fatal for a white man. All water must be boiled before drinking. All food must be thoroughly washed, if possible in water freshly drawn from a stream. The Prefect's clothes, soaked in perspiration, were changed each day and laundered in some convenient river. He was always scrupulous about personal cleanliness, even in the depths of the bush.

At night, he was often invited to stay in the chief's house or compound. Otherwise, he slept in the open air or in some unoccupied hut or shelter. He was never molested by any human enemy but the animals and insects were less considerate. The mosquitoes were exceptionally aggressive in the Amagunze area. He described them as 'big black lads, that stood back and took a good look before diving at you'. When he took refuge in his bed it was the turn of the sandflies, who slipped easily through the mosquito net. In the morning his hands and ankles were covered with little lumps which itched very painfully all through the day. Meanwhile, on the ground the ants were chewing up socks, books, and anything else that had been left lying around.

Occasionally he found himself wakened by sounds of revelry among his carriers. If the food was better than usual that evening, they might decide to have a meal in white man style after he had gone to bed. They would sit at a table if one were available and use whatever plates and cutlery had been brought along. Sooner or later they would start imitating some of the Fathers in French and English, with special emphasis on their eccentricities. 'Oui, oui, mon père,' they would say amid mounting hilarity, or 'Sale cochon' or 'Tiens, tiens'. The climax came when the cook gave his famous impersonation of the Prefect himself. He wrapped a white cloth round himself as a soutane and stuck some kind of false beard on his chin. Then he walked up and down in the moonlight, lecturing some imaginary chief on the value of school and book. He had all the Shanahan mannerisms to a T, from the thoughtful stroking of the beard to the murmured 'True enough, true enough' with which he was wont to show agreement. This always brought the house down and even the victim could hardly suppress his laughter. He thought it wiser, however, to pretend that he had slept soundly through it all.[4]

It may have been on this trek that he had a distinctly frightening experience in a disused hut. He awoke in the early morning to see a huge snake coiled in the only doorway, its head raised as if prepared to strike. For what seemed a very long time, the two looked at each other. He was trying to work out some way of killing the snake and he presumed the snake was thinking along similar lines. Suddenly he heard a patter of feet outside. A little boy appeared in the doorway, gathered up the snake, wound it round his naked body and made off again, staggering under the heavy burden. It transpired afterwards that the snake was a sacred snake, a good friend of the villagers who used to keep it supplied with food. It occasionally slept in the hut and was probably as much surprised to see Shanahan as he was to see it.[5]

Somewhere beyond Abakaliki he decided that it was time to return to his base in Onitsha. He had accomplished what he had set out to do. He had crossed the whole Ibo homeland and made invaluable contacts all along the way. His efforts to sell the schools had been if anything too successful. He had rashly promised teachers to far more places than he had any hope of supplying. But that was a problem that need not be faced just yet.

The year 1908 was coming to its end as he swung into more familiar territory near the banks of the Niger. It was the season of the harmattan, the cold harsh wind that blows from the Sahara, filling the air with a dusty haze and dulling the brightness of the sun. The carriers shivered and grumbled but the Prefect welcomed the cool dryness that absorbed the perspiration before it could settle on the skin. He came striding into Onitsha, tired but happy, the Great Trek behind him. He had planted the good seed across the whole breadth of Iboland. It was for God to give the growth.

6

Gods and demons

The new year opened with a retreat. Ten of the priests gathered in Onitsha on 3 January 1909 for their annual week of prayer and reflection. Father Xavier Lichtenberger was the preacher and he probably followed the traditional pattern by speaking of sin and its punishment in the opening conferences. Shanahan recorded his feelings in his novitiate notebook.

> On this 6th day of January 1909 I once again happened to take up this little notebook. With aching heart I read over what I wrote on three previous occasions. Strange, is it not, that each record seems not only to confirm the former one, but to add to the darkness of the picture. Instead of holiness being the keynote, it is sin, and the habit of sin, that alone dominates. My God, how long is that to last? Will I ever improve? If I don't, what will the end be? ...
>
> Forgive me, my God, I am really sorry, more sorry than words can express; more sorry than years and tears can ever suffice to tell Thee. Oh, I do promise once again to do my best, to lead a pure and good life; to take suffering as it comes, in atonement for my delinquencies.

The emphasis on sin takes the reader by surprise. This was a man who seemed to have refused God nothing. For the last two years he had travelled endlessly, he had preached and ministered, he had endured hardship and exhaustion, he had faced constant danger from people and animals, he had pushed himself to the limits of human endurance. Even as he wrote, he was planning to set out on further travels once the retreat was over. If he was so great a sinner, what does it take to be a saint?

Once again, it is impossible to probe his conscience. It may be that he was too sensitive to small faults, too scrupulous in judging himself. It may be that great souls are wounded by the tiny daily infidelities that lesser souls do not even notice. He does not name the sins. The only clue is the word 'pure', which suggests an element of sexual guilt. In his journeys through the bush, he saw many things that must have made him aware of his own sexuality, ranging from the innocent charm of bare-breasted young women to the deliberately erotic dances that accompanied many rites and festivals. The rigid moral theology of the time taught that a deliberate look or even thought contrary to chastity could be mortally sinful. This may be the source of the guilt that still had power to cause him so much pain.

The year 1909 was to mark what might be called the end of the beginning. During the year Shanahan compiled his second general report for the mother-house in Paris. He had no spectacular progress to announce. The number of missionaries had risen slightly. Three years ago the prefecture had twelve priests and nine brothers, now it had fourteen priests and ten brothers. The two lost missions of Dekina and Nsugbe had been replaced by three new ones and the number of catechists had risen from thirty-three to forty-two.

These modest gains do not in themselves account for the note of optimism that breathes through the pages of his report. To Shanahan the seeming lull was a time of germination. The seeds so painstakingly sown would soon be producing a rich harvest. He hymned the future in a purple passage which loses a great deal when translated into the matter-of-fact English language.

> The future! Does not the missionary love to paint the mysterious picture of the future in the most glowing of colours! He loves Africa, because he quickly forgets the difficulties and the miseries. He lies down at night with his soul wearied by thoughts of gloom. When he wakes, serenity and hope return with the morning sun.[1]

The three new missions were at Nteje, Ozubulu and Ibariam, all in Ibo country and none of them far from Onitsha. Nteje was a replacement for Nsugbe, where Shanahan had met with little success and which he closed down after his appointment as Prefect. Nteje was one of Nsugbe's out-stations and it had a promising school so he decided to establish a missionaries' house there in 1907. In March of the following year he visited the new mission and baptised the first converts, fourteen pupils of the school.

The second of the new missions was Ozubulu, one of the places which had attracted Father Duhazé during his pioneering trek in 1906. The local chiefs wanted a school to rival the Protestant school built in a neighbouring town and the enthusiastic young priest was happy to take up the challenge. He brought Shanahan to see the place and obtained his consent to the project. Within a short while the people had built a mission consisting of a large school, a house for the priest and a house for the catechist. It was sited on a hill that nobody else wanted since it was largely covered by bad bush, the name given to forest which was reputed to be the haunt of evil spirits and where newborn twins and other abominations were abandoned.

To counter the influence of Ekwenzu, the evil spirit of Ibo belief, Duhazé dedicated the new mission to Saint Michael the Archangel, conqueror of the forces of Satan. A large statue showing the saint crushing the demon was brought from Europe and solemnly installed on 14 January 1909. Shanahan, just finished his retreat, came to Ozubulu to bless the statue and preside over the celebrations. The statue proved to be a tremendous attraction and crowds continued coming to see it for weeks afterwards. Sadly, Duhazé himself was absent. Three weeks earlier he had collapsed and was brought back to Onitsha, showing the first signs of the tuberculosis that was soon to take his life. Friends brought a full account of the great day to the invalid and he wrote it up in his journal.

> The Prefect was there, with Father Léna and Father Bindel, now in charge. Up to three thousand inhabitants of the forest passed before the magnificent statue and the cry 'O maka, O maka!' (Splendid, splendid!) was heard thousands of times. The devil intrigued them considerably and Father Bindel had to remove the vases of flowers at the foot of the statue so that they could study at their ease the fearsome mouth, the fiery tongue and the burning eyes of the Lord of Hell.[2]

Shanahan was back in Onitsha on 15 January and left again the next day, this time heading north with Father Vogler. They passed through Nteje and Aguleri and arrived at Ibariam on the 18th for the formal setting up of the third of the new missions. There was already a school and a catechist in the town of Ibariam and the chiefs had now asked for a resident priest. Shanahan agreed to the request and appointed Vogler to the new mission, with Brother Valentin to help in the building of a mission house. In the meantime, the missionaries had to live in a thatched hut which up to that had been the shrine of a pagan idol. Shanahan stayed some days with them in the hut, where they shared their living quarters with the ju-ju, an unnerving concoction of wooden beams, creepers, feathers and scraps of cloth. Entrance was made through a low door, which they had to negotiate on their hands and knees, taking care not to hit their heads off the thick tree trunks that held up the roof.[3]

Each of the three new missions was to have its problems. Shanahan was to find out that Ekwenze was a formidable enemy, that ju-jus had strange and unaccounted powers of evil, that bad bush was not given its name without good reason. The longer he stayed in Africa, the more conscious he was to become of Satan as a living and active force opposed to the work of the missionary.

There were many villages where he could sense the presence of evil as soon as he entered. There was one village which he was physically unable to enter. It was a place which was wholly given over to the worship of malevolent ju-jus, with slavery and human sacrifice being openly practised. Shanahan's offers of a school were contemptuously rejected.

> After a long wait, I decided to try again, thinking that the example of other towns might make it easy to get in a school, which would also serve as a church. The moment I reached the confines of the town, I felt myself surrounded; it was as though a curtain of hatred had fallen over me. I was beaten and knew it. The few people who listened to my words were completely uninterested. The defeat rankled. It was a disgrace to see a missionary so helpless. Back with me again later on, full of fight. The shadows of evening were beginning to fall as the outskirts of the town rose before me. Just as I reached the first trees, something halted me dead. My legs refused to move forward. I felt a fool, but was only a little bit frightened. Nothing that I could do would get a stir out of my legs. I turned to come back and found that as easy as ever. I went around the outskirts till I met another path going in. On trying to follow this, I was stopped dead a second time. So I came away and left the place to Satan. He has ruled there ever since.[4]

At the same time, he continued to respect all that was good in the Ibo religion and to treat its shrines and holy places with reverence. He saw nothing to admire in the actions of those missionaries who overturned idols and scattered votive offerings laid out to honour the spirits. These things represented religion to the native mind, and any disrespect to them was disrespect to religion.

> So we toppled his idols no more. Instead, acting with respect for all existing native customs, we told them quietly where these things were wrong, and that there was a way of conducting religious observances laid down by God himself. Idols topple by themselves when they cease to be propped up by anxious human hands.

These treks to Ozubulu and Ibariam were probably made by bicycle. There were still very few roads in the country but he had acquired a push-bike and he found it was possible to cycle without much difficulty on most of the bush-paths. It is certain that he used a bicycle for the treks he made from Calabar later that year. The Great Trek had brought him through most of eastern and northern Iboland but he had not yet explored the southern coastal regions or the Efik tribal lands beyond the Cross River.

Together with Father Léna, the superior in Calabar, he set off to investigate the areas on both sides of the Cross River. On the west bank most of the people were Ibo, though they spoke a different dialect from the one he knew in Onitsha. They gave the impression of being distinctly warlike, but they received the two cyclists with courtesy. On the east bank they encountered a variety of different tribes. Most of the people were able to speak Efik, the language of trade in the area. As they made their way north, the two men visited a succession of remote villages where ancient and barbarous practices lived on. Léna reported on their impressions.

> We were able to see for ourselves that cannibalism is still in fashion. The courtyards of the village kings were paved with human skulls, and in order to enter their houses one had to walk on paths made of human bones. One of the chiefs we met had a crown made of leopards' claws and rare python bones. It appears that no white men have ever been in these regions; they do not travel anywhere in this country, except under strong escort. Our knowledge of Ibo

> and Efik opened all doors to us. North of the river there is the vast and rich country of the Munchis. We wanted to enter it but the soldiers were conducting a campaign there and they advised us to wait.[5]

Back in Calabar after three weeks in the saddle, Léna took a well-earned rest but Shanahan headed off on yet another expedition. This time he was accompanied by Father Krafft and they went westwards through the coastal regions as far as Bonny, one of the ports in the Niger delta. Here they met a number of Catholics who asked for a priest and a teacher. All that Shanahan could do was promise that a priest would visit them from time to time by steamer from Calabar.

By this time, he was becoming more cautious in making commitments. His resources of men and money were very limited. He was no longer satisfied when a town agreed to have a school. He had to be sure that they were committed to making a success of it. Some places accepted schools but failed to send their children regularly. Others sent only slave children and kept the rest at home. He now began to lay down certain conditions for the founding of a school. The village had to build the school-house and a house for the catechist. They had to promise to pay the catechist's salary, or at least make a contribution towards it in keeping with the size of the village. He found from experience that unless the people were involved in the building and running of the school they had little respect for it.

Once the arrangements had been agreed and the school built, the next step was to install the teacher. This was conducted with the greatest possible solemnity. The teacher was introduced to the assembled townsfolk by one of the missionaries, often by Shanahan himself. There was a gasp of surprise and admiration when they saw the teacher, an African like themselves, but dressed in spotless shirt and trousers and perhaps wearing a pair of shoes as well. The admiration deepened still further when Shanahan told them that the teacher had been taught book for many years by a white man in Onitsha. He could read book of all kinds, including the mysterious book known as newspaper. He could tell what was happening in all parts of the world from newspaper.

Under the teacher's guidance, it would be only a matter of time before their own children would be able to read and write as well as any white man. Then they would be important people, working for the government. But this could only happen if the people supported the teacher and sent their children to school. If not, the school would be closed and the teacher taken away and everyone would laugh them to scorn. The teacher would teach in another town and it would be the children of that town who became important people.

To drive home his point, the Prefect would produce a telegram with a dramatic flourish and read and explain its contents. 'Brother Healy, Onitsha. Send me six good boys for clerical work. Marine, Lagos.' This was what book had done for the boys of Onitsha. Did they want the same for their own town? They all agreed they did.

Then the Prefect would grow more serious. The teacher would teach their young people about something much more important than book. He would teach them about Chukwu, the Great Spirit. What the teacher said should be listened to by everyone, by grown men and women as well as children. Those who did not listen would be punished in the world of spirits. Chukwu did not want to punish anyone. He wanted them to live happily with him for ever. But they must not ignore him as if he were a small boy. Did they agree with that? They agreed with that too.

Agreement was not so easily reached on practical questions, such as the amount they were prepared to pay the teacher. It would be unseemly to the Ibo mind to settle such a delicate matter without lengthy bargaining and negotiation. Every now and then the village elders would say, 'We go consult', and huddle in a little circle to discuss the latest proposal. A matter which a European would settle in five minutes might drag on for hours. On these occasions Shanahan showed extraordinary patience and even enjoyment. He respected the authority and the traditions of the chiefs and elders and made no attempt to rush them or bully them. For this they respected him too. 'He has the fashions of proper big chief,' they would say, 'though he does not do things by strong.'[6]

* * *

As the number of missionaries gradually increased, so did the number of Irishmen. By the year 1909 seven of the twenty-two were from Ireland. Brother Otteran was in Calabar and Brother

Kevin in Nteje. In Onitsha Ogboli were Father Ward and Brother David. With Shanahan in Onitsha Waterside were Brother Osmund and the recently arrived Brother Adelm, Shanahan's uncle.

Adelm's coming was the result of a long and persevering campaign. Away back in 1896 he had been sent to Rockwell after the breakdown of his health in Sierra Leone. In the fresh air of his native Tipperary he made a good recovery and began to pine again for Africa. When his nephew was appointed Prefect Apostolic, he thought his wish was about to be granted. He was ready to go, Shanahan was ready to receive him, where was the problem? The problem was that his superiors were not willing to release him, either because they still feared for his health or because they needed him in Rockwell.

In the summer of 1908 Shanahan wrote to the authorities in Ireland, saying that Brother David was exhausted by his work in Ogboli where he had to look after a school of 450 children. He was in urgent need of a trip home to Ireland to recover his health.

> Now in Rockwell is a veteran West African campaigner pining away for a glimpse of the scene of his former labours. Brother Adelm is the man. A thousand times he has written to me on the subject. Could he not be spared to take Brother David's place?[7]

It is not clear whether David returned to Ireland or not. If he did, it was only briefly, for he was back in Ogboli before the end of 1909. But Adelm was granted his wish and allowed to leave for Nigeria. He was welcomed with delight by his nephew and assigned to the mission in Onitsha Waterside, where he taught in the school and looked after the vegetable garden.

Saint Patrick's Day was celebrated that year in Onitsha as it had never been celebrated before. Brother Osmund began the day by presenting the successful pupil-teachers with their certificates. He followed this with a sermon on the glories of Saint Patrick, mingled with dark warnings about the dangers of a godless education. Then he gave them the rest of the day off. 'The thought of Saint Patrick makes me so happy,' he said, 'that I can't stand here looking at you fellows.' That evening there was a special dinner in the community house, followed by an impromptu concert. Adelm had the time of his life. 'Despite his fifty-six years,' the Community Journal recorded, 'Brother Adelm danced Irish jigs all evening.' No doubt the Prefect produced a bottle of Irish whiskey to keep the proceedings flowing smoothly. The prohibition on alcohol could not apply to the feast of the National Apostle.[8]

No doubt he also remembered another Saint Patrick's dinner in Onitsha which had ended very differently. He was always conscious of the tension between the Irish and the French. As an Irishman he had often felt himself looked down on by his French confrères both in France and in Nigeria. He could sympathise with his fellow-Irishmen who were going through a similar experience. At the same time, he could understand the attitude of the French missionaries. They had founded the Nigerian mission, they had given the lives of many of their best young men to the cause. Now they found themselves being gradually supplanted by foreigners and newcomers, who knew nothing of their history and traditions, who brought with them history and traditions of their own. These newcomers had the ear of the Prefect, who was one of their own. They had the ear of the colonial authorities, whose language they spoke and of whose country they were citizens. The French would hardly have been human if they had not felt some stirrings of resentment.

Shanahan understood and sympathised. He had a special sympathy for the Alsatians who, according to Brother Kevin, were the most opposed to the Irish.[9] Their home province of Alsace had been annexed by Germany after the defeat of France in 1870. They suffered a conflict of loyalties between the two great nations which both claimed them. They must have found the celebration of the Irish national feast especially painful, they who had no national feast and no nation.

From his years in France, Shanahan knew that the biggest day of the year for an Alsatian was his name-day, the feast of the saint after whom he was named. He kept a list of all their name-days in his diary. If he was in the bush, he would walk or cycle back to Onitsha, buy a couple of bottles of wine and a box of cigars from a French trading post, select some fresh vegetables from his garden, put the lot into an empty kerosene tin on the carrier of his bicycle, and set off again to find the Father, ten or twenty or even thirty miles away.

That evening as the sun was setting, some Alsatian exile, sitting on the mud verandah of his house and thinking a little sadly of his far-off home and family, would be suddenly startled by an unexpected voice: 'Bonne fête, mon Père, bonne fête.' He would leap to his feet to welcome the Prefect and the two would greet one another with a warm and a very un-Irish embrace. The treasures would be unloaded, the canvas chairs drawn up, the bottles uncorked, and the health of the patron saint toasted and drunk in the sun-filled wine of France. They would talk far into the night, reminiscing about Cellule and Chevilly, Paris and Strasbourg, telling the old stories, singing the old songs. Next morning the Prefect would say an early Mass and head off again on his bicycle before the heat of the day, leaving behind a confrère whose heart had been touched and spirits raised by an act of unassuming kindness.[10]

There was nothing forced or artificial about these encounters. Shanahan enjoyed the company of others, especially the company of brother priests. He seized any opportunity for a social event, the patronal feast of a mission, the opening of a new church or school or priests' house, the ceremonies of Baptism and First Communion and Confirmation and the examinations that preceded them.

As the missions became more firmly established during 1910 and 1911, these occasions became more frequent. A change was coming over Southern Nigeria, especially over Iboland. When he entered a village, it was no longer as a stranger. Children ran to meet him, women smiled, men greeted him as Fada Onyisi. The network of schools was increasing, the Mass-centres were more thronged. There were even a few Christian marriages, which he welcomed as the foundation of Christian families and the hope for the future.

The examination that preceded Baptism was held in public and was a major event in the life of a village. The *ekwe* or tom-tom was sounded to summon the candidates, their families and all the people of the village. A table and chair were placed outside the church or school and here the Prefect was formally installed. The candidates, almost all of them children from the school, were called one by one to answer his questions. All around in a large circle their parents and neighbours listened intently to everything that was said.

The examination might last for two or three days. It was more than an examination, it was a course of instruction in Christian teaching for all those present. Questions, answers and explanations were listened to with hushed attention. When a candidate answered correctly, the crowd murmured an appreciative 'Ha-ha'. If the answer was wrong, it was greeted with a despondent 'Ndo'. Sometimes Shanahan invited a candidate to read out the correct answer, and the sight of their child reading from the white man's book caused parental hearts to burst with pride. At the end, the favourable judgement 'You have passed' was greeted with a roar of joy and congratulation from the whole assembly.[11]

The day of the baptism was an unforgettable experience. One old Ibo teacher, Ernest Olisa, was baptised by Shanahan in the village of Umuoji around this time. Describing it almost eighty years later he could remember every detail of a red-letter day.

> As ours was the first baptism in the town, the Bishop told us that there would be a feast so we brought our gourds. Our parents were invited to witness everything, but they did not recognise which one was their son, because we were given clothes to put on. When we were baptised, it was as if our eyes were opened and we saw things in a new light.
>
> After the ceremony we were lined up and asked to put our gourds down in front of us for food. We were given rice and tinned fish. We never saw that fish before and thought that it was eke (python) which is not eaten, so we left it. But the mission boys who came out from Onitsha knew better but did not want to tell us, so they ate it all themselves afterwards. Now I think it might have been sardines or mackerel.[12]

The baptism of Louis Chukwanna Obiajulu in Ozubulu a few years later was memorable for a different reason. For him the day was a disaster. He arrived on the morning with his 'Pass' card in his hand, all prepared for the great event. Through some mistake, he was given the job of keeping the other candidates in line and as a result missed being baptised himself. He went to the headmaster and then to the priest, Father Correia from Portugal, who thought he had come late through his own fault and sent him away.

The celebrations went on all day and in the afternoon there were sports and wrestling matches, presided over by the Prefect himself. Louis was wrestling for Ozubulu and succeeded in getting into the final.

> I wrestled with Raphael Ozulumbaike from Akuma, who was much bigger. I got my head under his chin and eventually threw him as all the people shouted encouragement. Father Correia came and lifted me above the crowds and proclaimed me the winner. Other sports events then took place but all the time I was not happy because of my baptism.
>
> At the end all the results were called out and I was asked to go to the throne where Father Shanahan's helmet had been placed. He asked me to sit on the throne and praised me and crowned me king of the wrestlers, putting his helmet on my head and giving me the name Eze Nwokolobia (king of the young men who were wrestlers). He asked the people to sing 'God save the King' and they did. Then as he gave out the prizes to the other boys he would say, 'Eze Nwokolobia asks me to give you this.' He gave me three yards of cloth. When I gave him back the helmet he said, 'No, it is yours.'
>
> But I was still sad that I was not baptised so I went again to the headmaster asking him to keep the helmet till I was baptised because I came for baptism not for helmet. Paul Anakwe wrote a message on a slate and asked me to take it to Father Correia and I did. He became annoyed because I had called him out of the house where the Fathers were. He asked me to kneel down and I did, thinking it was part of the baptism, but instead he caned me.
>
> Father Shanahan opened the door and looked out and saws the boy he had crowned being caned. He was upset and closed the door quickly. I continued to follow Father Correia asking for baptism. I said I now had got baptism of desire and baptism of blood but still wanted the one of water. He got some local people to take me away by force.
>
> The school had two days holidays to celebrate. When Father Shanahan was back in Onitsha he wrote a letter to Father Correia to ask why the boy he crowned had not been baptised. So Father came to the school during the week and asked where was that foolish boy that had kept pestering him for baptism. Paul Anakwe then explained what had

> happened and then Father Correia wrote a letter to Father Onyisi, when he saw it was not my fault. Father Shanahan sent another letter and told him that I was to be baptised in church the following Sunday and wrote the name Leonard for me. But Father Correia changed it to Louis, saying he was a king too, the King of France, and his name was good for the king of the wrestlers. He used my case to instruct the people, saying that I had suffered that I could be baptised. Then all were very happy.[13]

Shanahan comes to life in that story. His enjoyment of the sports and the wrestling, his evident admiration for the young winner, his impulsive generosity in giving away his helmet, show the extrovert side of his nature. His more sensitive side is seen in his handling of the aftermath. Though obviously angry with Correia, he avoided an immediate and damaging confrontation. He waited until the situation had cooled down before taking action. Correia was corrected without being humiliated and was allowed to right the wrong in his own way.

The story also shows the faith of the young wrestler. He was the son of a dibia, a traditional priest, and was intended to follow his father's calling. His decision to become a Christian was not lightly taken. He was a sign of what was happening in the schools. Young men were asking for baptism not because the priest or the teacher told them or because they were following the herd, but because they truly thirsted for the *mili Chukwu,* the water of God.

* * *

Towards the end of 1912 Shanahan compiled another general report on the state of the prefecture for Bishop Le Roy, the Superior General in Paris. The number of missionaries had scarcely increased: seventeen priests and eight brothers. But the progress on the schools was striking. In three years the number of teachers had increased from 42 to 124 and the number of pupils from 2,591 to 6,578.[14]

It was good news and it was bad news. The increase in the schools meant an increase in the Catholic population, but this carried with it an increase in the responsibility that weighed on the Prefect. Where would he find the missionaries to look after the new catechumens and converts? Where could he find the money to maintain and expand the church and school network? He had the feeling that a moment of grace had come for Southern Nigeria, a moment of opportunity that must be seized now or lost for ever. The harvest was ripe. Where were the labourers?

In addition to his reports to Le Roy, Shanahan had to send regular information to Cardinal Gotti, Prefect of the Congregation for the Propagation of the Faith in Rome. Le Roy provided the men, Gotti provided the money. Every year Gotti sent the subsidy which was the mainstay of the mission. It averaged about £2,400 a year and was a substantial sum at that time, given that the annual salary of a teacher was £12.

The Roman subsidy had strings attached and these were a problem. About a third of the money came from anti-slavery collections. It was meant for the liberation of slaves and for no other purpose. Gotti believed that this money should be used to buy slaves and to set up Christian villages for them to settle in. Shanahan believed that the expanding of the educational system was a much more worthy cause. Never a man to be bound by petty legalism, he had no compunction about spending the anti-slavery money on teachers and schools. His reports to Gotti contained impressive statistics about the number of schools built and pupils taught but were suspiciously silent on the subject of slaves.

In 1912 Gotti wrote to Shanahan and politely asked for a detailed account of how the anti-slavery subsidy was being spent. 'It is solely for slave work', he reminded him, 'that the subsidy is allocated by this Sacred Congregation.' Directly challenged, Shanahan wrote back what amounted to a major apologia for his school policy. On the principle that the best form of defence is attack, he criticised the policy of buying slaves and settling them in villages. This was only scratching the surface of the problem. The school was the one real and permanent bulwark against slavery.

> Already we can see the results existing schools have brought. Because of them the children are no longer forced to sacrifice to idols, or to take part in immodest dances, or to indulge in diabolical rites. Pagan parents allow them full liberty to practise the Christian religion. The very slave-

> dealers are afraid of them, because they can speak a little English. This of itself will prevent them from being taken as slaves and will save their families also.
>
> So far we cannot but congratulate ourselves on the fidelity of the children, and on the goodwill of the pagans. The school keeps the missionary in contact with the people, because the children give him free entry into every house. He is no longer a stranger but a member of the family. This fact alone makes what he can effect, and what he can prevent, really incalculable. He is known everywhere and he alone can go through the country without danger. Other Europeans dare not move about the country unescorted. But at the moment of writing, our presence is being demanded in some fifty towns. Yet traffic in human flesh still goes on. Our method of opposing it is to make known the truth through the medium of the school.

The argument was ingenious rather than convincing. The people who gave money for the emotive purpose of freeing slaves hardly expected it to be spent on teaching school-children. However, Gotti did not press the point. He knew that the money was going on a good cause and he allowed himself to be convinced. The subsidy continued to be paid.[15]

The problem of manpower was not so easily dealt with. As Shanahan collated the reports from the different stations, one message kept coming through, the need for more men. From Calabar: 'Let us hope that a new contingent will soon arrive and that we can carry out our plans for expansion.' From Ozubulu: 'It is true the results are not very brilliant; lack of personnel is the main cause.' From Ibariam: 'To open more schools, we are waiting for the building work to be finished and also for our personnel to be increased.' From Nteje: 'In the town of Nteje alone, there is work for four missionaries. May God send them to us!'[16]

The reports were duly sent to Paris. Paris acknowledged them in the usual way, and in the usual way did nothing about them. New missionaries arrived in ones and twos when they should have been coming in boatloads. Hardly had one man landed when another had to return to Europe on sick leave. Did nobody know what was happening? Did nobody understand? Did nobody care? 'The year 1913 stands out in my mind as a year of agony', he said later. 'Right before our eyes, we watched a whole people, with the most wonderful qualities of any people in the world, slip from our grasp through lack of priests.'[17]

He decided to go to Europe in the spring of 1914. The trip had a twofold object. The first was to restore his health. He was tired and rundown after eight years of continuous work in an alien climate and environment. He always advised his missionaries to look after their health and to go home on leave if necessary. Now it was time for him to do the same. The second object was to make one more appeal for men. Perhaps his personal presence could achieve what his letters had failed to do. There must be no repetition of the heartbreak of the 1906 trip. This time he would have his arguments prepared, his facts and figures ready to produce. This time he would go straight to the top and take his problem to the Pope himself.

Before he left, he shuffled his missionaries around once again in an effort to staff all the missions. A new mission had been established at Emekuku in 1912, which meant that there were now seven in the western part of the Prefecture. In the southern and eastern area there was still only the single mission in Calabar. On Saint Patrick's Day, 17 March 1914, he made the decision to raise Anua, one of the Calabar out-stations, to the rank of a full mission with a resident priest. Hopefully he would return from Europe with the reinforcements needed to staff all nine existing missions and enable new ones to be founded.

On 17 May 1914 he landed at Liverpool and made straight for Rome.[18] Our only account of his efforts in Rome and elsewhere comes from Father John Jordan's biography, based on Shanahan's own reminiscences a quarter of a century later.[19] He planned his approach to Pius X very carefully. The Pope was known for his love of children, which had led him to reduce the age for receiving First Communion to seven years. He would surely be sympathetic to the work being done by the schools in Nigeria and the way that they were turning their pupils into little missionaries.

The audience started well. The Pope received him kindly and listened with great interest and sympathy to his description of the Nigerian mission. Shanahan told him how open the people were to the Christian message and how the children in the Catholic schools were acting as apostles to their parents. At the word 'apostles' the Pope nodded his approval. 'Yes, yes, that is what they should be.' When Shanahan knelt to ask his blessing, the Pope unexpectedly knelt down beside him to thank God for what was happening in Nigeria. As they rose, he gave Shanahan a present of his own crucifix.

Shanahan seized the opportunity to make a direct appeal.

'Holy Father, where am I to get the priests I need for my people?'

'You are a Holy Ghost Father. Go to your Superior General. Tell him I sent you.'

'Holy Father, he has missions to supply throughout Africa. He will say that many other prefects and bishops have greater needs.'

'He must not. Your needs come first. Tell him I sent you.'

It was not exactly the answer Shanahan had been hoping for. He left the Vatican conscious of the Pope's support and good will but uncertain as to how these could be translated into living, working missionaries.

Obedient to the Pope's suggestion, he headed for 30 rue Lhomond in Paris, the mother-house of the Holy Ghost Congregation. Once again, he prepared himself carefully for the interview. The Superior General was himself a former African missionary and loved to hear of new ventures and new pastoral approaches in Africa. Shanahan was always a convincing speaker and a fascinating raconteur. This time he excelled himself. He told stories, he drew maps, he wrote out statistics. He spoke of the devotion and self-sacrifice of the missionaries. As he went on, he forgot his prepared agenda and spoke from the heart with increasing emotion. Le Roy was obviously touched. The time had come for the direct question.

'Father, if we get ten more priests our conversions will be multiplied. Will you not give them?'

The General paused before answering. 'I can't. They don't exist.'

'But the Holy Father said —'

'The Holy Father can't expect me to work miracles. There are no men to give.'

It was Le Roy's turn now to put his case. He produced letters from superiors in Gabon, Malagasy, Sierra Leone, Mauritius, Martinique. All contained the same arguments that Shanahan had used and made the same plea. What was a superior to do? He could not take priests from other missions and send them to Nigeria. There was only one suggestion he could make. Shanahan should approach the Provincial in Ireland and ask him if he could spare some men from the colleges there. He promised to write to the Provincial himself and urge him to go to the limits of sacrifice.

Shanahan arrived in Dublin in the glorious summer of 1914, which would long be remembered as a golden time of warmth and sunshine before the massacre began. His good friend Father Ebenrecht, now seventy-seven years of age and in failing health, made an entry in the Blackrock journal on 18 June. 'Father Shanahan arrived last evening from abroad. He went to Maynooth. If only he could get a few vocations!'[20]

The Provincial at the time was Father John T. Murphy and the provincial headquarters had been moved from Clareville to Kimmage Manor on the south-west edge of Dublin. By this stage Shanahan's hopes can hardly have been very high, but he met the Provincial and put his case once again. The response was predictable and familiar. There were too many commitments and not enough men. Other missions had equally strong claims for consideration. There was an undertaking to supply priests for the United States. The three Irish colleges, Blackrock and Rockwell and the most recent addition, Saint Mary's in Rathmines, Dublin, all had to be staffed. When Shanahan argued that a missionary order should not be engaged in educational work in Ireland, the answer was that the colleges helped to maintain the faith and encourage vocations. Without them, there would be no missionaries at all.

Shanahan had to face the fact that he had failed once again. He was to sum it up later in a few words.

> The Pope said, 'Go to your General'. I went. The General said, 'Go to your Provincial.' I went. At the end I had nothing to show except the merit of obedience. Yet God works through obedience.

He remained in Ireland for another three months, taking his well-earned holiday, recovering his strength, visiting family and friends. He continued to look for missionary helpers, women as well as men. He had an encouraging meeting with the Mother General of the Irish Sisters of Charity, who promised to ask for volunteers. She circularised the convents and a number of sisters expressed their interest in going to Africa. Unhappily, the outbreak of the First World War in early August caused her to cancel plans for a visit to Nigeria and the project was shelved indefinitely. It was one more disappointment.[21]

For much of the time his headquarters were in the small town of Maynooth, about twenty miles from Dublin. The attraction was not Maynooth College, the national seminary of Ireland, but the hospitable home of his sister Mary. She had married a Maynooth businessman, Joseph Dawson, who owned a general shop and garage in the town. Their home was to be Shanahan's home on this and many subsequent visits to Ireland.

His father, Dan senior, had died in 1911. His mother was still alive and living in the old home at Clohinch with the youngest son, Daniel junior, who had taken over the house and farm after his father's death. The rest of the family were now scattered all over the world. The youngest, Margaret, had died while at school at Salford in England. Louis Patrick had emigrated to America. Michael, John and Jeremiah had all gone to Australia, a less usual choice than America. It is very likely that their decision was influenced by the fact that their uncle, Brother Adelm, was stationed in Ballarat near Melbourne from 1888 to 1892. Dick had completed his medical studies and was now practising as a doctor in England. The remaining daughter, Bridget, had married James Kelly from Borrisoleigh in 1913. Her husband was a primary teacher and owned in addition a small pub in Borrisoleigh village.

Shanahan's visit to the home in Clohinch was a happy one. In addition to seeing his mother again, he was introduced to his new sister-in-law. Dan had married Jane Hogan in February of that year and they were awaiting the birth of their first child, a boy who would be given the name of Daniel and who would in due course inherit the house and farm himself. A further pleasure was the arrival of Louis Patrick who had come from America to see his aging mother and who was much closer in age to Shanahan than was Daniel. The Prefect and Louis Patrick became Joe and Paddy again as they reminisced about their bygone youth and visited familiar places. Tipperary looked more beautiful than ever on those days of brilliant sunshine as Dan drove his two older brothers along the winding road from Templederry to Borrisoleigh and up the little boreen to the original family home at Glankeen, Joe's birthplace.[22]

Shanahan left Ireland on 30 September. An entry in the Blackrock journal for that day reads, 'Father Shanahan left this morning for Liverpool to try to secure a passage for himself, Father Con Liddane and Brother Carthage, newly professed.' The entry is not in Father Ebenrecht's familiar hand. The old man had died after a short illness on 20 August. Shanahan himself was the celebrant of his funeral Mass in Blackrock College chapel, after which his burial took place in a vault under the altar of the church which he had designed and built almost fifty years before.

The slaughter was already under way on the battlefields of Europe when Shanahan sailed for Nigeria. The two missionaries who accompanied him were no more than replacements for those others who were sick or on leave. They were all he had to bring with him after such strenuous efforts, and they would have come anyhow. There were some consolations. His health had been renewed, his physical and spiritual batteries recharged. What if he had nothing to show except the merit of obedience? God works through obedience.

7

The thousand-mile walk

Despite the outbreak of war, the journey back to Nigeria was uneventful. Later on, the build-up of the German submarine fleet made travel between Europe and Africa increasingly hazardous, but communications were never cut off completely. There were always a few ships willing to run the gauntlet for the sake of the financial reward.

Nigeria had its own small share of the Great War in the form of the Cameroons campaign. The German colony of the Cameroons was sandwiched between British Nigeria on the west and the French central African colonies on the east and south. British and French armies invaded the Cameroons and engaged the German army. All three armies had European officers but the unfortunate soldiers were Africans, who had even less idea than their counterparts on the Western Front why they were killing and being killed. The German forces were defeated and the colony was portioned out between the victorious French and British. All German nationals, including the missionaries, were interned on the off-shore island of Fernando Po and the territory was left without priests.

The situation in the Cameroons was to be a cause of great concern to Shanahan at a later stage. When he arrived back in Onitsha in late 1914 he had problems nearer home to worry about, the chief one being the shortage of priests in his own prefecture. There were two ways in which the problem could be tackled. One was to load yet more work on to the shoulders of the few priests he had. The other was to involve the Catholic laity more fully in the work of the apostolate.

The priests were overworked as it was, with nine principal stations and scores of out-stations to look after. There was one method, however, of lightening the burden of endless travelling from one out-station to another. Six years earlier, Shanahan had taken to the bicycle. Now he discovered the merits of the motorcycle. Roads were gradually being built to link the main centres of population along the Niger and the sea coast. It had become possible to travel from Onitsha to Calabar by land. Primitive though these roads were, they could be traversed without much difficulty by a sturdy motorcycle.

Shanahan's first motorcycle is said to have been a Multi-Rudge.[1] It is remembered as a great, growling, shuddering monster which spread terror and confusion on its first appearances in the villages of Iboland. Even in cosmopolitan Calabar, women dropped baskets of fruit and fled down side alleys when the iron devil first came roaring down the street. When the Prefect disappeared into the priests' house, some of the more daring youngsters edged their way up to the now slumbering machine and touched it gingerly. Their worst suspicions were confirmed. 'Ha! He is hot like proper devil.'[2]

Often he was accompanied on his journeys by a missionary or catechist on a bicycle. To speed up the proceedings he would tie a rope from the saddle of the motorbike to the frame of the pushbike and tow the cyclist along behind him. The trouble was that as the journey went on he tended to forget about his companion. The unfortunate cyclist found himself being bounced along at twenty miles an hour or more, his brakes useless against the power of the motorcycle, his cries of protest unheard over the engine's roar. Once while towing Father Bindel on a rather long rope, Shanahan crossed a river and had to take a sharp turn as he came off the bridge. As he shot off in the new direction, the bicycle and its passenger found themselves suddenly plunged in the water.[3] After this, the other missionaries began to acquire their own motorcycles, in self-defence if for no other reason. By 1917 the number of motorcycles in the prefecture had risen to eight.

Most of the priests and brothers were men of outstanding character and dedication but there were occasional scandals, hushed up at the time and still largely inaccessible to the researcher. Temptation was always present in the form of alcohol and in the ready availability of black women. Another temptation, strengthened by the example of many colonial officials, was to treat the Africans as an inferior branch of the human race. Brother Kevin mentions one of the Alsatian brothers whose ungovernable temper led to the death of two Africans. He gives no details of the incident except to add that the brother was sent home by Shanahan as a result.[4]

There were many other occasions when relations became strained between the missionaries and their often unruly flocks. The turbulent history of Nteje is a case in point. The mission, founded in 1907 as a replacement for faithless Nsugbe, soon developed problems of its own. When Shanahan returned from Europe, he found that most of the people of Nteje had stopped going to church and had taken their children away from the school. The resident priest, Father Bubendorff, attributed this to an unfortunate accident when the schoolboys were clearing an area of bush. One of the boys accidentally struck another on the leg with his machete and the victim died a few days later, though Budendorff claimed it was not as a result of the blow. The people demanded the death of the other boy in accordance with their tribal law. When Bubendorff refused to hand him over, they stopped attending church and school in protest.

That was Bubendorff's version. The people's version was rather different. They said they had asked the priest not to touch the bush because it was bad bush, the haunt of evil spirits. He rejected their request as superstitious and said that the land must be cleared in order to extend the school. According to an Ibo chronicler:

> School children were employed to do this work, while the Reverend Father occasionally came to inspect the work, usually in his boots. As the work went on, the children contracted various diseases. Some of them died; some were very sick; and others, such as Paul Nwafor Nnose, were paralysed.[5]

This has the feel of an eye-witness report. Bubendorff's boots are precisely the kind of detail that would be remembered by one of the bare-footed schoolboys, at the mercy of the snakes, rats and other creatures fleeing from the threatened bush. The diseases that struck them down were equally dangerous, though whether they were due to evil spirits or to natural causes or to the force of suggestion is open to debate. The power of the ju-ju and the fetish is one of the perennial unsolved mysteries of African life.

In incidents of this kind there were faults on both sides. The priests could be arrogant and impatient, especially when suffering from the bouts of malaria and dysentery that were a regular part of their lives. The people could be fickle in their allegiance, ready to change their religion with bewildering suddenness. Even Shanahan's own Ogboli saw a mass return to paganism at this time, led by the advocates of polygamy. At an assembly of the townsfolk, one of the speakers asked mockingly, 'What do you call a man with only one wife?' An old man with several wives shouted out, 'A dog.' He was answered by a young man who said proudly, 'A Christian.' The tide turned. King Sami, who had been among the lapsed, publicly repented and burnt his idols. The waverers returned to the fold.[6]

These were the Catholic laity on whom Shanahan had to depend if the work of spreading the gospel was to develop and expand. He decided to trust them. Where other missionaries saw only shallowness and unreliability, he discerned a deep underlying goodness. He brought out that goodness and used it to the full. He trained and sent out catechists in ever increasing numbers. He set up high schools in Onitsha and Calabar. He started a teachers' training college in Ibariam. In one of his most original innovations, he announced the holding of a Catholic Congress in Onitsha in January 1915 and invited all the missions to send delegates.

In his report to the mother-house on the Congress, there is a slightly defensive note, as if he does not expect his readers to take seriously the idea of African lay Catholics discussing the affairs of their Church. Yet it is clear that the Congress was taken very seriously indeed by the delegates and by Shanahan himself. Thirty-five stations and out-stations sent representatives, and these included women as well as men, a further innovation. The three subjects that attracted most discussion would have meant little or nothing to Europeans, but they were the things that concerned these men and women in their lives as Nigerian Catholics: namely, titles, spirits and marriage customs.

Reports were made on the various subjects, speeches were delivered, decisions taken. Knowing the Ibo love of open-ended discussion, the Prefect thought it necessary to limit the number of speakers and the time allotted to each. On the question of the titles, tribal honours which involved taking part in pagan rituals, they agreed unanimously that these were to be condemned by Christians. They also condemned the custom of honouring the *Muo* or spirits by means of masquerades, in which men wearing grotesque masks engaged in obscene posturing and dancing. Shanahan notes that this debate aroused the curiosity of the women delegates to a high pitch, since by tribal law they were allowed to know nothing about these masquerades.

The discussion on marriage customs was the most urgent of

the three. The practice of polygamy was one of the main obstacles to the spread of Christianity in Nigeria. A man had to pay a costly dowry to the bride's parents before he could marry, and this meant that most men could only afford one wife. But village chiefs and other wealthy men could have all the wives they could pay for. The system was unfair to men and both unfair and degrading to women, who were bought and sold with little reference to their own wishes. A young girl could be given as the fourth or fifth wife to some rich old man because the young man she loved could not afford the dowry. Once she was married, her husband owned her and could force her into prostitution if he wished. The delegates decided that the only solution was to educate young people from an early age in the Christian teaching on sex and marriage.[7]

The conclusions of the Congress strengthened Shanahan's own conviction about the importance of the schools. The Church could be built only upon a foundation of Christian marriages and families. To bring this about, the mothers as well as the fathers must be believers. He used to ask the schoolboys to promise that they would get married in church when the time came, and he was prepared to reduce the normal three years' catechumenate before baptism in the case of brides. But he knew that there would be an imbalance in the Church as long as the educational system was geared only to boys.

He had hoped that the Sisters of Saint Joseph of Cluny in Onitsha and Calabar would take the lead in developing schools for girls. His hopes were disappointed. The rule of their order was in the traditional French mould, binding the sisters to an enclosed life and making it hard for them to undertake the running of schools. Moreover, all of the sisters in Nigeria were French and had little or no English. For these and other reasons, the convent in Onitsha was closed in 1908, and it was uncertain how much longer the convent in Calabar with its five sisters would continue.

In his report to Rome in 1917, Shanahan wrote at length and with feeling about the needs of the women of Nigeria. It is clear that the idea of starting an order of sisters with a rule specially geared to meeting these needs was beginning to crystallise in his mind.

Christian families are being formed under most trying

> difficulties. There is only one convent of almost 'cloistered' sisters to look after the girls and women to be found among 40,000 Catholics and catechumens. Protestants have several well-equipped schools for girls, under the charge of Lady Missionaries. The latter undertake also, on a large scale, missionary work in the different Protestant catechist stations. They are to be met with in the most out-of-the-way places and in all kinds of weather. They are our principal opponents for unfortunately they have a horror of all things 'Catholic'. Their influence is undoubted. A pity their genuine zeal and conviction are not spent in the service of Truth! For I honestly believe their good faith is beyond doubt.
>
> Why not missionary Catholic sisters, to emulate the zeal and self-sacrifice of those Protestant ladies? It is difficult to establish Christian families without having the future mother's heart and soul formed to habits of virtue ... Our young men have to choose their companions for life from among pagans.[8]

The failure to draw the girls into the educational net could not take away from the remarkable progress being made in the work of the mission as a whole. In the year 1917 the number of Catholics in the prefecture rose above the ten thousand mark and there were a further thirty thousand catechumens preparing for admission to the Church. While Shanahan agonised over missed opportunities, his superiors in Rome and Paris were becoming aware of the fact that Southern Nigeria now had one of the most fervent and fast-growing churches in the world.

* * * *

A new and heavy responsibility landed on the Prefect's already over-burdened shoulders in February 1917. A document from Rome appointed him Administrator of the Prefecture of Adamawa in the Cameroons. Adamawa was the part of the Cameroons which adjoined Southern Nigeria and which had been placed under British rule after the Germans were driven out. The missionaries in Adamawa had been German priests of the Sacred Heart Congregation. With their departure the prefecture was left completely without priests. Shanahan was asked to visit the region and report on the state of the Church there.

He took this new commission very seriously and began to make plans for a visit to Adamawa. Unfortunately his health began to trouble him again. It was a difficult time for white people in Nigeria. The disruption caused by the war meant that supplies of medicine and European food were drastically reduced. Many of the missions tackled the food question by planting vegetables and keeping cattle and poultry, but the shortage of drugs remained a problem. By 1917 most of the missionaries were very run down and Shanahan himself was seriously ill for a good part of the year. He does not name the illness but in view of later developments it was probably amoebic dysentery, a disease which is very weakening and difficult to cure completely. As a result he had to postpone his planned visit to Adamawa until the following year.

Brother Adelm was another whose health was causing problems at this time. In March 1917 Shanahan wrote to the Irish Provincial to tell him that Adelm was dangerously ill in hospital.

> The poor old man is now in his 65th year. During his nine years here he has seldom been one day absent from his hard daily work in school for five hours a day. He also looked after the plantations, the garden, the housework, etc., etc. At last he has broken down completely. I appeal to your charity to give the poor man some little corner in Rockwell where he may prepare for death. It is the last and only ambition of his life.
>
> Out here we are like the men in the firing line. So long as we are able to keep on our legs, well and good; but the day we fall ill, our lot is to be removed away behind the lines, though many of us if not all would prefer to die where we stand. And old Brother Adelm is one of the many. Unfortunately there are so few of us left and we are so poor that we are unable to look after our own wounded much as we should like to do so.[9]

There is something almost eerie about this letter in the light of what was to happen later to Shanahan himself. It is clear that he was unhappy about sending an old man home just because he had outlived his usefulness. But he went ahead with the arrangements and when Adelm came out of hospital he found that his passage to Ireland had been booked and his ticket bought. He went to his nephew and begged him with tears in his eyes to let him remain in Nigeria for what little remained of his life. Shanahan was touched by the appeal, perhaps imagining how he himself would feel in the same situation. He gave in and allowed Adelm to stay on in Onitsha Waterside, no longer teaching but still tending his garden and providing fresh vegetables for the community table.[10]

The visitation of the Cameroons still remained to be tackled. In May 1918 he made his first expedition into the country, travelling by sea from Calabar to Victoria, on the Cameroons coast. He visited three former mission stations at Victoria, Engelberg and Einsiedeln, and ministered to the neglected Catholics of the coastal area. He could see that he was merely scratching the surface. A vast tract of mountains and forests stretched hundreds of miles northwards from the coast. It was clear that it could be explored only by a fully-equipped land-based expedition. He returned to Onitsha to plan his campaign.[11]

Once again his plans were to be disrupted. In that same year an epidemic of influenza swept the world and caused many millions of deaths. In Southern Nigeria it coincided with an outbreak of smallpox. The lethal combination carried off many thousands of the Ibo people and was especially severe in the Onitsha area. Shanahan and his fellow priests were called out at all hours of the day and night to the homes of the dying, to anoint the Christians and to baptise those who were still catechumens. It was a consoling ministry but it further depleted his reserves of strength and energy.

A strange incident happened to him one evening on the road from Calabar to Onitsha. He was travelling alone when his motorcycle developed some mechanical trouble and he had to abandon it. He set out to walk to the nearest mission, which happened to be Ozubulu, several miles away. As he walked he began to become confused and disoriented. He imagined all kinds of menacing shapes in the bush around him, wild animals, lions, even tigers. He arrived at the mission house in a state of total collapse and remained ill and fevered for quite some time afterwards.[12] It was a sign that his system was near breakdown, but he chose to ignore it. Whatever else happened, the long-postponed visitation of Adamawa must go ahead before the end of the year.

* * *

Shanahan estimated that the trek through Adamawa would take three or four months and cover about a thousand miles through some of the most difficult and rugged terrain on the African continent. It would be even more arduous than the Great Trek of ten years earlier. He was now forty-seven years of age, weakened by long service in the tropics and not fully recovered from his recent illness. None of these factors lessened his determination to carry out his mandate and visit the abandoned missions of Adamawa.[13]

He left Onitsha with an escort of twenty carriers in early December 1918 and marched three hundred miles across country to the Cameroons border, which he crossed on 22 December. His motorcycle was left behind, as it was worse than useless in the roadless mountains and valleys of Adamawa. Once or twice he was able to use a canoe and for a few days he experimented none too successfully with a mule. 'We never became friends, because when I wanted to go one way, it always decided to go the other.' For the rest of the thousand miles he went on foot, walking on rough bush tracks, climbing up steep slopes or slithering down them, wading through shallow streams and being carried across deep ones, swaying on rope bridges across ravines with a drop of hundreds of feet below.

On Christmas Eve he arrived in Ossidinge, where the German priests used to have one of their missions. They had been in Adamawa only three years before they were expelled and Shanahan was uncertain whether any of the people had become converts or, if they had, whether they still remained faithful. His carriers had scarcely laid down their boxes in the market-place when a couple of Catholics discovered who he was and laid his doubts at rest.

> They began to dance and sing with joy, clapping their hands wildly and embracing each other. When their first transports were over, they flung themselves on their knees, kissing my feet and the ground before me as though I were a great king. It brought to my mind the way the shepherds of Bethlehem fell down before the divine child, and I wished from my heart that I was not so unworthy.

The mission buildings in Ossidinge had been demolished by those hostile to the Christians. Nothing remained. The bricks had crumbled into dust and the site returned to bush. There was a rumour that the bells had been preserved but nobody was able to find them. It did not matter. Drums were beaten and horns blown and messengers sent to neighbouring villages to summon the people to midnight Mass. A two-roomed rest-house was swept out and set in order for the Prefect. Behind it an open-air altar was set up under a palm-leaf shelter and decorated with wild flowers and shrubs. In the moonlight it looked like a Christmas tree.

The congregation for midnight Mass was small. There were the Ibo carriers from Onitsha, a few Catholic traders from the coast towns of Douala and Victoria, and a handful of local Catholics and catechumens. They made up in joy what they lacked in numbers. From the consecration of the Mass until the communion, they continually kissed the ground in their tribal greeting for a king. They sang the *Adeste Fideles* with touching fervour. At the end of Mass they were overjoyed when Shanahan told them that he intended to stay in Ossidinge for a week and that he would turn one of the rooms of the rest-house into an oratory with the Blessed Sacrament reserved in it for their adoration.

During the following week he used Ossidinge as a base, making visits to the surrounding villages during the day and returning home each night. All week long the little makeshift oratory was never without its group of worshippers, their eyes fastened on the wooden tabernacle. 'We were praying', they told him, 'that Our Lord will send us priests to stay with us.' Some of them had come three or four days' journey over rough and dangerous tracks to receive the sacraments.

They told him of the ill-treatment they had been subjected to since the priests were taken away. The British authorities obviously saw them as a threat because of the ties of loyalty that bound them to the German missionaries. A number of the leading Christians were taken to Fernando Po and interned there with the Germans. Those who remained were persecuted in various petty ways by the local chiefs at the instigation of the British administration. The churches and schools were closed and in most cases deliberately destroyed. The children of the internees were forced to discard the clothes that marked them out as Christians and were then distributed among pagan families. In all his travels through the area, Shanahan saw only two Christian girls.

After leaving Ossidinge, he headed west into the mountainous heartland of Adamawa. Some of the Christians travelled with him to show him the way and to attend the Mass with which each new day began. Others met him at various points along the route, sometimes by accident, and added themselves to the company. He was deeply moved by these encounters.

> Never in my whole life did I experience such emotion as when, on the roads leading to their villages, I met these children of God, with the familiar Christian greeting on their lips, 'Laudetur Jesus Christus'. With what joy they welcomed us! They could not tear themselves from our side, and yet we were aliens in race and tongue. With what earnestness they prepared themselves for the sacraments, these poor souls, so loved and protected by God! And in the little hut where the morning Mass was celebrated, it was real saints that were praying. I could not help thinking of the catacombs.

The steep climb up the escarpment tested him severely. The tracks were rough and narrow, with sheer mountains on one side and plunging ravines on the other. At heights of five and six thousand feet the air became thin and breathing more difficult. Added to the weariness in his legs and the pressure on his lungs, he became aware of growing abdominal pains. He pressed on. He was determined to visit every one of the six former German mission stations and as many other villages as he could.

On 6 January 1919 he celebrated the Feast of the Epiphany near the village of Bamao on the top of the escarpment. In the darkness of the early morning, he could hear the native drums beating out the message of his arrival and see the lights of the Christians winding along the mountain paths on their way to Mass. The devotion of the little congregation matched that of the Christmas congregation at Ossidinge. As he stood at the altar on that high mountain-top he felt that he was standing halfway between heaven and earth.

From Bamao he continued on in the direction of Bali, and was met on the way by one Francis Fongoh. When Francis learnt that the white man was a priest, he was delighted to announce that he himself was a Catholic and he led the group to Bali. The first Mass ever said in the village was celebrated in an abandoned Protestant mission and was attended by eight local Catholics. When he resumed his journey in the direction of Bamenda, Christian Junia travelled with the group 'for show road for other places them'.

Bamenda was the administrative centre of the area. Here he was received kindly by the British District Officer, who showed him twenty-two boxes of church furniture taken from the defunct missions. He pushed on, still going west, and reached Kumbo, which had been a flourishing mission station four years earlier. The chief was friendly and was keeping the priests' house in good repair, but the convent, the schools and the catechumens' house had all vanished. He intended to go on to the former station of Wum, to the north of Bamenda, but was unable to do so because of unrest in the area. It was the only one of the six stations that he missed.

South of Bamenda were the missions of Bakom and Babaju. There was no trace left of the mission buildings in either place. Despite this, Shanahan continued his practice of spending a week or two in each station to give time for any Catholics in the area to learn of his presence and come to receive the sacraments. He urged them to meet together in one another's houses on Sundays and to say the Rosary and other prayers until the priests were allowed to come back.

Two Christians came to him one day and told him they had travelled three days from their village to see him, a distance of up to a hundred miles. They wanted him to give them absolution from all their sins. When he agreed to do so, they started reeling off a long list of offences, each with a large number of times attached. He tried to stop them as there were others listening, but they said it didn't matter as everyone knew about these sins.

They carried on with their list, helping one another with nods of affirmation and occasional prompts. Shanahan grew mystified and suspicious at the number and variety of the offences and began to question them. It soon emerged that they were not just confessing their own sins. They had been sent to confess the sins of all the Christians in their village and to bring them back absolution from the Father. Shanahan was touched by their faith but taken aback by their theology. Nothing in his seminary lectures had prepared him for this. He decided that it was no time for niceties.

> I said to them, 'Tell the people I have given them absolution in the name of Jesus. Tell them to kneel down and say a good act of contrition.' I prayed to the Lord to make the absolution carry. And I believe it did.[14]

In one station he discovered that the teacher-catechists had continued their work in secret after the priests had gone. They had led prayers on Sundays and taught the catechism to children and adult catechumens. These were so well grounded in the faith that Shanahan was able to baptise them. He stayed two weeks in the village and during all that time there was continuous adoration of the Blessed Sacrament in the mud house where he was staying. When the time came for him to move on, there was desolation. A loud wail arose from the people as he removed the sacrament from the tabernacle and with dreadful finality blew out the little light.

They followed him down to the river bank, where a canoe was waiting to bring him on the next stage of his journey. 'Stay with us, Father', they begged him. 'You brought us Our Lord, how can you take him from us?' He stepped into the canoe, the oarsmen dipped their paddles in the water and started a rhythmic chant as the boat moved out into midstream. Above the sound of their singing, he could still hear the cries of the people on the bank. 'Come back again and bring Our Lord', they called after him. 'Come back again and bring Our Lord.'

It was a scene that would have moved a far stonier heart than his. But the sadness of partings like this contained hope for the future. The conclusion of his report to Rome struck a firm note of optimism.

> Catholicity is still alive in Adamawa. The Christians fully expect to see the priests return to them again. They remain devotedly attached to them. Their constancy during the four years of severe trial has been admirable. There is a splendid future before a mission which after two or three years of existence has been able to produce such splendid souls.

His optimism was justified. After the peace settlement, Adamawa remained under British administration. The mission was entrusted to an English Congregation, the Mill Hill Missionaries, who built up a flourishing church on the foundations so well laid by their German predecessors.

It was now March 1919 and Shanahan's task was finished. In spite of altitude, age and exhaustion, and in the face of pain that was becoming more frequent and more intense, he had visited all the stations except the inaccessible Wum. Day after day he had forced himself to keep going by sheer willpower. Now that his mission was accomplished, he suddenly collapsed. He was in the heart of the bush, hundreds of miles from civilisation. Racked by pain, he seemed likely to die.

It was his faithful Ibo bearers who saved his life. They managed to carry him the long journey to the sea coast, and after an agonising week he arrived at the port of Douala in the French part of the Cameroons, where there was a Holy Ghost mission and a hospital. He was taken into the hospital, put to bed and ordered to remain lying flat. He was suffering from an amoebic abscess on the liver, a common and often fatal complication of amoebic dysentery. The abscess could burst at any time, flooding the peritoneum with poison and leading to almost certain death. Hence the injunction to lie flat and avoid movement, especially sudden movement.

He endured it for three days, while the doctors tried to treat him. Then he decided that lying flat on his back was no life for a missionary. With characteristic impulsiveness, he gripped the bars of his bed and suddenly hoisted himself upwards and out on to the floor. What the doctors had warned about happened. The abscess burst, but providentially it burst outwards through the abdominal wall and the poison escaped harmlessly.

He was released from hospital and cared for by the French Holy Ghost Fathers, who spoke afterwards of the extraordinary impression he had made on them. As soon as he was strong enough, he took the boat for Calabar. The priests there were shocked at his appearance and he himself feared that his health had been damaged beyond recovery. He even began to speak of the possibility of resigning from the position of Prefect. The others would not hear of it but urged him to return to Europe as soon as possible to recuperate.

He was due to go to Europe in any event. As superior of the Southern Nigeria mission, he had been called to attend the General Chapter of the Holy Ghost Congregation. It had been postponed because of the war and was now scheduled to take place at the end of August. This would provide him with an opportunity for recovering his strength, beginning with the sea voyage and ending with a period in Ireland for convalescence.

He returned to Onitsha to make preparations for his journey and to attend a ceremony that gave him great joy. It was the ordination to the priesthood of Joseph Delaney, a former Irish Christian Brother who had spent nearly ten years in Nigeria as a lay missionary helper and catechist. He had been a great support to Shanahan in the setting up of the schools, and had undergone more than his share of hardship and adventure. In one famous escapade, he escaped from a group of cannibals just as the pot intended to cook him was coming to the boil. The ordination took place on Sunday, 13 July 1919, and the ordaining prelate was Bishop Broderick, Vicar Apostolic of Asaba in Western Nigeria.

It was the first ordination of a Catholic priest in Shanahan's prefecture. He hoped that it would not be too many years before the first African priest was ordained. He had already sent one promising young man, John Anyogu, to be educated in the Holy Ghost College at Castlehead in Lancashire. Despite his weakness and weariness, he was in good heart as he boarded the boat for Europe.

The delegates for the General Chapter assembled in Chevilly on Sunday, 24 August 1919, for the week's retreat. The following Sunday the Chapter opened and one of its first acts was to elect Le Roy for a third term as Superior General. The Chapter ended on 11 September. The list of delegates who attended does not include Shanahan's name. A note explains that he was detained in Ireland by illness.

The sea voyage had done him little good. On arrival in Liverpool towards the middle of August, he was too weak to think of going on to France. He crossed over to Ireland and was admitted to Saint Vincent's Hospital in Dublin for observation and treatment. There was a possibility that an operation might be needed to drain the liver abscess and ensure that all poison was removed from his system. The general feeling was that he had come very close to death in the Cameroons.

In September he was out of hospital for a while and staying in Saint Mary's College in Rathmines, to which the headquarters of the Irish province had been moved. Though still decidedly shaky, he contacted the Mother General of the Irish Sisters of Charity and renewed the request for sisters he had made on his last visit. He even paid a visit to the Charity Convent in Foxford,

Co Mayo, to see Mother Arsenius, who wielded great influence in the congregation and was strongly in favour of sending sisters to Nigeria. In mid-October he was back in the hospital again, where he had a meeting with a delegation from the Sisters and put his case to them with all the power at his command. Once again he was unsuccessful. They listened sympathetically but were unable to help him. As one of them put it:

> We told him that our chief difficulty was that we had not sufficient members and those offering to go were not, with a few exceptions, those you could send as pioneers. Some of them were decidedly odd and not living the common life at home.[15]

Meanwhile, the doctors decided that surgery could no longer be avoided. The operation took place on 20 November and was considered to be a success.[16] In early January 1920 he was out of hospital again, renewed in health, full of vigour, determined to return to Southern Nigeria with a large new contingent of missionaries. If the Holy Ghost Congregation or the Sisters of Charity could not provide them, there were plenty of other places he could look.

8

Bishop Shanahan

The year 1920 was a turning point in Shanahan's life. In this year he became known throughout Ireland under a new and resounding title: Bishop Shanahan of Southern Nigeria. In this year for the first time he used to the full his formidable powers of eloquence and inspiration, touching the hearts of individuals and moving the minds of masses. In this year he forged alliances with some of the most remarkable figures in the younger generation of the Irish Church. Edward Leen, Thomas Ronayne, Marie Martin, Patrick Whitney and Mary Charles Walker all fell under his spell and offered themselves in his service. All five were destined in their different ways to bring him both joy and sorrow. In this year he started the process which would lead to the founding of no fewer than five new religious congregations, the Holy Rosary Sisters, the Medical Missionaries of Mary, the Handmaids of the Holy Child Jesus, the Sisters of the Immaculate Heart of Mary and the Missionary Society of Saint Patrick.

He began the year with yet more attempts to secure sisters for Nigeria. He had now failed twice with the Irish Sisters of Charity, though during his visit to Mother Arsenius in Foxford the previous September he had made an important contact through his meeting with a member of the community, Sister Mary Charles Walker. She expressed her wish to go to Nigeria and he told her she would be very suitable for the school in Calabar, soon to be deprived of nuns. The meeting probably made little impression on him at the time; it made a deep impression on her.

Sister Charles was aged thirty-eight at the time, an Englishwoman who had joined the Irish Sisters of Charity in 1901. When the original call for volunteers for Nigeria was made in 1914, she was among those who sent in their names. It was said that some of these volunteers were 'decidedly odd and not living the common life at home'. The criticism could have applied to her to a certain degree. She was a woman of deep spirituality and genuine culture, a talented writer, a teacher and educationalist of outstanding ability. But the other sisters in Foxford felt that she never fitted in completely with the community. One of her contemporaries wrote:

> All were unanimous in agreeing that she was what nowadays would be described as a dedicated religious, silent and a strict observer of Rule. Any adverse criticism was that she was not a good mixer, she did not seem to have contributed much to their recreations.[1]

The Sisters' decision not to take on the Nigerian mission was a great disappointment to Sister Charles but she saw it as no more than a temporary setback. She began to investigate the possibility of going to Nigeria on her own, if no-one else would go with her.

In the meantime, Shanahan had just received news that the last three Cluny nuns had left Calabar, leaving the prefecture without a single sister. He stepped up his efforts to try and find a replacement. The most promising response came from the Franciscan Missionaries of Mary, a French order which had a convent in Loughglynn, Co. Roscommon, and which regarded service on the foreign missions as its principal work. He was given reason to hope that a group of their sisters might be willing to return with him to Nigeria later in the year.

In Saint Mary's College he renewed his acquaintance with Edward Leen. As a small boy in Rockwell, Leen had been one of the young Father Shanahan's most ardent admirers and had watched from his bed as his hero set out for early morning rugby practice. On leaving school, Leen joined the Holy Ghost Congregation and was ordained priest in 1916 at the age of thirty-one. Having revealed exceptional ability in his study of philosophy and theology, he was appointed to Saint Mary's College to teach these subjects to students for the priesthood. His biographer, Father Michael O'Carroll, describes him as he was at that time.

> He was impulsive, eager to inspire others to a life of idealism; an intellectual with a scholastic record that truly merits the much abused word brilliant. No member of the Congregation had ever reached such academic success; none since has quite equalled it. Apart from extraordinary grace, such things tend to make a man intolerant and arrogant. From arrogance Father Leen was saved by fidelity to the religious rule, which he had accepted at profession, and perhaps also by ill-health, which was probably due to intense intellectual activity and the pace at which he had

> driven himself. Was he intolerant? In those days he did not suffer fools gladly; half-truths and misconceptions offended him and drew from him prompt, even blunt rebuttal.[2]

Meeting Shanahan again after so many years and in such a different relationship, the brilliant young theologian might well have found that his idol had feet of clay. What happened was the opposite. He found himself more impressed than ever. It was true that Shanahan was not an intellectual but that was of no importance. He did not need to study theology: he lived it. He was the kind of inspiring leader that Leen would be happy to serve under, if he could secure his release from the Irish province. In later years he tried to analyse what it was that gave Shanahan his extraordinary charisma.

> He saw all things in terms of God and God's outpouring of himself on souls. Every aspect of life was for him sacramental, and raised his thoughts to the divine. His very appearance betrayed that he dwelt in the world of grace. In repose there was an 'inwardness' about his looks that caused the term 'Christlike' to come spontaneously to the lips of people who met him. Habitually he wore that look of 'inwardness' and self-control. To all his advantages was added that of a splendid physique, a mobile and very expressive countenance, and a voice that charmed. He looked what he was, a prince of the Church and a priest of the most high God.[3]

Leen was not the only one in Saint Mary's to be deeply impressed. The students and the younger priests were enthralled by his conversation. One of them gave an account in his diary of an evening Shanahan spent with them towards the end of January 1900. They sat around the fire while he told them 'stories of every description, comic, tragic, pathetic' about his experience in Africa. They were so spellbound by his description of his trek through the Cameroons that the bell-ringer forgot to ring the bell for the end of recreation and a whole hour of study was lost.[4]

It was a time when the Catholic people of Ireland were becoming suddenly conscious of the missionary dimension of their religion. The period was one of great idealism in the fields of nationalism and religion, fields which lay very close together in those days when to be Irish and to be Catholic seemed the same thing to many people. 1916 was the year of the Easter Rising, the beginning of the armed struggle which was to lead to the setting up of the Irish Free State six years later. The same year saw the birth of the Maynooth Mission to China, the first formal commitment of the whole Irish Catholic Church to the work of preaching the gospel to all nations.

It began very inconspicuously on the evening of 4 September 1916 with a meeting of three young priests in the presbytery in Monkstown, a Dublin suburb. The host was Father Tommy Ronayne, a priest of the Dublin diocese, and he introduced to one another two of his friends, who shared with him a deep interest in the missions. Father Edward Galvin was a missionary home on leave from China. Father John Blowick was a theology professor in the national seminary in Maynooth. The three talked into the small hours of the morning, sharing their dreams and their plans. It ended with the decision to establish a society of Irish priests committed to the work of spreading the faith in China.

Blowick was given the task of obtaining the approval of the Irish Bishops. He put the plan to them at their meeting in Maynooth in October and met with a heartening response. They approved the projected Maynooth Mission to China and authorised the setting up of a seminary to receive and train students for the society. From then on progress was rapid. In 1918 the society was formally established under the title of the Missionary Society of Saint Columban, with twenty priests already committed to membership and thirty-one students in its new seminary. Galvin returned with the first volunteers to China, where he later became Bishop of Hanyang. Blowick remained in Ireland as the first Superior General of the Society of Saint Columban. Ronayne, to his great disappointment, was refused permission to join by his superior, Archbishop Walsh of Dublin.

The success of the new society was viewed by Shanahan with mixed feelings. He rejoiced in the wave of enthusiasm for the missions which was beginning to sweep through the country. At the same time, he worried at the fact that the enthusiasm seemed to be directed solely towards China and was ignoring Nigeria, where the needs and opportunities were so great. He decided to make his own assault on the great citadel of Maynooth from a slightly different angle.

During the course of his frequent visits to his sister in Maynooth, he had come to know many of the professors in the seminary and had become particularly friendly with the president, Monsignor McCaffrey. He discussed his idea with McCaffrey, who listened sympathetically. Shanahan had noticed that a number of Irish dioceses had too many priests, with the result that newly ordained priests had to spend the first few years of their ministry in Britain or America until a position became vacant for them at home. Here was a new source to be tapped. There must be many young priests who were not willing to make the lifelong commitment required by the Columbans but who would be happy to spend a few years on the missions while awaiting an appointment in Ireland.

A meeting of the Irish hierarchy was due to take place shortly in Maynooth. McCaffrey arranged for Shanahan to be invited to dine with the bishops as an honoured guest, and he put him sitting beside the Archbishop of Armagh, Cardinal Logue. It was a position not greatly sought after, due to the Cardinal's habit of offering his snuff-box to whoever sat next to him. Shanahan valiantly accepted the snuff for the sake of the cause and between sneezes outlined the main points of his scheme. Logue was so impressed that he called for silence and invited him to put his case to all those present. Shanahan made the most of the opportunity and spoke with such eloquence and conviction that the Bishops were completely won over. He was given permission to speak to all the students in Maynooth and appeal for volunteers.[5]

Shanahan's address to the Maynooth students was long remembered by those who heard it. He described the state of the Church in Southern Nigeria, the small number of priests, the huge number of Catholics and catechumens, the even greater number of pagans. 'The time is particularly ripe,' he said, 'for paganism is collapsing throughout Nigeria and the people are eager to hear the Gospel of Christ.' He suggested a five-year period of service to any young priest whose bishop was prepared to release him. 'The moving appeal of the tall apostolic man with the long white beard and flashing eyes produced a profound impression', one witness noted.[6] Among those most impressed was a final-year student, Patrick Whitney, due to be ordained that summer for the diocese of Ardagh.

In the spring of 1920 Shanahan paid a visit to Paris. One

purpose of the visit was to seek missionary priests and nuns for his prefecture. Another purpose, not publicised, must have been to discuss his forthcoming appointment with the Superior General. Fifteen years previously Lejeune had recommended that Southern Nigeria be made a vicariate with its own resident bishop. If the case had been strong then, it was now overwhelming. Even the official Bulletin of the Congregation referred to Southern Nigeria as 'the fairest of all our African missions'. It was high time the mission had a bishop and it would be hard to imagine a better man than Shanahan for the post.

While in Paris he got a letter from a nun friend in Dublin urging him to go to the town of Lisieux in Normandy and pray at the grave of a young Carmelite nun, Sister Thérèse of the Child Jesus. Shanahan had heard of Thérèse, who was gaining a reputation as a miracle-worker, but he was not inclined to make the journey. He felt the antipathy that any normal middle-aged cleric could be expected to feel towards a nun whose cult had not been officially approved, about whom extravagant and even hysterical claims were made, and who was referred to by her devotees as The Little Flower. And anyhow, were there not plenty of genuine canonised saints who could answer prayers just as effectively? But a second and even stronger letter arrived from the nun in Dublin and he decided to go.

Accompanied by a priest friend, he took an early train from Paris. They arrived in Lisieux and made for the cemetery. Thérèse's grave was easily found, festooned as it was with medals and objects of piety. Shanahan began to pray.

> I shall never forget to my dying day the impression both of us got at the grave. We felt we were in a supernatural atmosphere, surely in the presence of something strange. We prayed there for a while, and it was while there I realised for the first time how this little girl, who had never left her convent, was nevertheless a great missionary and an exceptional friend of missionaries in pagan lands. I asked her to place the cause of Nigeria before Our Lord.[7]

On leaving the cemetery, he suggested they pay a visit to Thérèse's convent, where her three sisters were still living. His friend objected on the grounds that their visit would become known and they would be made the butt of ridicule from their confrères. But Shanahan insisted and they went to the convent and spoke to Thérèse's sisters. When he apologised for his earlier scepticism they merely laughed. Then he spoke of his need for missionaries and they told him of their little sister's love for the missions. They assured him that she would obtain the favour he asked for. He left Lisieux strengthened and consoled.

On his way home, a letter from Ireland reached him in London. It was from a priest, volunteering for the Nigerian missions. Already it seemed to him his prayers were being answered.

* * *

On 17 April the official announcement came from Rome. The Prefecture Apostolic of Southern Nigeria was to be made a Vicariate Apostolic. The present Prefect Apostolic, Joseph Mary Shanahan, was to be appointed Vicar Apostolic of the new Vicariate and raised to the episcopate as titular Bishop of Abila. It was customary for a bishop who was not in charge of a diocese to be given the title of some ancient and long defunct diocese. Abila, wherever it was, was one of these.

Shanahan was visiting Castlehead, the Holy Ghost College in Lancashire, when the news was announced. After a modest but heartfelt celebration put on by the community there, he hurried back to Ireland to make arrangements for his consecration, the name used at that time for the ordination of a bishop. He had decided that he wanted it to take place in the college chapel in Maynooth. Monsignor McCaffrey was happy to make the chapel available for the ceremony and the date was fixed for 6 June.

It was an unexpected and surprising decision. The obvious choice would have been the chapel in Blackrock College, where other Holy Ghost bishops had been consecrated in recent years and where he himself had been ordained to the priesthood. No doubt there were many in the Holy Ghost Congregation who were disappointed at his choice and some who interpreted it as a rejection of his own order. It was hardly a rejection but it certainly suggested the beginning of some kind of alienation. He no longer saw the Congregation as the only source of men for Southern Nigeria. He now looked to Maynooth, to the Irish bishops and secular clergy, to make up the shortfall.

To emphasise his message still further, the consecrating prelate was to be a member of the Irish hierarchy, Dr Denis Kelly, Bishop of Ross, a native of Shanahan's home parish of Templederry. There was a Holy Ghost bishop on leave in Ireland at the time, Bishop Neville of Zanzibar, but he was only given the subsidiary role of co-consecrator, along with a retired Oblate missionary, Bishop Miller. Everything was carefully planned in such a way as to strengthen the newly forged links between Maynooth and Southern Nigeria and to make the greatest possible impact on the minds of the students. Not for the first time in his life, Shanahan showed that for the sake of a good cause he could combine the wisdom of the serpent with the simplicity of the dove.

The excitement of the preparations did not cause him to overlook other matters. He got in touch with the priest who had sent the letter to Paris. He was none other than Father Tommy Ronayne, who had brought together Blowick and Galvin and then been refused permission to join the Columbans. This time he was more successful and he got permission to go to Nigeria from Archbishop Walsh, who was nearing the end of his long life.

Ronayne was not a complete stranger to Shanahan, since he had been a boy in Rockwell while Shanahan was dean. Meeting him eighteen years later, Shanahan was favourably impressed by his obvious spirituality and commitment to the missions. Though he had only just turned thirty, he was in considerable demand as a spiritual director and was an excellent judge of souls. Among those he was guiding was a young lady from his parish, whom he believed to be a specially chosen soul. He suggested that Shanahan should meet her, as she might be willing to go to Nigeria as a lay missionary. She came from a wealthy Dublin family and her name was Marie Martin.[8]

The historic meeting between Shanahan and Marie Martin took place in Ronayne's presbytery in Monkstown on 29 April. For the second time, Ronayne was to be the means of bringing together two of the giant figures of the modern Irish missionary movement. It must be said that it would be hard to imagine anyone who looked less like a giant than Marie Martin. Just twenty-eight years of age, she was small and frail. A bout of rheumatic fever in childhood had left her with a weakened heart and delicate constitution. But she had a humorous eye and an engaging toothy grin and a toughness of spirit that would more than make up for any physical weakness.

There was an immediate meeting of minds and souls between herself and Shanahan. The challenge he offered was exactly what she had been looking for. She told him she was beginning a course in midwifery in Holles Street Hospital and would be qualified early in 1921, a skill which would be of use in Africa. By the time they parted, they had decided that she would come to Nigeria as soon as she had qualified and help in the school in Calabar. It is not clear if Shanahan had given much previous thought to the possibility of having laywomen as missionaries. It may have been Marie's obvious suitability for the role that caused him to make the decision. A few days later he wrote to her from Maynooth, 'It is quite evident that you are called by the Holy Ghost to co-operate in the most beautiful and heavenly of all works: the divinisation of souls.' He ended by saying, 'From this day I consider you as one of the Nigerian missioners.'[9]

There was more good news in Maynooth itself. One of the final year divines, Patrick Whitney, had volunteered for Nigeria and had been given permission to go by his bishop. He would be ready to travel to Africa with Shanahan and Ronayne later in the year. In his very different way, he was as impressive a figure as Marie Martin. A very vivid pen-portrait of Pat Whitney has been left by Bishop James Moynagh, who knew him well. He describes him as 'a man of extraordinary faith and unlimited courage — the faith concealed under a rugged, rather rollicking but extremely shrewd personality.' According to Moynagh, he had a rather undistinguished academic record in Maynooth, not from want of ability but because it was considered bad form by 'the boys' to show any excessive interest in study.

> Father P.J. would be typical of that background: pucks of brains, happy, jolly personality, ever cracking jokes, treating life as great fun, shrewd knowledge of men, deep unshakeable faith, but a rather ruthless strain to his character with a touch of craft which prompted him to enjoy getting what he wanted or thought necessary for the work by rather devious ways rather than by honest straightforward request .... Add to all this a towering presence (he must have been six foot two or three), a massive striking face with alert smiling eyes, a face ever on the verge of breaking up into vast furrows of mirth, a deep bass voice ready to issue in gusts of jollity, all beneath a shock of beautiful jet black hair,

> immense physical strength — all add up to a very unusual intriguing personality.[10]

There was good news from Shanahan's own spiritual family, the Holy Ghost Congregation. They were releasing two of their best men for service in Nigeria, one of them his very good friend Edward Leen. He was considered to have a brilliant future before him as a writer and scholar and his going to Africa would be a big loss to the Irish province. Both Shanahan and Leen must have used a good deal of persuasion to bring about this happy outcome. The other was a very able young man, Father Phil O'Connor.

On top of this, more good news came from Rome from the acting Mother General of the Franciscan Missionaries of Mary. They had definitely decided to undertake missionary work in Southern Nigeria and they would have six sisters ready to sail with him when he returned there in the autumn.

He began to count his blessings. Ronayne, Whitney, Leen, O'Connor, four new men of exceptional calibre. Along with them there would be five French and Alsatian missionaries, Nigerian veterans returning from leave in Europe. Add to these the six Franciscan sisters, and later on Marie Martin, and perhaps other laywomen as well. The Little Flower was certainly living up to her reputation.

* * *

The consecration ceremony took place as planned in the college chapel in Maynooth on 6 June 1920, just two days after Shanahan's forty-ninth birthday. He chose as his episcopal motto the prayer of the blind man in the gospel, *Domine ut videam,* Lord, that I may see.

The chapel had been completed not long before to a design by the eminent Victorian architect, J.J. McCarthy. It is one of the finest Gothic revival churches in Ireland, with its tall spire, rich stained glass and lavishly decorated interior. The long nave is lined by rows of handsomely carved choir stalls, rising in four tiers on either side of the central passageway. These stalls were filled to overflowing by the six hundred students of the college, who made an impressive spectacle in their surplices and soutanes.

Room was also found for the family and friends of the bishop-elect. His mother had died in 1916 but the rest of the Irish branch of the family were there in strength. Of his five brothers who had left Ireland only Dick, now practising as a doctor in London, was able to attend.

When the congregation had taken their places, the procession of ministers entered the chapel. The bishop-elect was accompanied by his two chaplains or assistant priests; he had chosen Fathers Ronayne and Whitney for this honour. Behind him came the co-consecrators, Bishops Neville and Miller, and last of all the principal consecrator, Bishop Kelly. After the readings of the Mass had been concluded, the rite of consecration began with the singing of the ancient hymn to the Holy Spirit, *Veni Creator Spiritus.* The bishops laid their hands on the head of the bishop-elect and said the prayer of consecration. Then the principal consecrator anointed him on the forehead with chrism, presented him with the book of the gospels, and solemnly invested him with the insignia of his office, the ring, the mitre and the crozier.

The Mass of consecration continued in the accustomed way and ended with the new Bishop's blessing. He made an extraordinarily impressive figure as he turned to face the congregation, tall, dignified, white-bearded, the mitre on his head, the ring on the third finger of his right hand, the crozier grasped in his left. Many of those present were irresistibly reminded of the traditional pictures and statues of Saint Patrick.

As the procession left the church, the students paid a suitable tribute to the Bishop and to the Holy Ghost Congregation by singing the *Chant du départ* or Song of Departure, the Missionary Hymn of the Congregation. The Gounod melody had recently been provided with English words by Father James Burke, CSSp.

Go ye afar,
Go teach all nations;
Bear witness unto me,
On earth in every clime,
And I with you shall be,
Until the end of time.

The vigorous singing of six hundred young men filled the church, bringing tears to eyes and lumps to throats. Monsignor

McCaffrey, the president, declared afterwards that the college had never seen a more beautiful episcopal consecration.

Lunch followed afterwards in the college refectory and ended with various toasts and speeches. McCaffrey paid a glowing tribute to Shanahan, attributing the great success of his ministry to the way in which he had identified himself with the people entrusted to his care. The Lord Mayor of Dublin reflected the struggle for national independence then reaching its climax and mingled religion and patriotism in his speech. 'Ireland stands', he said, 'with the crucifix in one hand and the flag of Irish nationalism in the other.'

In his reply, Shanahan gracefully accepted the tributes on behalf of all his missionary colleagues in Nigeria. 'There is not one among them', he said, 'who does not wish at the end to rest in the land of Nigeria where he has worked and will go on working, following the example of Irish missionaries of every age who were resolved to rest in the land where they fell in the service of God.' It was a wish which would eventually be granted to him in an unexpected way.[11]

In the afternoon, he posed for photographs outside the college with his family and friends. Ronayne and Whitney feature more than once. Shanahan himself appears completely recovered from his illness, and even though in many of the pictures he is seated while others stand, he is always the dominant figure. One quality which people remarked about him was that he drew all eyes to himself. In modern show business they call it star quality. Unconsciously, unintentionally, he upstaged everyone else. In Ireland as in Nigeria, people wanted simply to look at him.

There was much detail to be arranged in connection with the voyage back to Nigeria. Sixteen passages from Liverpool to Calabar had to be booked on the Elder Dempster Line at a total cost of £1,600. He never worried about money and he spent it as freely as if he had an endless supply. In the long run everything always worked out. The only thing that mattered was to get the workers into the harvest. 'Sixteen missionaries for Nigeria!' he wrote exultantly to Ronayne. 'Never in the history of Africa did so many set out together for the same missionfield!'[12]

In September he travelled to Rome and on the 12th had an audience with Pope Benedict XV, who had succeeded Pius X in 1914. The Pope listened with great satisfaction to his account of the Nigerian mission and sent his blessing to the missionaries and to all the Christian people. 'If I could,' he said, 'I would be glad to go and give them my blessing in person.' He presented the new Bishop with a generous donation of 100,000 lire so that he could start building a cathedral in his Vicariate.[13]

The conversation turned to another subject, which Shanahan did not mention in his letters at the time but often spoke about in later years. The Pope asked for information about the troubled situation in Ireland and the name of Terence McSwiney, Lord Mayor of Cork, came up. McSwiney was in prison in Brixton Jail in London and he had gone on hunger strike in protest against the British presence in Ireland. There was much controversy about the morality of his action. Was a hunger strike a legitimate form of protest? Or was it a form of suicide and therefore immoral? The Pope did not enter into the controversy but he said to Shanahan, 'Tell him I sent him my blessing.'

On his way back to Ireland, Shanahan stopped in London and managed with some difficulty to get into the prison. He spoke to the hunger striker, who was now very weak, and gave him the Pope's message. McSwiney was greatly comforted by the blessing. The fact that the Pope had not condemned him set his mind at rest. He died soon afterwards.[14]

The tickets were finally booked for 24 November. Unhappily, only ten were needed. Word came from the Franciscan Missionaries of Mary that their sisters would not be ready to travel until the new year. This was a great disappointment, but he had become used to disappointments of this sort. The priests held firm, and he organised a get-together for the four Irish newcomers and the five French old-timers before they sailed. It took place in Blackrock College from 16 to 21 November, ending with a solemn Mass and a special dinner organised by the college authorities.[15] The next day he crossed to Liverpool, accompanied by Leen, O'Connor, Ronayne and Whitney from Ireland, and Douvry, Groetz, Bindel and Treich from France. The fifth Frenchman, Feral, had been unable to come to Blackrock but he met them in Liverpool. The ten of them boarded the *RMS Ekari* for the journey to Nigeria.

9

The ladies from Ireland

As the *Ekari* steamed its way down the west coast of Africa, Edward Leen kept careful note of his feelings and impressions. The previous year he had been appointed the first editor of *Missionary Annals,* a new missionary magazine published by the Irish province of the Holy Ghost Congregation. Now he was no longer a desk-bound missionary. He was about to become the real thing.

The ship made its usual stop at Freetown in Sierra Leone. The group went ashore and were greeted by Bishop O'Gorman and the other priests in the town. To Leen it felt like a homecoming.

> At about 11 o'clock on Monday morning, the 6th December, four of us set foot on the soil of Africa for the first time. The others perhaps can describe their emotions. I find it impossible to pen my own. One feeling dominated all others — it was the feeling of being at home at last. You will find that astonishing — it surprised myself — yet there it was. The mighty stretch of 3,000 miles that lay between us and Ireland were annihilated as if by magic.[1]

A group photograph was taken of the travellers and their hosts. The Irishmen, young and clean-shaven, are easily distinguishable from their bearded and venerable elders. During the following years, the four Irish priests were to grow beards and then, in a daring break with tradition, shave them off again. It was a sign that a new breed of missionary had arrived.

On 15 December the ship brought them to their final destination, the port of Calabar. Even the veterans among the group were astonished by the warmth of the reception that awaited them. The whole town was celebrating the arrival of Southern Nigeria's first Catholic bishop. Flags were flying everywhere and the harbour was festooned with bunting. As the ship slowly manoeuvred its way towards the quayside, it was surrounded by small boats, bobbing up and down in the water, packed with cheering, waving townsfolk. As soon as it docked, a message was sent asking Shanahan to delay going ashore until after 4.00 p.m. as those who were at work during the day did not want to miss the welcoming ceremony. Leen describes the celebrations with the zest and freshness of a new arrival.

> As the hour approached, the crowds began to gather, and a little after the time appointed the shore was literally (this time) black with people. The Bishop, arrayed in rochet and mozetta and followed by his priests, descended the gangway at 4.30. The young men of the Church Society were the first to welcome him and kiss his ring. It was intended that the Fathers should immediately follow His Lordship, and that the crowd should follow them in processional order. But nothing could beat the enthusiasm that took possession of the people at the sight of their long-absent, much-loved father and their first bishop. Sweeping the priests aside, they took possession of the bishop. I found myself in the midst of a very much excited and radiantly happy throng. From time to time it was possible, as the crowd parted here and there, to get a glimpse of the bishop's purple moving slowly in front: joy and gladness shone from every countenance.
>
> The procession was of immense length and was being continually swelled by the number of people that lined the road and fell in as their great chief passed. The heat that came from that densely-packed mass of human beings, with the rays of an African sun pouring down on it, was overpowering, the dust raised by the trampling feet was stifling, but still one should be made of stone not to have one's heart filled with exultation at the sight of this magnificent display of Catholic loyalty.

After a walk of two miles, the procession arrived at the Sacred Heart Mission. The gate was guarded by African police, appointed to limit the numbers entering. They were powerless to stem the crowd, who poured into the church and filled both it and the grounds around it to overflowing. At the church door, the Bishop was greeted by the priests of the parish, two Irishmen, Fathers Howell and Mellett. He walked up the aisle to the altar, knelt before it and intoned the *Te Deum,* which was taken up by the congregation inside and outside. Then, after a few words expressing his joy at being back again among his people, he gave them his blessing. Leen found his first few hours in Nigeria an overwhelming experience. 'To witness that,' he concludes rapturously, 'was in itself sufficient reward for having left home and country.'[2]

Shanahan stayed in Calabar for Christmas and then made his way to Onitsha where he was given an equally enthusiastic reception. On behalf of the Christians of Southern Nigeria he was presented with two motorcars, a remarkably generous gift from a people whose own standard of living was so low. Further gifts came from the priests and people of Onitsha: a handsomely wrought gold chalice and a substantial sum of money 'to assist in the maintenance of the two cars.'[3] The cars were to be of great use to him in his travels, though the scarcity of roads meant he still had to make many of his journeys by motor-cycle or bicycle or even on foot.

One well-loved face was missing from the welcoming crowd in Onitsha. Brother Adelm had died on 23 July, after a short illness. He was aged sixty-seven. He had lived long enough to rejoice in the honour paid to his nephew but not to congratulate him in person. All Shanahan could do was visit his grave on the Niger bank and pray for his soul.[4]

Now that the reinforcements had arrived, his first concern was to disposition his men. The nine he had brought with him did not mean an overall increase of nine, since others were waiting to go on leave, some on extended sick-leave. Still, the twenty-three priests now at his disposal was the largest number he had ever had in the mission. His respect and regard for Leen had deepened steadily over the past weeks and he decided to keep him with him in Onitsha Waterside. He assigned Ronayne to Calabar, Whitney to Emekuku, O'Connor to Anua. He appointed two of the older men, Douvry and Mellett, to start a new mission in far-off Ogoja, on the borders of the vast and primitive region where the Munchi tribe lived.

Shanahan himself has left us an eye-witness description of the departure of the two men from Calabar on the long trek to Ogoja. Douvry made the first part of his journey by boat.

> He went off in a canoe from Calabar with a canoeful of every possible utensil you could think of. Jellicoe did not look half so imposing as Father Douvry, shouting orders right, left and centre, as he started up the Cross River, a 200 miles pull, amid the cheers and blessings and good wishes

> of his fellow-missionaries and Christians on the bank of the river.
>
> An open canoe, under the African sun during the day and exposed to the cold damp dew of the night, with legions of mosquitoes to disturb one's rest, is not precisely pleasant. Father Douvry weathered the difficulties all right. He got up to Ogoja in tip-top form with all his paraphernalia. Before getting there he had to march 100 miles after leaving the river.

Mellet took a more roundabout way, as he wished to say goodbye to the people among whom he had been working. Shanahan decided to go with him, as part of his visitation of the Vicariate. From his description of their trek, it is obvious how much he enjoyed being able to take to the trail once more.

> Father Mellett went by another route. He paid a final visit to his Oban Christians on the way. They are lost away in the immense virgin forests and mountains of the Oban Hills. It took him over three weeks on foot from the time he left Calabar until he reached Ogoja. I trudged along with him half the way, giving Confirmation to his poor people in their delightful little villages hidden away in the mighty forest.
>
> It was very touching to see the extraordinary welcome they had for their Father, a welcome all the warmer because he spoke not only Efik, the language of the predominant race in Calabar, but also Ekoi, the language of these poor bushmen, who had been driven by their powerful neighbours to take shelter under the friendly protection of the wilderness.
>
> When they learned that this was his final visit to them, as he was travelling away north to regions as yet untrodden by the missioner, to regions where the name of Christ had never yet been heard, these poor Ekois flocked round me, weeping and imploring me not to break their hearts by sending or rather taking away from them their own special Father and friend. I told them that another would take his place, that the country he came from would send them more Fathers and friends in his stead. These scenes were repeated in village after village as we passed along. It was touching, more than words could say.

> At night after the long day's march, or after the day's examinations, Confirmations and instructions, Father Mellett and myself sat and talked far away into the night, before taking our rest in our camp beds, placed under the same little roof in the same small hut. These were happy hours. They were far too short and flew away all too soon. On such an occasion, you know well that two Irishmen cannot forget the old country or the friends far away.
>
> We parted one morning after Mass, I to return to Calabar through the forest, he to go away North after a last farewell to all his friends and children, the Ekois. He had far to travel, all alone and through a country where he had never been. He had the camp bed and the two extra-special pairs of no. 11 brogues that his friends in Ireland provided him with for the journey.
>
> Without saying a word, we shook hands and turned our faces in opposite directions, to conceal the emotions that neither of us dared to show. We parted and soon lost sight of one another in the forest. It will be many months before we meet again.
>
> Among missionaries, is it any wonder that there grows up friendship stronger than bands of steel?[5]

From Calabar he returned to Onitsha, which he used as a base from which to visit the missions in the western part of the vicariate. One of his first visits was to the leper village a short distance from the town. In those days leprosy was thought to be highly contagious and sufferers from the disease were isolated from the rest of the community.

He did not flinch as the lepers crowded round him and begged him to examine them for Confirmation. They wanted him to come and give them the Holy Ghost, and they wanted him to be sure to wear the new robes they had heard about, with the shining gold head-dress and the beautiful stick, more magnificent than the spear of any tribal chief. He examined them and found that the level of theological competence left something to be desired, but he could not refuse any of them their request. A few days later he returned on his bicycle, with a boy to carry his mitre and crozier. The priest who looked after the lepers, Father Geoffrey O'Sullivan, has left us a description of the scene.

The church is packed. The female visitors from Onitsha who are to be sponsors, the servers and the other non-leper members of the congregation are quite close to the Bishop. It is no use to expect that those who are to be confirmed will come two by two as the ceremonial demands. The book of ceremonies was scarcely made out for people who are some of them without feet and some of them without hands. The horror of leprosy seems to be absent. The flowing robes hide most of the wounds and deformities, and there is little that is really repulsive to the sense of sight or smell.

The Bishop speaks. It is an intimate chat, in which he tells them what and whom he brings to them. The ceremony proceeds, the invocations are intoned and the responses given. And then arrives the crucial moment; down goes the Bishop's thumb into the holy chrism and he makes the sign of the cross on the poor disease-eaten forehead, touching the leprous skin: 'I sign thee with the sign of the cross and I confirm thee with the chrism of salvation, in the name of the Father and of the Son and of the Holy Ghost.' And once again does the Bishop's hand touch the leprous face, the cheek: 'Pax tecum – peace be with thee!'

After another short instruction, filled with comfort for those poor sufferers, the Bishop goes up the little path to the right, over the boulders, past the huts, to a door where one is waiting, not indeed a Job covered with sores, but one as patient in her suffering, a poor young girl wrapped in a blanket, her sweet though dusky face badly attacked and eaten with ulcers. Once more the ceremony to her and she too has the stamp of the soldier marked indelibly on her soul to help her to fight her fight on to the end. A lesson in real Christianity.[6]

* * *

When he travelled to other villages for Confirmation, he was more exacting in his examination of the candidates. He took Leen with him on most of these journeys and he amazed the younger man by his ability to cycle sixty or seventy miles in a day when the occasion demanded. Sometimes the examinations took several days, each one filled with excitement and drama, jubilation for the successful, desolation for those who failed. In the evening, when the two men were relaxing in the rest-house, they often found themselves besieged by unsuccessful candidates begging for a second chance. In one village, they were called out to investigate a sudden commotion and found that those who had failed were giving a beating to their teacher, whom they blamed for their misfortune.

The day of the Confirmation was a day of celebration. Even those who had been rejected could console themselves with the knowledge that there would be another opportunity next year. The Bishop's stately presence made him the focus of all eyes and the people's love and reverence for him was almost tangible. When the ceremony was over and it was time for him to go, Leen watched the villagers vying with one another as they showered him with gifts.

> The presents are for the most part in kind — goats, fowl, yams and eggs. These are no mean presents, for a goat will fetch anything from fifteen to thirty shillings, eggs are a penny each, and a person will have done good marketing if he brings home three yams for a shilling. One is irresistibly reminded of the patriarchs of old as the Bishop, with his white hair and venerable beard, passes through the kneeling crowds, followed by a long train of bleating goats and a retinue of boys carrying the yams in baskets on their heads. When he has passed, the kneeling crowds spring to their feet and follow as far as they can — the hardiest and the swiftest keeping pace with the bicycles until they are completely out of breath.[7]

What he remembered most vividly about those days with Shanahan was not the public events, but the talks they had together as they travelled on to the next village, or strolled in the evening air when the examination was over, or sat at night on the verandah of the little rest-house. Shanahan would discuss with him the different questions and answers that came up during the examination of the day and in doing so would reveal the strength of his faith and the depth of his spirituality. The young Doctor of Divinity confessed afterwards that he learnt more from him in two years than any university could have taught him in ten. At the same time, Shanahan profited by exchanging ideas with a trained theological mind. As their relationship developed, they began to put together a framework of the fundamentals of Christian belief as they saw them. Intended to serve as a basis for instructing their Nigerian catechumens, it grew into a vision of Christianity as being essentially the presence of God's life in the soul.

Leen distilled the essence of these discussions into an article entitled 'Catechetical Instruction in Southern Nigeria', which was published in the Maynooth theological journal, the *Irish Ecclesiastical Record.*[8] In it he criticised existing catechisms for their heavy emphasis on sin and morality and the sacrament of penance. As a result, many Christians had a mental picture of their religion in which 'the Ten Commandments bulked centrally and hugely, shading away on either side into a penumbra of dogmatic scraps, the penumbra on one side being illuminated darkly by the lurid glow of the fires of hell.' Instead he proposed, on behalf of Shanahan and himself, a format which would begin with 'the creation of man in the supernatural order by the gift of sanctifying grace.' After this would come the loss of sanctifying grace through the fall of Adam and its restoration through the Incarnation. The Church would be presented as the institution for distributing sanctifying grace, the sacraments as the channels for its distribution, prayer and the commandments as the means of preserving it in the soul.

It is easy to trace the influence of both men in this synopsis. Shanahan's letters show that the presence of God in the soul was central to his thought. This presence gave life to the soul, made it God-like, divinised (a favourite word of his) the soul. To him there was nothing more beautiful than a soul in which God had his dwelling-place. The precepts of the moral law were important to him only as the means of preserving and strengthening that presence. This broad and optimistic view was a useful corrective to Leen's approach, which tended to be strict and legalistic. Before he met Shanahan he would hardly have put the commandments so low on his list of priorities.

Leen's contribution was to provide a theological framework and terminology for Shanahan's intuition. This was not altogether a benefit. It cramped his thought and even distorted it. Shanahan did not normally speak of sanctifying grace or the supernatural order, perhaps because these terms were not easily translated into Ibo. He preferred to speak of God's life and God's presence, closer to the language of Africa and to the language of the New

Testament. Moreover, he did not see the contrast between the natural and the supernatural as sharply as Leen did. He felt that nature was something to be enjoyed rather than suppressed. Hidden here were the seeds of a conflict which would not become apparent for many years.

* * *

All this time Shanahan was increasingly worried about the women and girls. The girl's school in Calabar, the only one in the vicariate, had virtually closed down after the withdrawal of the sisters in 1919. All the boarders had been sent away and there were only a few day-girls being taught by African male teachers. He now had over five hundred schools for boys and just one barely surviving for girls.

All his efforts to recruit new sisters seemed doomed to failure. On 30 March 1921 he wrote in something like despair to his faithful friend and supporter, Mother Arsenius of Foxford, to tell her of his latest disappointment.

> By the same mail came a letter from the Rev. Mother General of the Franciscan Missionaries of Mary with the bad news that she would have to postpone for an indefinite period the departure of her sisters for Nigeria. Alas! for promises made and reiterated! Perhaps it is Holy Providence that is making other arrangements. Nigeria is once again open for the Sisters of Charity. Would they accept to come out on trial for three years if they wish? Or do they definitely renounce work in this mission?

The indomitable Mother Arsenius, now in her eightieth year, responded to the appeal. The General Assembly of the order was meeting in Dublin in May and she got a motion put on the agenda urging them to accept Shanahan's offer and send six sisters to Nigeria before 1 November. The debate was heated and many expressed the view that the needs of Ireland and England must come before the needs of Africa. When the motion was finally voted on, it was rejected by seventy votes to seven. Even Mother Arsenius had to admit defeat. 'Nigeria is quite off and definitely dead', she noted sadly.[9]

There was still one last resort. Marie Martin had finished her midwifery course and was as interested as ever in the missions. What was more, she had met a medical student, Agnes Ryan, who was also willing to come to Nigeria. Even before he heard of Mother Arsenius' failure, Shanahan sent Marie a telegram. 'Sisters departure considerably delayed your presence Calabar much needed try come when colonial outfit completed writing Bishop Shanahan.' The letter which followed explained the situation in detail and gave practical information on what was meant by a colonial outfit.

> Don't forget your passports. Get a good lady's sunhat or pith helmet. They are to be had at the Junior Army & Navy Stores, D'Olier St. Pillows, pillowcases, sheets, table linen etc. etc. needed; also light jaeger khaki blankets. All bills etc. to be sent to Father Meagher on my account. Don't forget a good deckchair. Come on the monthly Calabar steamer.

The two women arrived in Calabar on 14 June 1921. Shanahan was unable to leave Onitsha and had to content himself with sending a welcome telegram. Father Tommy Ronayne, who had known both of them while he was in Dublin, was at the quayside when they docked and had a guard of honour of boy scouts drawn up to greet them. They were brought to Saint Joseph's, the old convent of the Sisters of Cluny, and they found the house in good condition, with a number of Catholic girls looking after it. They set to work at once to get the school re-organised.

Since the school had been run by nuns, it was decided to confer honorary sisterhoods on the two new teachers. Agnes became known as Sister Agnes, Marie as Sister Mary. Agnes Ryan had teaching as well as medical qualifications and she took over as principal teacher. Mary Martin taught religion and English and looked after the housekeeping.

The news that the sisters had returned spread quickly and pupils began to flock to the school. The lower floor of the building was used for classrooms and the upper floor provided living quarters for the sisters and dormitories for the boarders. When Shanahan finally managed to get to Calabar in August, he was delighted to find the school running smoothly with 160 pupils on the rolls. He appointed Mary Martin sister-in-charge and before long was referring to her as Reverend Mother. She herself, having been a nurse during the Great War and having recently completed her training in midwifery, felt she would like to use her medical skills. She asked him if she could attend the sick in their homes and in the local hospital and he gave her written permission to do so 'in urgent cases'. There is the first hint here of a difference in emphasis that would later grow more marked, he more interested in education, she in medicine.

It was obvious both to him and to her that if the work were to continue and expand, more volunteers would have to come from Ireland and some kind of formal structure would have to be set up. Once again, the idea of setting up a religious order presented itself to his mind, this time with more immediacy. As yet he had only two potential members, and one of them, Agnes Ryan, was suffering from malaria which she seemed unable to shake off. But there was an encouraging number of inquiries coming from Ireland and there was reason to hope that more volunteers would soon be arriving in Calabar. And there was Mary Martin. His respect for her qualities deepened, for her spirituality, her judgement, her tenacity, her resourcefulness, her courage. In spite of her frail appearance, she was the rock on which a great edifice could be built.

He left Calabar to return to Onitsha and resume his visitations of the Vicariate but he continued to discuss his plans with her by letter. In September he sent her the Book of Rules of the Franciscan Missionaries of Mary as a possible model for their own projected congregation. 'I feel quite certain you will be delighted with them', he wrote. 'They are the best I've ever seen.'

Later that month he wrote again to her on the occasion of her making a commitment of herself to the work. 'Please accept my sincerest congratulations on the great decision you have taken: the perpetual sacrifice of yourself to service of God as a religious and in Nigeria.' But the news was not all good. Agnes Ryan's health was worsening. He reluctantly came to the decision that she would have to go back to Ireland. In October he made the journey to Calabar to say goodbye to her and thank her for all she had done.

Now Mary Martin was alone and all the responsibility of the school fell on her shoulders. It did not seem to worry her. She organised classes, supervised the work of the teachers and the pupils, and attended to their material needs. When the Christmas holidays came, she headed for Onitsha with four of the schoolgirls for another meeting with the Bishop. He offered her the use of the old convent building and of the mission car during her visit. It is not known whether she used the car (in later life she was to be notorious for her reckless driving) but she certainly stayed in the convent, deserted since the Sisters of Cluny left it twelve years earlier. Shanahan was happy to see the building in use again and saw in it a foretaste of better times to come.[10]

In the new year, 1922, he decided it was time to start drawing up the constitution of the new congregation. He had many other duties to attend to and it was not until after Easter that he could come to Calabar and get down to serious work. A series of meetings were held in the evenings on the verandah of the priests' house in Calabar, meetings that were to live long in the memories of those that took part in them. They all felt they were present at the beginning of something new and exciting and filled with endless potential. A door was opening in Southern Nigeria. Leen wrote:

> The members of the group differed one from the other in many respects — in temperament, experience, education, mentality — in almost all that contributes to impart psychological stamp to a human being. They were drawn together and unified in one particular: they all shared in an absorbing passion for the welfare of souls, for the thronging multitudes that peopled the land of Southern Nigeria.[11]

The priests' house was a two-storey building on a hill high above the town, free from the mosquitoes that swarmed along the waterfront. The verandah, a wide balcony on the upper floor, was a pleasant place to sit and talk in the cool of the evening. There were four people in the group that met on that verandah in Calabar: Shanahan, the inspirer and father-figure; Leen, the clear-minded theologian; Ronayne, the gifted and sensitive director of souls; and Mary Martin, whose practicality and common sense made sure that even when their heads were in the clouds their feet stayed on the ground. She described the outcome in a letter to her mother.

> Two weeks were spent on Rules and Constitution. I was chosen as Foundress; it may pave the way for someone more

> worthy. The Order could not be founded before 1927, as five years are required to have novices trained and professed, to obtain approval from Rome and sufficient candidates. You, as President of the Mission League, are to interview candidates and refer them to the bishop and myself. Only those hoping to become Sisters are to be sent out in future.

By the time her letter reached Ireland, three new volunteers were already on their way. They were Catherine (Katie) Meagher, a schoolteacher, Joan Murtagh, a civil servant, and Elizabeth (Bessie) Ryan, a medical student, no relation of Agnes Ryan. They had not been very well briefed on the situation in Calabar, and when they arrived there in May they expected to see only sand and savages. They were surprised to be met by the Bishop in person, along with the priests, European officials, and Christians of Calabar, to the accompaniment of flowers, bands and dancing. It was Katie Meagher's first meeting with Shanahan and she was tremendously impressed. He seemed to her like Saint Patrick come to earth again. She piled up epithets to describe him: Christlike, manly, apostolic, shrewd, gentlemanly, intelligent, generous. He told her and her two companions that all he asked of them was to live as real Christian women and to let the African women see what this kind of living meant. He then returned to Onitsha and left them to get on with their work.

They were a little taken aback to discover that they were expected to stay for five years and that it was proposed to form the volunteers into a religious order. This was rather more than they had bargained for. But they set to work in the school, where they had six classes to teach and no assistance apart from two not very helpful African male teachers. In the afternoons they gave special training to some of the girls who were hoping to become teachers themselves. In the school they wore a simple habit, consisting of a white dress, a white headscarf and a blue sash. In the open air, the inevitable pith helmet was put on over the headscarf.

Katie Meagher was not impressed by her companions. She thought them somewhat flighty, over-interested in the social life of the European community with its dances, parties, and At Homes in the Governor's House. Though she herself had no more intention than they had of becoming a nun, she felt that the calling of a lay-missionary did not combine very easily with the social round of the colonials. She was not surprised when the other two began to have second thoughts about staying in Nigeria.[12]

Shanahan re-appeared in Calabar in July. He had decided to return to Ireland and Leen was to go with him. His principal reason for going was a deterioration in his health. There had been a worrying recurrence of the pains that had heralded his liver abscess three years earlier. In addition, he was having trouble with his sight and one of his eyes might need surgical treatment. A spell in Europe would also give him an opportunity to recruit some more missionaries.

To his dismay, Bessie Ryan and Joan Murtagh asked if they could go back with him. The six weeks they had spent in Nigeria were small return for what he paid on their passage out and back but he was realist enough to know that an unwilling worker would do the cause no good. He consented with a good grace and during the whole of the three-week voyage was unfailingly kind and considerate to them both. Bessie has left us a description of the voyage.

> On the journey home we sat at the doctor's table in the dining saloon — Bishop Shanahan, Dr Leen, a Government Officer of the Howard family, and the two of us. Both the Bishop and Dr Leen manifested their capacity for doing everything well, even during those short three weeks. Their whole mornings were given to reading and the study of how best to give to the catechumens and the new Christians an even deeper understanding of the nature of the new life in their souls and an appreciation of it. They read and discussed *La Grâce et la Gloire,* and seemed to go into a kind of ecstasy about it. Sanctifying grace seemed to unfold new and deeper meanings to both of them at this time.
>
> When the work of the morning was over, they set out to enjoy the journey and they did it well. The fun was fast and furious at table and there were enjoyable talks, mostly by the bishop, on deck in the evenings.[13]

They landed in Liverpool on 13 August. Bessie had been so won over by three weeks of Shanahan's company that she declared she wanted to go back again to Nigeria and become a religious. Her wish was to be granted, but not until very much later. For the time being, they went their separate ways, Shanahan and Leen to Paris, Bessie and Joan to Dublin.

In Calabar, Katie Meagher continued with her teaching work to the best of her ability but she too began to develop health problems. In December the doctor told her she would have to leave and she returned to Ireland in the new year. Mary Martin was alone once again.

10

The house on the hill

Shanahan intended to spend no more than six or eight months in Europe. But nothing turned out as planned, one complication led to another, and in the event it was to be the better part of two years before he saw Nigeria again.

From Liverpool, he and Leen went to the mother-house in Paris. They took part in the annual retreat at Chevilly, which lasted from 15 to 22 August. Shanahan saw the Superior General, now promoted to Archbishop, and made his usual report on the situation of the Church in Southern Nigeria.

The meeting did not go altogether smoothly. The idea of bringing in secular priests for limited periods was a novelty for Le Roy, but whatever his misgivings he did not oppose it. But when Shanahan spoke of his intention to found a sisterhood devoted to the needs of Southern Nigeria, Le Roy produced an alternative proposal. He told Shanahan that he himself was setting up a new missionary order of women, which would be linked with the Holy Ghost Congregation and called the Holy Ghost Missionary Sisters. He suggested that instead of starting a completely separate order, Shanahan should send recruits from Ireland to train with the Holy Ghost Sisters in France.

There were good reasons for accepting Le Roy's proposal. First of all, there was Shanahan's loyalty to the Superior General and the Congregation. Then there was the fact that the long and complicated process of getting papal approval for the new order would be avoided, since it would be handled by Le Roy. Against this was Shanahan's fear that he would have no control over the appointment of the sisters and could find them being sent anywhere in the world. Moreover, he distrusted the French influence which would be dominant in the new order. He had found that the strict rules of the Cluny Sisters had made it difficult for them to work effectively in Nigeria.

Shanahan turned down Le Roy's offer. It was not easy to state his reasons without giving offence, especially since Le Roy was unwilling to take No for an answer. They parted on somewhat strained terms, with Le Roy saying that he would like to discuss the matter again. Shanahan returned to Ireland, upset by the confrontation but still determined to go ahead with his original plan.[1]

On 1 September, he was back in Blackrock College, which was to be his headquarters for this and all his subsequent visits to Ireland. For some reason, his entry into hospital was delayed. Instead, he embarked on a round of lectures and sermons which would have taxed a man of the most robust health. He was in great demand as a preacher and speaker and he rarely turned down an invitation. He spoke in churches, halls, seminaries, convents, colleges, schools, anywhere he could find an audience. On every occasion, he spoke about the work of the missions and the duty of all Christians to be involved in the spreading of the faith. Wherever he went, his impact on the young was immediate and lasting. He made less impression on some older listeners, especially those in ecclesiastical authority. He discovered to his disappointment that the Irish Church was not yet as fully committed to the cause of the missions as he had hoped.

He was invited to preach at the Mass which marked the opening of the academic year in University College, Dublin. One of the students in University Church that morning was Catherine O'Carroll, drawn by the preacher's growing reputation. She was a little disappointed by the content of the sermon. He spoke about the missionary's work of bringing divine life to souls instead of telling exciting stories about darkest Africa. But she was not disappointed by the man. 'I was impressed by his appearance, his dignity, his obvious sanctity — a real missionary!' Four years later she was to join the sisterhood he founded.[2]

The new Archbishop of Dublin, Dr Edward Byrne, was also at the Mass and Shanahan took the opportunity to have a chat with him about Nigeria. Byrne asked him if he had any secular priests in his Vicariate. Shanahan said he had, including one from Byrne's own diocese, Father Ronayne. 'He is the last you will get', said Byrne crushingly. Shanahan wrote sadly to Mary Martin:

> The Archbishop of Dublin is dead against missioners and foreign missioners in particular taking any vocations from his diocese. He will not do much for us. If he only knew that special blessings are in store for the archdiocese the day he declares openly for mission work among pagans.[3]

The Archbishop of Westminster, Cardinal Bourne, was more sympathetic to the cause. Shanahan was among those invited to speak at the Missionary Congress held in London towards the end of September. He addressed a large gathering including the Cardinal, bishops, priests and laity in Caxton Hall on the 29th of that month. 'The Bishop was asked to speak on educational problems in Africa,' wrote Leen, who was with him, 'but he spoke only of his own experience. It was very effective.'[4]

Shanahan had a more immediate problem to discuss with Bourne, the strange case of Sister Charles Walker. She was the friend of Mother Arsenius from Foxford who had volunteered to go to Nigeria with the Sisters of Charity in 1919. The following year she was moved from Foxford to Bray, in the diocese of Dublin. When the Sisters finally voted against Africa in 1921, Charles decided she wanted to go on her own. The Sisters of Charity were aghast, the canon lawyers were aghast, the Archbishop of Dublin was most aghast of all. Sister Charles was told that nobody except the Pope could grant her permission to leave her community in such circumstances. Sister Charles said she would be quite happy to ask the Pope.

In 1922 the Mother General transferred her to the Charity convent in Chiswick, London, to be near her dying father. A secondary reason was to place her under the jurisdiction of Cardinal Bourne, who was likely to be more sympathetic than Archbishop Byrne. Shanahan was pleased to discover that her application had gone to Rome and that Bourne was giving her his full support. It is very likely that he visited her in Chiswick to encourage her in her resolution. He intended her to play an important role in the new sisterhood, possibly as Mistress of Novices.[5]

He returned to Ireland to resume his campaign on behalf of the mission. On 5 October he addressed a meeting of the Holy Ghost African Missionary League, a mission support group founded by Mary Martin's mother. To great enthusiasm, he made the first public announcement of his intention to found an Irish missionary congregation of sisters who would care for the spiritual and material needs of the women of Nigeria. A full account of the meeting appeared in the *Holy Ghost Missionary Annals* and it gives a vivid impression of the way he could sway a sympathetic audience. The slightly over-wrought style seems to catch exactly the mood of those who heard him.

> His Lordship Bishop Shanahan then rose to speak. A thrill passed through the crowded hall when the venerable missionary faced the audience. Perhaps more even than his imposing presence — for Bishop Shanahan, tall, robust, with the glory of hair grown white in the service of God, with his features browned and tanned by the suns of more than twenty years under the African skies, is nothing if not imposing — it was the halo that for those familiar with the African missions surrounds his name, the memory of his energy and devotedness, the tremendous impetus the very vigour of his personality has given to missionary work all along the west coast, the almost legendary progress of the faith in his vast Vicariate, and much more that was in our minds that thrilled us as the great missionary looked down on us from the platform. Few of us that were there that evening will ever forget that moment when Bishop Shanahan began to speak.[6]

His next target was his own Congregation. On 1 November he gave a lantern slide show followed by a talk in Blackrock College. The talk hit hard against the educational policy of the Holy Ghost Congregation. Now that there were other religious orders involved in education, he said, was it not high time that the Holy Ghost colleges in Ireland flew the missionary flag of Africa, which was the flag of the Congregation? Should they not devote themselves exclusively to the education of missionaries? He sent a summary of what he had said to the new Irish provincial, Father Joseph Byrne, and commented, 'I tremble for those in authority who would keep priests doing schoolmasters' work for any other reason than that of absolute urgent necessity, where God's honour and glory and the salvation of souls is concerned.' To soften the sting he added, 'Won't you pardon an old missioner for writing *tamquam auctoritatem habens'* — that is, as one having authority.

The old missioner received a diplomatic but basically unyielding reply from the young Provincial.

> It is a splendid ideal and we shall think of it and work towards it and perhaps eventually attain it, but you'll forgive a young administrator if he feels nervous in the face of such an abrupt break with all the ideas and traditions of the

> Province. For the moment and at this critical stage, I'd prefer to try to combine the works and direct all to the main end. Developments will come in God's good time.[7]

One more opportunity to influence the Congregation came in the form of an invitation to speak at the annual dinner of the Holy Ghost past pupils, which took place in the Metropole restaurant in Dublin. It was perhaps too much to expect that the alumni of the three colleges would welcome a proposal which would mean the closing down of their schools as they knew them. Shanahan and Leen both wrote to Mary Martin about it. 'The audience was unsympathetic', Shanahan told her. Leen was more optimistic. 'They listened, at least, politely. Anyhow we are driving home the fact that we are a missionary congregation above and before anything else.'

Shanahan went into Saint Vincent's Hospital in mid-November. Four days later he was operated on for his liver condition, which was found to be more serious than expected. The operation was considered a complete success. After a couple of weeks of recuperation, a second operation was performed, this time to remove a cataract from one of his eyes, and it too was successful. 'He has not been so well for years', Leen told Mary Martin, but added, 'It was somewhat startling to learn that he was in danger of sudden death every time he rode a motor bicycle in Africa or exerted himself violently in any other way.'

* * *

Recovered from his operations, Shanahan started house-hunting in early 1923. He was looking for some roomy old house which could be used as the first convent of his new sisterhood. He had definitely decided against any liaison with the French sisters, strengthened by a very firm letter from Mary Martin. He had asked her for her candid opinion on Le Roy's proposal and she told him she was totally opposed to it.

> We would be always under a French rule and Spirit, which I am and have all my life been against. The French training system is very bad. They are very narrow in themselves. This reacts in all their works and they are not able to cope with the broad work of a missionary life. They forget Christ's beautiful prayer for his disciples, a thing that strikes me very much, when he prayed, 'I pray, not that Thou shouldst take

them out of the world, but that Thou shouldst keep them from evil.'

In February he heard of a house for sale in Kimmage, near Dublin. It seemed ideal. The house and its grounds were of a suitable size and it was close to Kimmage Manor, the College where Holy Ghost students were educated for the priesthood. This meant that priests would be available to act as chaplains and spiritual directors to the sisters when he had returned to Nigeria. It was also within easy reach of Blackrock College, where Leen had been appointed to the teaching staff as Dean of Studies.

The Provincial's decision to keep Leen in Ireland was a blow to Shanahan, as it deprived him of the companionship of the man who had become closer to him than anyone else. Yet he could see a silver lining in the cloud. As Dean and later as President of the college (for he was obviously destined for the higher office), Leen would be in a very influential position in the Irish Province. He might even become Provincial in due course. In him, Nigeria and the missions would have a very powerful and committed advocate. Furthermore, he had played a central role in the planning of the new sisterhood and would be the ideal man to supervise its development when Shanahan went back to Nigeria.

Since the house was in the archdiocese of Dublin, Shanahan approached the Vicar General, Monsignor Hickey, for permission to bid for it. Hickey assured him that there would be no objection from the Archbishop and Shanahan went ahead with his plans to buy it. All went well until the day of the auction. That very morning a written message arrived from Monsignor Hickey to say that the Archbishop would not hear of Shanahan buying the house.

It was a pattern that was to repeat itself all through the long frustrating year that lay ahead. He quickly found out that as a Nigerian bishop he had no rights in Ireland. He could do nothing without the consent of the local bishop and that consent was simply not forthcoming. He thought of getting some land from Rockwell College ground and obtained the permission of the Archbishop of Cashel, but for some reason the project fell through. Then he spent a week with Bessie Ryan's family in Abbeyleix and found that nearby Durrow Castle was both suitable and available. He applied to the Bishop of Ossory for permission to buy but the Bishop, while not refusing outright, showed a marked lack of enthusiasm. All he brought back from Abbeyleix was a happy memory of the Ryans' hospitality and of the bluebells that filled the surrounding woods. He does not say how many other bishops he approached without success, but he gives the impression that they were many. They all feared that the new house of sisters would adversely affect their dioceses, which might have to support it, or their priests, who might have to service it, or their local vocations, which might be diverted away from home.

* * *

Around this time, a crisis blew up in Calabar which added to his worries. The priests there discovered that there were widespread abuses in their apparently flourishing Catholic community. Many of those who came devoutly to Mass and the sacraments were deliberately living double lives. Some were polygamists, some were prostitutes, some were practitioners of pagan rites. Everyone in the town knew about it except the missionaries. Naturally, the priests reacted and even, especially in the case of Father Ronayne, overreacted. Something resembling an inquisition was set up. All the Catholics were individually questioned by the priests and had to prove their good faith before being admitted to Mass and the sacraments. The task of questioning the women was given to Mary Martin.

Shanahan began to feel guilty about his prolonged absence from Nigeria. The Calabar crisis would have happened in any event, but if he had been there it might have been handled more sensitively. He was particularly concerned about Mary Martin and the unpleasant new responsibility that had been thrust upon her. There was an American girl in Dublin called Veronica Hasson whose brother was a Holy Ghost priest in Southern Nigeria. She had volunteered to go to Calabar and Shanahan rather hastily sent her out so that Mary would have a companion to share her burdens. Mary was not over-pleased. She had already given Shanahan a respectful but firm warning about sending out unsuitable candidates.

> My Lord, we cannot be too particular. Be very hard and exacting. Your mind and heart are far beyond the average woman. Women would take advantage of your generosity and your desire to open a door to any soul that you really believe wants to serve God on the missions.

Within a short time she was writing to her mother, 'Miss Hasson is not the right sort of person to send here without training. Only an exceptional girl will stand the strain of living here as a religious and according to rule.'

Meanwhile, the case of Sister Charles was being examined in Rome. In April, Shanahan heard that permission for her to go to Nigeria was about to be granted. It was not until June that the formal document arrived in London. 'Sister Charles is free!', he wrote jubilantly to Mary Martin and started making travel arrangements for her. He decided that in view of the fact that she was now attached to the Vicariate of Southern Nigeria rather than the Sisters of Charity, she should take a new religious name. She chose the name Magdalen in memory of a recently dead Sister, and during all her time in Nigeria was known as Sister Magdalen.[8]

In July he went to Rome himself to get approval for the new sisterhood and to report on his Vicariate to the new Pope. Pius XI had been elected Pope in February in succession to Benedict XV and was still something of an unknown quantity. He was to emerge as a man of strong character and a determined opponent of both Hitlerism and Stalinism. He was deeply committed to the missionary work of the Church in Africa and Asia. He was to encourage the independence of local churches and the ordination of native priests and bishops, in the face of considerable opposition from within the Roman establishment. His encyclical letter *Rerum Ecclesiae* in 1926 was to be a major influence in developing the missionary policy of the Church.

Shanahan found him very different from his predecessors. The meeting was not to be confined to broad outlines and generalities. This Pope was interested in all the details and prepared to discuss them. He pored over all Shanahan's photographs of Nigeria and carefully studied the statistics, reading them aloud. He gave his enthusiastic approval to the scheme for bringing out secular priests on temporary contracts. 'It will have a double benefit', he said: 'the missions will profit from it and they will no longer be unknown territory for the secular clergy.'[9]

Shanahan then spoke of his plan to start a new sisterhood for Nigeria. The Pope was fully in favour of the project and gave it not only his consent but his encouragement. After all the difficulties, it was an intensely emotional moment for Shanahan when the Pope gave his *Fiat,* his 'Let it be'. He saw that word not merely as a granting of approval but as a giving of life. In that moment he became the father of a great progeny. In that moment he was bound to them and they to him by a mystical bond that could never be broken. Many years later he was to speak of it in a letter to Sister Catherine O'Carroll.

> That was a solemn moment for me on my knees before the Holy Father upon whose will depended your very existence; and our Holy Father said 'Fiat'. Can I ever forget that moment! For one can never forget that little scene where an old missionary Bishop, carrying you all in his heart, asked on his knees Our Lord to give you life through the lips of another old man, His Vicar on earth. From the moment the Holy Father's fiat was pronounced, I became conscious of its quasi-sacramental effect. From that moment I carried you all, living now as God's consecrated spouses, in my soul, conscious that I was united to each of you by a special bond of spiritual paternity. Hence my profound spiritual love for each one of you, for the whole Congregation.

True to style, Pius was not content with giving his approval. He went into considerable detail in regard to the setting up of the new sisterhood. Shanahan took careful note of all his suggestions and when he got back to Ireland he wrote a full account of them to Mary Martin.[10]

> Our Holy Father, when granting me the privilege of organising a missionary sisterhood in Nigeria, said:
>
> 1. that no girls should be taken out to Nigeria until their missionary and religious vocation had been tested by experienced religious at home;
>
> 2. that a Mistress of Novices should be found to look after the missionary novices in Nigeria;
>
> 3. that, the girls' vocation being tested, they should take the habit and go to Nigeria as novices, there to continue their missionary and religious novitiate for a period of from three to five years;
>
> 4. if after that period a certain number of novices had persevered, I could establish a canonical novitiate and admit novices to profession;
>
> 5. the rules and regulations to be made from lived experience as we went along;

> 6. when, finally, the little order seemed well on its feet, he would give it pontifical approval.
>
> In a nutshell, this is how we stand. There is full liberty to go ahead on lines we judge best. There could not be any greater liberty given, and we have our Holy Father's approval to experiment and go ahead and report as we go along.
>
> Sister M. Magdalen was given by our Holy Father to Nigeria to act as Mistress of Novices.[11]

Sister Magdalen, the former Sister Charles, left for Calabar on 12 September. With typical courtesy, Shanahan travelled over to Liverpool to see her off. She arrived in Calabar on 3 October and was welcomed in the midst of a tropical downpour by Father Ronayne, Mary Martin and Veronica Hasson. 'We first went to the parish church, then to the schools, lastly home to the convent. I am delighted with all I have seen', she wrote to Mother Arsenius. It was decided that as soon as she had familiarised herself with the situation, she would take over full direction of the school.[12]

* * *

The search for a house in Ireland went on. Father Pat Whitney had shown a remarkable talent for organisation in Emekuku, so Shanahan decided to bring him back to Ireland to publicise the new sisterhood and raise funds for their future convent. Whitney did not disappoint him. He travelled around Ireland on a battered motor-cycle, giving slide-shows and lectures on Nigeria. Money and inquiries began to flow in.

For Shanahan himself it was a time not only of frustration but of indecision. He was now over a year absent from his vicariate and he was feeling increasingly guilty. Yet if he returned, all the work of the previous year might go for nothing. There were half a dozen girls who were eager to join now, but who might go elsewhere if the delay continued. He could not find a house where they could live in Ireland. He was now convinced from experience that it would be premature to bring them out to Nigeria. His letters show him toying with various possibilities, none of them satisfactory.

One possibility was that they would accept an invitation to go to the convent of the newly founded Columban Missionary Sisters in Cahircon, Co Clare. He decided against this, perhaps fearing that his small group would be submerged and lose its identity. Another possibility was that they might be received as a group in some convent boarding school and there receive basic training in the religious life. He explored this possibility with the Dominican Convent in Cabra on the northern outskirts of Dublin, one of the leading convent schools in the country. The response from the Prioress, Mother Colmcille, was gratifyingly positive. Within days of his return from Liverpool, he had come to an arrangement with her which seemed to meet all his immediate needs.

He shot off letters at once to all those who had expressed interest in joining the sisterhood. The first two names on his list were the two Ryans, Agnes and Bessie. His letter to Bessie was written on 17 September.

> There is news at long last. I didn't care to write to you until there was news. And here it is. On the 1st Oct, this coming month, the Cabra Sisters are granting me the exceptional favour of taking into their convent the first seven postulants of the Nigerian Missionary Sisters. This was settled two days ago and it is to be kept quiet for a hundred and one reasons. Needless to say, Agnes is no. 1 on the list and you are no. 2.
>
> Now write to me immediately before you say anything to anybody and tell me what you think of it. Are you still ready for the great sacrifice and are you feeling physically fit for it? You know what I mean and what the year in Cabra will mean. The religious habit will be given at the end of the year. Then Nigeria and a further period of from two to three years Novitiate as missioners before taking vows, so that the sisters may well understand their vocation and see whether they have one or not.
>
> I am most anxious to have a long talk with you before you speak to anybody about it. During all those months since the bluebells came and went I often thought of you and often wished I could go down to where the bluebells grow. I will try to get down some time next week, as early as possible. I'll wire you or write. Tell me where I may find you.[13]

Now at last, after a long period of stagnation, everything began to happen at once. He wrote to the others on his list and arranged to meet them. He sent a letter to Calabar asking Veronica Hasson to return at once and join the group in Cabra; Mary Martin, of whose vocation he had no doubt, was to stay on until Sister Magdalen had firmly established herself.

On 1 October the first four arrived in Cabra. The veteran of Calabar, Agnes Ryan, was the eldest and was given the honour of being regarded as the first member of the new sisterhood. They were provided with a sitting-room and a dormitory apart from the boarders in the convent so that they could live their own community life without disturbance. The Dominican nuns arranged a programme of religious formation, which included instruction in doctrine, in plain chant, in spiritual reading and in mental prayer.

Two of the first four came from Co. Cavan. Shanahan arranged to meet them and bring them to Dublin but the plans miscarried and when he arrived at their homes he found they had already left. It was a fortunate blunder. Finding himself with time on his hands, he decided to pay a courtesy call on the Bishop of Kilmore, Dr Patrick Finegan, whose cathedral and house were in Cavan town. The Bishop received him hospitably and invited him to dine and stay the night with him.

During the course of their conversation, Shanahan spoke of his efforts to find a house and the number of bishops he had asked in vain. He was saying a novena of Masses for the Holy Souls with that very intention in mind but he had almost given up hope. 'You didn't ask me', said Finegan. He not only gave Shanahan full permission to buy a house in his diocese, but suggested a number of suitable properties and offered him the use of his own car to inspect them.

He began house-hunting again with renewed hope. Many owners of large country houses were anxious to sell because of the current political unrest and especially because of the number of young men who were anxious to prove their patriotism by setting fire to as much as they could of the country's architecture. He had the good sense to enlist the help of his sister, Mrs Mary Dawson, whose womanly eye was quick to point out defects that escaped his notice.

He was especially taken by Virginia Lodge, magnificently situated on the shore of Lough Ramor. When he rhapsodised about the view, his sister pointed out how much it would cost to make the house habitable and said sharply, 'Nuns can't live on scenery.' She was better satisfied with Drumullac House, substantial and in good repair, built on a hill near the village of Killeshandra, about ten miles from Cavan town. The owner wanted £5,500, a substantial sum at that time, but Shanahan always treated money as the least of his problems. A little negotiation got the price reduced to £5,000 and he borrowed the amount from the Ulster Bank, confident that Father Whitney would soon succeed in paying it off.[14]

During October two more joined the group in Cabra. One of them was Bessie Ryan. Shanahan called to Abbeyleix to collect her. Years later her brother recalled the family standing around awkwardly in the hallway as she was leaving and the distress shown by their father. He never forgot the way Shanahan spoke to the old man. 'Don't be sad, Pat. I'm not taking her away. It's you who are giving her to God.'[15]

Veronica Hasson arrived from Calabar, returning on the same boat that brought Sister Magdalen out. She joined the group in Cabra on 20 November and made up the full complement of seven. An eighth applied and seemed so suitable that the Dominicans agreed to find room for her and she was admitted in early December. During the Christmas holidays the eight remained in Cabra and Father Whitney set them to work sending out raffle tickets to schools all over the country. The response was very encouraging. The names of Nigeria and Bishop Shanahan were beginning to take root in the hearts of the Irish people.

A multitude of things still remained to be settled. One was the name of the new sisterhood. Shanahan intended to call them the Missionary Sisters of the Holy Ghost but when he sent the name to Rome he was told that there was already another order of that name, the one that Le Roy had founded. It was the Prioress of Cabra, Mother Colmcille, who suggested the name by which they were to become known: the Missionary Sisters of the Holy Rosary.

He turned to Mother Colmcille for the solution to a more serious problem. Now that he had the house, he was having second thoughts about sending the postulants to Nigeria for their novitiate. It seemed far more sensible to keep them in Ireland for three or four years until they had made their first profession, and then send them to Nigeria when they were mature enough to cope with the new challenges they would find there. In order to carry out this plan, he would need experienced sisters to take charge of the new house for a period of three to five years. Could Mother Colmcille possibly provide them?

It is a tribute both to Shanahan's charisma and to Mother Colmcille's generosity that the Dominicans granted his request. Four of the sisters were selected to supervise the new Holy Rosary Convent in Killeshandra for a period of five years. Mother Xavier, a former prioress, was to be the superior, and Mother Aquinas, the Mistress of Studies in Cabra, was to be Mistress of Novices. The two others were Sister Ursula and Sister Anastasia. It would have been difficult to find four sisters more ideally qualified for the work. It was a real sacrifice on the part of Cabra to part with them.

One obstacle remained. They had to obtain the permission of the Archbishop of Dublin before they could leave Cabra. It should have been a formality, but the Archbishop's responses were unpredictable. However, he made no difficulty about granting the permission. 'I am giving you the best nuns in the Archdiocese', he said, dazzled by the spectacle of his own magnanimity. Everything was now settled and a telegram went out to Mary Martin in Calabar: 'Return Dublin earliest enter novitiate. Shanahan.'

The formal possession of the new house took place on 25 February 1924. Three car-loads left Cabra after Mass that morning. The motorcade included Shanahan, Mother Colmcille and the four nuns who had been chosen to supervise the new foundation. Edward Leen was there to see them off, but when one of the cars returned for Shanahan's breviary, he yielded to a sudden impulse and got in. They were the advance party, charged with preparing the house for the arrival of the main group.

On arrival, they were received by Mrs Dawson and her daughter May, who had gone ahead to open the house. Mother Colmcille had a statue of Our Lady with her and her first act on entering the house was to place it on a table in the hall. Unconsciously she was establishing a tradition that was to be followed in all subsequent Holy Rosary foundations. That evening Leen blessed the house and the following morning Shanahan said the first Mass there.

The feast of Saint Thomas Aquinas, the great Dominican theologian, falls on 7 March. This was the day chosen for the arrival of the seven from Cabra. Once again Shanahan was there to accompany them on their hundred-mile journey. He drove one of the cars and his nephew, Michael Dawson, drove the other. The day was very cold and there was snow on the ground. The first sight of the house, black and stark against the white hillside, was not reassuring but the welcome they received when they went in was warm. The girls were now officially postulants and the nuns helped them to put on their black dresses and veils. Then they went to the newly fitted-out chapel to sing the *Veni Creator* and make their Act of Oblation. Shanahan gave them a talk on the meaning of the religious life, which they must regard as the framework which would support them in their work as missionaries. They returned again to the chapel for Benediction. It was the birthday of the Holy Rosary Sisters.[16]

There was nothing to keep Shanahan any longer from his vicariate and he booked his passage for Nigeria. He had not yet left when Mary Martin arrived, returning from Calabar on his instructions. She had been accompanied on the voyage by Father Ronayne, coming home to recuperate after a bout of malaria and general nervous exhaustion. As she herself was also somewhat run down, it was decided that she would not enter Killeshandra until June.

Shanahan saw another change in her that was more worrying. She seemed to have lost some of her zest for the work. He was inclined to blame this on Ronayne, who had sunk in his esteem as a result of the events in Calabar. He was still Mary Martin's spiritual director and must have had every opportunity to influence her during the voyage home. However, Shanahan was confident that once she had recovered her strength and joined the community in Killeshandra, she would regain her old enthusiasm and fulfil her role as corner-stone of the new sisterhood.[17]

Before leaving, he appointed Leen as his official representative in all matters relating to the convent. Whitney was to continue as chief fund-raiser. Ronayne was given the post of convent chaplain, in which his main duty was to say Mass each day. Shanahan sounded a warning note about him in a letter to Mother Colmcille: 'The less the chaplain or any outside person has to do with the Aspirants the better for them. Use your own discretion.'[18]

On 23 April 1924 he boarded the *RMS Ekari* in Liverpool and started on his long overdue return to his vicariate.

11

Personality problems

The Bishop had been expected to land in Calabar as usual. Instead he disembarked at Port Harcourt, which was nearer to Onitsha and was growing in importance as a sea-port since the opening of the railway line to Enugu. He made his way north, visiting different missions on the way and meeting the priests. He was more than a little on the defensive after his absence of twenty-two months but to his relief he was well received everywhere he went. He described his arrival in a letter to Leen.

> At Onitsha there was a reception to cheer the heart of a saint, whatever it might do to the heart of a sinner. It looked as if I had been over to Saint John's and just returned. It was really delightful.
>
> I got all the *chers confrères* down to dinner and we had a really great day. All without exception were anxiously inquiring about you — not for your blood, mind! — real genuine *amour fraternel.* They all looked what they are: fit, fat, hardworking lads. Now that I'm back everything is normal. The Mission is not 'bust up', neither is anybody in it. All is well. That's good news you'll like. You can easily fancy my delight at being again at my post, the one assigned to me by Providence. I never felt better. I'm fit for any amount of work. This took everyone by surprise. I'm so glad for I felt all the time like a coward and a deserter at home. I felt humiliated — and as you know that too was good for me.[1]

The letters he wrote to Leen over the next few years are perhaps the most unbuttoned in all his vast output. He was always a prolific letter-writer but his list of correspondents grew to epic proportions after the founding of Killeshandra. He wrote letters of guidance in answer to questions, letters of encouragement in times of difficulty, letters of condolence to those bereaved, letters of spiritual direction to those with problems. He wrote letters of congratulation on all festive occasions, such as the receiving of the habit or the taking of vows. He wrote letters of gratitude for favours received and services rendered. None of the letters give the impression of being routine or perfunctory. He wrote to people as he spoke to them, giving each one his full and undivided attention. Every night he sat at his desk in the mission-house in Onitsha, sometimes until three o'clock in the morning, covering page after page with his flowing script. Many of the letters were treasured by the recipients until their dying days, for their charity, their wisdom, their humanity, their affection, their compassion, and the unaffected spirituality that lit up every page.

The letters to Leen had all these qualities and something more. They showed a side of the writer that was hidden from everyone else. It is so rare to find the slightest word of criticism of anyone in any of his letters that one might suppose he viewed the human race through an irremovable pair of rose-coloured spectacles. The Leen letters disprove this. According to the moral theologians of the time, the law of charity did not prevent a person from revealing the faults of others to a prudent friend in order to obtain advice or consolation. Leen was the friend to whom Shanahan turned, his safety-valve when he was under pressure. He told him of the problems he was meeting from his fellow-missionaries with much candour and a good deal of wit. The words 'Personal' or 'Confidential' are written over some of these letters and could well have been written over them all.

The show of unity and goodwill that greeted Shanahan on his return was not as solidly founded as he imagined. His absence had been increasingly resented as the months lengthened into years. Small problems had grown into big ones because there was no-one there to deal with them. As he became aware of this, his feeling of guilt increased. Yet he remained convinced that by staying in Ireland to set the sisterhood on its feet he was doing what was ultimately in the best interests of the Church in Nigeria.

One of his first actions was to make the 'changes', the periodic re-shuffle occasioned by missionaries going on leave or returning or various other reasons. He sent the details to Leen.

> Here are the changes, made without any *Conseil* or any notice to anybody prior to the official formal one without explanation. People are anxious for strong government — it is certainly the easiest and best for the man that governs.[2]

He was within his rights in making the appointments without referring to the Council of Priests, and without offering any consultation or explanation to those appointed. It was the traditional way that bishops dealt with their priests in those days. It was the way Lejeune had dealt with him and he had obeyed without a word, in accordance with his promise of obedience. But not all his priests were as biddable as he had been and in the strained atmosphere resulting from his long absence he might have been wise to adopt a more consultative approach. Some of those who were discontented with their new appointments began to complain that the Bishop was becoming unduly autocratic.

Having visited the missions in the western part of the vicariate, he set off for Calabar. The situation had stabilised there, helped by Ronayne's departure for Ireland. The new priest there was Phil O'Connor, who had come out in 1920 and had quickly earned Shanahan's respect.

He was worried about Sister Magdalen being left alone in charge of the school in Calabar but his worry was groundless. She had got on well with Mary Martin during their four months together, but she was quite happy to be on her own. Using senior pupils to help her with the teaching, she was raising standards in the school to a very high level. Though reserved and awkward in her dealings with adults, she could relate easily with even the youngest children. Her aim was the same as Shanahan's. She was against a system that would produce semi-educated women, who were at home neither in their traditional culture nor in the wider international one. She wanted to educate them to be fully integrated and fully Christian and to take their proper role in the building up of the Church in Nigeria.

An incident she relates in a letter to her great friend and supporter, Mother Arsenius, indicates the hold she had over her pupils. One of the girls had been misbehaving and she threatened to send her away. 'Never send me from you', the girl answered. 'If you are angry with me, strike me with your right hand, but draw me to you with your left.'[3]

Mother Arsenius was keeping her supplied with books for the senior classes and toys and Montessori equipment for the juniors. In addition she sent out the latest books on religion and education for Sister Magdalen's own use, and the convent gradually built up a small but well-chosen library. Many of the priests would call on her when in Calabar and borrow the latest Chesterton or

Belloc. They did not always remember to bring them back.

Shanahan had dropped his original idea of bringing out the postulants to Nigeria for their novitiate and appointing Magdalen their Mistress of Novices. But he had a new plan in mind for her and it is probably on this visit that he first discussed it with her. He had long hoped to found a sisterhood of Nigerian women but did not feel that the Church was well enough established to be able to produce and support the necessary vocations. The school at Calabar made him revise his view. He suggested to Magdalen that she might be prepared to help him in founding such a sisterhood, watching out for suitable candidates, and supervising their training as religious. He found that her views on the subject were the same as his own and that he would be able to rely on her full co-operation when the time came.[4]

He returned to Onitsha to deal with another aspect of the same question. Little progress had been made with his plans for establishing a native Nigerian priesthood. John Anyogu had come back from his European education and had then been sent for a time as catechist to the remote and difficult mission of Ogoja, probably as a test of his commitment. He passed the test convincingly, making the long journey there and back on foot, through country which was reputed to be the haunt of cannibals. He was now in Onitsha, living in the mission-house and continuing his studies in philosophy. At the same time he was teaching Latin to six other young men who were interested in becoming priests, using the corridor of the mission-house as his classroom. Shanahan decided the time had come to establish a proper seminary and he chose Igbariam as its location.[5]

Saint Paul's Seminary was formally opened in Igbariam on 19 July 1924. There were nine seminarians, John Anyogu, his six pupils from Onitsha, and two Irish seminarians who had come to help in the work of the mission. They were housed in the former teacher training college which had been closed six years earlier. Father William O'Donnell was appointed as its director and entire staff, since only one priest could be spared. He fell sick almost immediately on appointment and had to return to Ireland. Much of the duty of running the seminary fell on the shoulders of the ever faithful John Anyogu, who had to teach the others, see that the rule was kept, and even look after the kitchen. Shanahan wrote them an appreciative letter.

> The spirit of faith which I spoke of to you all before you left for Igbariam has been put to the test and not found wanting, thank God. Keep on trusting with absolute faith in God and all will be well no matter how hopeless things may appear, how utterly useless men, God's instruments, may seem to you. It is God who does the work, not men.

In December he brought one of the priests from Calabar, Father Charles Heerey, to be the new director. The seminary was to go through many more vicissitudes, including changes of name and location, in the years that followed, but it survived to become the alma mater of many priests.[6]

The mission at Ogoja remained to be visited. It was the furthest outpost of the Vicariate, founded by Douvry and Mellett in 1920, a hard two hundred mile trek from Onitsha. It was not the kind of journey to be enjoyed by a man of fifty-three with two serious operations behind him, but Shanahan looked forward to it with positive eagerness. On 8 September, the eve of his departure, he wrote a long letter to the superior in Killeshandra, Mother Xavier.

> I have visited all the central stations of the Mission and am once again in the run of things. From morning to night I'm seated at this old desk of mine, for it is at the desk the work that counts is done. I'm broken into work again. My two years idleness in Ireland had wrought havoc with my working powers. The old engine is tuned up again and fit for any old road, any old rough bush path.
>
> The Mission as a whole is doing very well. With the few Missioners we have it is almost impossible to do better. Now critics will pass around and find fault with this and that etc. etc. But God knows that a man can't do more than a man's work. When he has done that, especially if it is for God, then God Himself does the rest and does it well too, no matter what the critics may say ...
>
> I have to get my boxes ready for the long trek — and if there's one man glad to be off into the bush, I'm the man. I would wish to never again see a desk or an office. In Heaven there won't be any.[7]

* * *

Setting off into the bush, Shanahan was more worried about Killeshandra than he revealed to Mother Xavier. He was chafing at the impossibility of being in two continents at the same time. Whenever he was in Ireland, difficulties arose in Nigeria. Whenever he was in Africa, difficulties arose in Killeshandra. On the spot, he could deal with them easily. Absent, he could only imagine the worst. The same letter to Mother Xavier contained an enigmatic paragraph about Father Tom Ronayne.

> I knew Father Ronayne would be of great use to the cause as his health improved. You can scarcely realise how much he has suffered. God permits that his highly sensitive nature should suffer for and bring great blessings on any cause he embraces. He does not experience the great happiness most people have in working and suffering for a cause. He has all the more merit. Then again he cannot see from most people's viewpoint; and the result is more mental agony in having to do what his own mind tells him could be done more effectively some other way — his own way in preference. Well, I ought to know something of Father Tom's difficulties — but he's the best, sincerest and most loyal man and priest on earth.

This is, under the circumstances, a remarkably charitable description of Ronayne's personality. His nature was such that he could not refrain from interfering in everybody else's business, always with the best of intentions. He had never yet met a soul that would not profit by his direction or a situation that would not be improved by his intervention. He had now begun to do what Shanahan had feared by moving outside his duties as chaplain and trying to take over the running of the convent. Shanahan wrote in more forthright terms to his confidant, Leen.

> It seems Father T.R. is once more worrying over guarantees and all kinds of things in connection with the convent as if we were all a pack of fools, none of whom know the first thing about the work assigned to us by Holy Providence. Father T. has got to come along and coach us. Well, I'm positively tired of this perpetual interference of that well-intentioned holy humbug.[8]

Leen was in entire agreement with Shanahan, but he was at a disadvantage, living in Dublin and able to make only occasional visits to Killeshandra. Ronayne lived in the chaplain's house, the old gate-lodge, and was on the spot twenty-four hours a day. He set about ingratiating himself with Bishop Finegan and undermining Leen's position. He impressed on Finegan that as Bishop of the diocese in which the convent was situated he was its ecclesiastical superior. He referred to the document from Rome authorising the opening of the convent and pointed out that it was addressed to Finegan and not to Shanahan. He began to set himself up as the defender of Finegan's rights against Shanahan, Leen and the Dominican nuns, who were all conspiring to deprive him of these rights. Years later he recalled his own version of these events to Mary Martin.

> Dr Finegan regarded me as his personal agent to see that everything was done according to Canon Law. The Dominican nuns and Dr Shanahan regarded Fr Leen as their agent to see their private agreement was carried out. I never raised the question until the Mother Prioress General sent me a letter to say, 'You do not seem to understand your position in Killeshandra.' I then told Dr Leen, 'The nuns are under an illusion. Dr Finegan is the real authority.' He replied, 'Who will ever know?' I replied, 'It's Canon Law and therefore God's will.'

In March 1925 Bishop Finegan came to make his official visitation of the convent. Ronayne, Leen and Whitney were all present. Mother Xavier brought in a document for the Bishop to sign and he queried the inclusion of Shanahan's name, substituting his own. Afterwards there were angry words between Leen and Ronayne, with Leen saying, 'It's your fault', and Ronayne replying once again, 'It's Canon Law.'

Other complaints about Ronayne reached Shanahan. It was said that he had been going around criticising the Dominicans as unfit to direct Killeshandra and suggesting that a religious order more involved in the active apostolate should have been chosen. Most worrying of all to Shanahan was the news that Ronayne was giving spiritual direction to the young sisters, particularly to Mary Martin.

Mary had entered Killeshandra as arranged in June 1924 but she did not seem to have settled down. No letters describing her state of mind at this time appear to have survived and our only information comes from letters written by Leen and Ronayne. A number of factors were causing her to question her vocation to the Killeshandra Sisters. One was her interest in medical work rather than the educational work which was the main object of the new sisterhood. Another and diametrically opposed one was her attraction to a life of prayer of the kind that could be realised only in a contemplative order. The second attraction was uppermost in her mind and was encouraged by Ronayne, as he indicated in a letter about her which he wrote to her mother, another of his directees. He habitually addressed Mrs Martin as 'My dear child', though she was old enough to be his mother.

> She has an intense attraction for prayer and the life here gives very little opening for this attraction. I may tell you, I didn't yet tell her, that if her previous history had not been what it is, i.e. if she were simply a soul in an ordinary novitiate without any previous experience of mission life, I would tell her at once to enter the Carmelites. But she has great aptitude for work, she seems to be the one pointed out to head the work, everyone takes it that she is the backbone of it, so naturally at a superficial view everyone takes it that her place is here. Does it not seem that in retaining her here we are acting on considerations other than her own soul's interest, which should be the only factor to be considered? Now, child, this is only an opinion. I am not yet giving a judgment.

He adds that it would be better not to discuss this with Leen, as he would 'pooh-pooh the whole difficulty'. In this at least his judgement was correct. Leen knew all about the problem and in a long and detailed letter written from Blackrock he told Mary bluntly, 'You have neither the mental nor physical qualities that would make a good contemplative.' He ended with the words:

> This may seem to you a hard letter — it is really sympathetic. As I say, it is hard to judge at a distance — but this I know, that your supernatural outlook when you came here last September (or whatever time it was, I forget now) was wholly wrong and certainly not dictated by grace. I greatly fear that your present state is closely akin and really the outcome of restlessness, self-centredness and pride.[9]

It is impossible not to sympathise with Mary Martin in this situation, obviously deeply troubled and getting such conflicting advice from those to whom she turned for help. One has to sympathise too with Shanahan, watching helplessly from a distance as the person whom he had seen as the first mother-general of the new sisterhood seemed to be turning her back on the work. He decided that at all costs Ronayne must be removed from Killeshandra.

In March Finegan wrote to Shanahan, giving an account of his visitation of Killeshandra and asking that the authority question be finally cleared up. 'What I would suggest to Your Lordship', he wrote, 'is that you write to Father Leen and the nuns in Cabra that you recognise my canonical position as Superior of the new institute.'[10] Shanahan had no difficulty about conceding this point. Canon law was a mystery to him and he did not care who had the name of superior as long as the work was done. He knew that Finegan was inclined to be punctilious about legalities but he also knew that he was a man of honour and integrity and totally committed to the welfare of Killeshandra. He promised to write to Leen and to Cabra saying that he had nothing whatsoever to do with the canonical superiorship of the convent. Then he cautiously and diplomatically approached the subject of Ronayne.

> I fear you will find no small difficulty in consenting to his return to S. Nigeria. I would not ask for it were it not that his presence here with me in Onitsha is almost indispensable if I am to retain the use of my rapidly failing eyesight. The strain of continuous office work in addition to the burden of many other duties is so great that I begin, for the first time in my life, to fear that unless help comes soon the end of my work as a Missioner is within sight. In the interest of the Mission I wish this fact to be known to nobody except your Lordship.[11]

Ronayne left Killeshandra and returned to Nigeria, to take up his new duties as Shanahan's assistant and secretary. While he himself was in no doubt about the reason for his recall, everyone else thought it a sign of Shanahan's confidence and esteem that he should want him as his secretary. Even in such a situation, Shanahan respected his good intentions and did nothing that would damage his reputation.

* * *

Shanahan's need of secretarial help was genuine. A few weeks earlier Sister Magdalen had written to Mother Arsenius, 'In health he is well but his sight is fast failing. One eye is completely gone and he has to use the other far too much. He really requires a good secretary.' He was beginning to worry about his ability to cope with all the rapid new developments both in Nigeria and in Ireland. He wrote to the mother-house suggesting that a coadjutor be appointed for the vicariate, that is, an assistant bishop with the right of succession.

His morale was boosted by the celebrations for the silver jubilee of his ordination to the priesthood, which took place in April 1925. A pontifical High Mass was held in the church in Onitsha and was attended by twenty-four priests and ten seminarians from the vicariate, together with a large and enthusiastic congregation. From the Vicariate of Asaba on the right bank of the Niger came Bishop Broderick and four of his priests. Broderick preached at the Mass and mentioned that in the twenty years of Shanahan's regime the number of mission stations and out-stations in Southern Nigeria had increased from 13 to 1,200 and the number of Catholics from 2,500 to 45,000.[12] He might have added that there was an even larger number of catechumens awaiting baptism, bringing the total number affiliated to the Catholic Church to well over 100,000.

If Shanahan had died in 1925, his work would be regarded as one of the great success stories of modern missionary endeavour. The years that followed took nothing from that success but added to it, as the Church in Southern Nigeria grew steadily in strength and fervour. But for Shanahan himself the last two decades of his life brought a series of personal reverses that robbed him of much of the joy of achievement to which he was entitled. As the work flourished and the number of workers grew, so did disunity and distrust among them. The increasing sadness of his later years came not from the people to whom he ministered, but from those who were his fellow labourers in the ministry.

The trouble with Ronayne was only a foretaste. During the course of 1925 he had to face rising discontent among some of the priests of the mission. What added to his feeling of betrayal was the fact that it came from the Holy Ghost priests, not the secular priests, and that the most vocal among them were Irish. Their main complaint was about his policy of introducing secular priests from Ireland, which they regarded as counter-productive. They claimed that in bringing out Irish secular priests and in founding an Irish sisterhood he had acted against the wishes of the Holy Ghost Congregation. As a result he had fallen into disfavour and no new Holy Ghost priests were being sent to his vicariate. There was a subsidiary complaint about the fact that Holy Ghost and secular priests were being appointed in some instances to the same mission, which was against the community spirit of the Congregation. Even worse, in one or two cases, secular priests were put in charge of missions and Holy Ghost priests were subjected to their authority. They wrote to the mother-house and asked that the vicariate be divided in two and that one half be manned exclusively by the Congregation. In that way they would be sure of getting men for their own vicariate.

Shanahan wrote to Le Roy and asked him to make a written statement which could be circulated to the priests. It should say unequivocally that the policy of bringing out secular priests was approved by the mother house and that there was no question of the vicariate being boycotted by the Congregation. Le Roy obliged with a hand-written letter which Shanahan had photographed and sent to all the priests.

> At a time when we are everywhere trying to meet the most urgent needs, we are very saddened to learn that allegations dictated possibly by jealousy, certainly by narrowness of spirit, are being aired in your vicariate. There are some missionaries who reserve an area to themselves and will not admit that any others can do any good in their own field of the apostolate.
>
> We implore the missionaries of Nigeria to lay aside these personal preoccupations, national or otherwise. This regrettable narrowness of spirit is entirely contrary to the zeal of genuine apostles ...
>
> It is with our full approval and our most sincere encouragement that you have sought priests from Maynooth and missionary sisters for your Vicariate, and it is with the greatest happiness that we have seen your hopes being realised.[13]

It was not quite the vindication Shanahan might have hoped for. While it approved his introduction of secular priests, it did not deny that as a result of this Holy Ghost priests who would have come to Nigeria were now being directed elsewhere. Moreover, in a separate letter to Shanahan, the mother-house stated that the time had come to divide the vicariate, thereby indicating a certain sympathy for the dissidents. With some irony, Shanahan commented that this was their solution to his failing eyesight. 'It will need less power of vision to see half a vicariate than a whole one!' In the unkindest cut of all, Le Roy added a postscript to say that Shanahan was free to choose a coadjutor or to resign. He told Leen:

> I'm doing neither one nor the other. I'll hold on here at my post until I become blind and can't do any more work. By that time the convent will be on its legs. You will have got Ireland as a missionary province on its legs and facing its true destiny: Africa.

Towards the end of the year, the time came again to make changes in the personnel in the vicariate. Shanahan grasped the nettle with his usual firmness and sent Leen a list of the new appointments with confidential comments.

> Fr Howell is transferred to Ogoja. Fr G.O'S. — mad as ever only a bit more so — to Calabar. Ph. O'Connor to the seminary to help Fr C. Heerey. Fr Knaebel to Anua. Fr Graetz to Aba! Fr D.W. and G.O'S. have been on the warpath as usual. But all is very well. Nobody heeds red Indians nowadays even though they do walk about in war paint and with tomahawks at their belts. Fr C.L. cannot understand why he hasn't a station of his own etc. etc. — the sempiternal Irish failure to submit to authority and do their own bit of work without bothering how the man in authority is doing his.

Despite his air of confidence, Shanahan was deeply hurt by the dissensions among the clergy and the lack of support from the mother-house. To add to his trials, letters were going back to Ireland, particularly from Ronayne, painting a lurid picture of a vicariate on the brink of revolt. But the extent of the trouble should not be exaggerated. The priests continued to do their work faithfully and remained loyally obedient to their Bishop. An important witness to this is Sister Magdalen, who wrote home to counter the false reports.

> I know you may have heard adverse criticism of the workers and methods, especially from Fr Ronayne. I have been here now nearly two and a half years. I have travelled all over the mission, met all the Fathers except two and all the Brothers. I have worked with ten of them. I have seen them when they were on their guard and off guard, and I have seen nothing but what was edifying. In the newer stations especially their lives are very hard and they seem to forget even the necessaries of life in the eagerness of their work for souls. Personally, I think the Bishop is a saint. His humility and patient courage are a constant lesson to me. His kindness to me has been untold ...
>
> I know Father Ronayne has spoken of many things to you. He is a holy man and says what he believes. But he is also sick in mind and body. His nerves have got the better of him and I am afraid he has got the better of Marie Martin. It is a pity because she could have done splendid work here.

The new year brought further troubles. Early in January 1926 Shanahan had a serious accident. A fall from his motor-cycle resulted in a badly injured shoulder and he had to spend several weeks in hospital. The thought of resigning from the vicariate returned and this time he did not dismiss it. Notification came from Paris summoning him to the General Chapter of the Congregation, due to be held in July. It seemed to him a suitable opportunity to offer his resignation to the Pope. 'My general health and my eyesight in particular necessitate my resignation', he told Leen. 'I have little doubt about it being accepted.'

March brought two hammer-blows from Killeshandra. The convent had been flourishing since Ronayne left. The Dominican sisters reported an excellent spirit of prayer and community and a steady increase in the number of vocations. Father Pat Whitney's fund-raising efforts had been spectacularly successful and the debt for the purchase of the convent was completely paid off. His very success was to prove his undoing. He wanted to use the surplus money to buy a house which would serve as an Irish base for the secular priests in Nigeria. The Killeshandra nuns wanted the money to go to the running of the convent. A further dispute arose over his use of lay secretaries to do office work which the nuns thought could be done by the novices. A meeting with Bishop Finegan and the nuns in Killeshandra ended in a blazing row, with Whitney storming out of the convent. Finegan wrote to him forbidding him to do any further fund-raising and asked Shanahan to recall him to Nigeria.[14]

The second blow was expected but none the less shattering. On 8 March 1926 Mary Martin left Killeshandra for ever. She had spent almost two years there and was still unhappy. She had been veering between the two opposite possibilities, one of joining a contemplative order, the other of founding an order of medical missionaries for Nigeria. By this time she seemed to have discarded the idea of the contemplative life and come down in favour of the active apostolate. Mother Colmcille wrote to her from Cabra in a last-ditch effort to prevent her leaving.

> If your desire is to found a society for the conversion of the pagans in Nigeria, I would in all sincerity advise you to pause long and to pray earnestly before you embark on such an enterprise and this for the following reasons:
> 1. Because such a society has already been founded under the title of the 'Missionary Sisters of the Holy Rosary' and it has been approved by our Holy Mother the Church.
> 2. Because the Founder of the Society is a most holy Bishop whose zeal for God's glory and the salvation of souls is boundless, and who has had a long experience of missionary and religious life, and whose judgement therefore merits our most profound respect and confidence; consequently I would be fearful lest any means, other than those chosen by him, might not be in complete accordance with the Holy Will of God and might therefore lead only to disaster.[15]

The letter arrived on the afternoon of the day Mary Martin was leaving. She read it but did not change her decision.

Shanahan wrote her a dignified letter when he heard the news. He expressed his sorrow and the sorrow of all the Nigerian missionaries, but did not in any way quarrel with her action. He was generous in his praise of what she had done in the past.

> I will never forget that you inspired and were the chief instrument in the formation of the new missionary society.

> Were it not for you, I would never have taken the steps I took to get it started. Our Lord will never forget what you have done for his sake ...
>
> I will be very pleased — I need scarcely write it — to hear from you and to know what are your plans for the future. If there is any help I can give you, I will give it with all my heart.

Though he rarely referred to it again, it must have been one of the greatest disappointments of his life. In her he had found a woman of exceptional spiritual and intellectual qualities. She seemed sent to him by God so that she could use her unique gifts in the building up of a sisterhood for Nigeria. He could hardly hope to find her like again.

He left Nigeria for Europe in mid-May, possibly for ever. Now that he had made the decision to resign, he was tranquil and at peace. To Leen he wrote:

> Do you know, I was never happier in my life? I suffered somewhat at first when the Mission accused me of being the cause of the shortage of personnel, but now I see the whole situation in a new light. God simply has done with me all he could and now he wants me to retire and prepare for eternity. He could not bestow on me a greater favour.

12

Choosing a successor

Shanahan arrived in Liverpool in the first week of June and made straight for Ireland. He would have liked to have gone at once to Killeshandra to see for himself the progress of the sisterhood but there were matters to be attended to in Dublin. He needed to see the Provincial and Leen, both of whom were out of town at the time, and he had to await their return. He found a room in Saint Mary's in Rathmines and did not move to Blackrock College until later in the year.

It was not until a week after his arrival that he was able to make the journey to Cavan. He was driven in one of the Dawson motor cars by Father Whitney, who was to return to Nigeria on the ship that Shanahan came on. He stopped for a time in Cavan town to see Bishop Finegan and it was late in the evening when he arrived at Killeshandra. For Whitney it was a rather embarrassing occasion, his first visit to the convent since his dramatic departure three months earlier. For Shanahan it was pure joy.

The novices were in a state of high excitement when they heard he was on his way, none more so than Sister Philomena, formerly Isabel Fox of Philadelphia, a friend of Veronica Hasson.[1] She had joined the sisters in June 1924 and had never seen Shanahan, though she had heard much about him. She was one of those who peered out of the upstairs windows to catch a glimpse of him as he arrived, but though she heard the car she saw no sign of the great man himself.

She was told that he was spending the night in the gate-lodge but would be in the convent to say the Mass for the sisters the following morning. One of the older novices mischievously described him to her as very old and feeble and practically blind. As she knelt in the little chapel next morning, she pulled her skirt in close around her ankles, lest the venerable Bishop trip over it on his way to the altar. She was totally unprepared for the reality.

> The entrance from the sacristy was at the back of the chapel. It was a surprise and a delight to see this tall, majestic figure taking long, sure, striding steps up the centre aisle, head erect, the whole form full of grace and purpose. At the foot

of the altar he turned to greet the community with a radiant expression. The chapel came fully alive with the presence of this wonderfully human, Christ-like man.

In a strong, resonant voice, Bishop Shanahan spoke of his happiness to be back in the house on the hill. He was not an orator. The words did not come evenly but in a rather jerky fashion; yet he held everyone spellbound. Whenever or wherever he spoke, this seemed to be the case. One could say with the apostles, 'Our hearts moved within us.' Talking with easy, graceful gestures, he remarked on the wonderful progress and changes he had observed about the place since he had said goodbye in 1924. He described the eagerness with which the girls and women of Southern Nigeria were preparing for the coming of the sisters, of two girls in particular who were then in Calabar with Mother Magdalen, the Sister of Charity who had been excloisterised to work on the missions. These two girls, both from Ibo country, later became Sisters of the Most Pure Heart of Mary, a diocesan society trained by the Holy Rosary Sisters. The Bishop ended his talk by directing the thoughts of the sisters to the power of the Mass, telling them to let their prayers include all mankind from now until the end of time. Nothing was too great for God: 'Pray not only for Nigeria and for our own needs but for the whole world to be brought to Christ.'

On this occasion he stayed only a few hours but promised he would soon be back for a longer period. He returned to Dublin, where he saw Whitney off on his return voyage to Africa, and later in the month ordained three priests in Blackrock College chapel, the first priestly ordinations there since his own. In July he set off for Paris and the General Chapter, accompanied by Father Leen, who was representing the Irish Province.

His visit to Paris had a double purpose. He wished to have his eyes examined by some of the city's eminent ophthalmologists. Their report was discouraging. 'They tell me my left eye is lost beyond repair,' he told Mother Xavier, 'and that the optic nerve in my right eye is attacked. Unless there is direct intervention on the part of Divine Providence there can be no question of my resuming missionary work in dear old Nigeria.'

The retreat in preparation for the Chapter opened on 18 July and the Chapter itself opened on the 25th. The agenda was not very heavy, the main item being the election of a new Superior General. Archbishop Le Roy, aged and infirm, had now been thirty years at the head of the Congregation and had come very close to death the previous year. His re-election was out of the question. The delegates chose Bishop Le Hunsec, Vicar Apostolic of Senegambia in French West Africa, but it took several days of toing and froing to get the election approved by Rome, since there was some objection to the choice of an active bishop for the post. The Chapter closed on Saturday 31 July.

The following Monday Shanahan went to Lisieux with Leen to pray at the grave of Saint Thérèse, who had been canonised the previous year. On his first visit he had prayed for missionaries for Nigeria. This time his request was more personal: the restoration of his eyesight. They came back to Paris the following day with no miracle to report. 'His Lordship is quite resigned,' Leen noted, 'but those praying for him are still hopeful of a cure through the intercession of the Little Flower.'[2]

On 16 August he was in Killeshandra for the ceremony of reception of three new postulants and this time he remained on for a week, staying in the gate-lodge as usual. He spent as much time as possible with the novices and postulants, walking and talking with them in the grounds during the day, chatting with them in the parlour in the evening. He felt they were not getting enough air and exercise and he brought them on long walks through the fields, so that they could breathe the fresh air and enjoy the summer sunshine. These walks would usually end up with him enthroned on a bank or a tree-stump, while the rest sat around on the grass, listening spellbound as he told them stories about his experiences in Africa and described in glowing words the great work they could do for God and souls once they had joined him there.

None of them doubted his love for them, which he showed in so many ways, small and great. Nor could he doubt their love for him, so evident in the way they kept their eyes on him and hung on his every word. By the Pope's word he was their father and he had a father's love for them and a father's pride in them. They were happy to be his daughters and to drink in that love, so sincerely felt and so tenderly expressed. They were young and impressionable and none of them had ever met a man like him, a man who listened to them, valued their opinions, recognised their gifts, encouraged them to reach their full potential.

There could have been an element of sexual attraction in this as there can be in any relationship between a man and a woman. They felt the power and the charisma of the man, still handsome and vigorous and vital at the age of fifty-five. They were impressed by his charm and his courtesy and his attentiveness. Even so minor a trait as his physical cleanliness drew them. He was always immaculate in his appearance, his white hair and beard washed and trimmed, his hands manicured, his boots shining, his clothes neat and spotless. It was an age when washing facilities were neither as easily available nor as highly valued as they are now, and when most Irishmen regarded grubby nails and soup-stained waistcoats as a sign of masculinity.

But there was never any doubt about the real basis of the relationship. For him natural love was part of divine love. If God is love, then in every true human love God must be present. His presence was almost tangible in the Bishop's love, in the words he spoke and the stories he told, always filled with the awareness of God's nearness, always directed to his glory alone. This is what they saw and felt. This is what more than anything else they responded to. Sister Philomena said simply: 'I loved him. I wasn't in love with him — he was an old man — but I loved him. He was simply Christ for me.' What she said could have been said by all of them.

It was with great reluctance that he left them to prepare for his visit to Rome. His formal letter of resignation had already been sent in. Now he had to see the Pope and the officials at Propaganda Fide to make the arrangements for his retirement. He left Ireland by the evening boat on 26 August for the long journey by sea and land to Rome.

The audience with the Pope took place on Tuesday, 7 September. Shanahan spent most of that evening and much of the following day writing letters to describe what happened at the audience. To Finegan he wrote:

> I exposed the many reasons I had for requesting him to accept my resignation as Vicar Apostolic of Southern Nigeria. He would not hear of my resignation. He told me that I need not read or write but content myself with saying the Rosary. Then I should select a coadjutor to do the work of the Mission under my direction.

> If my eyes gave trouble I could return to Europe whenever I liked to get them attended to. The Propaganda told me to do exactly as the Holy Father had said.[3]

It was just what he had been hoping for. Though he had offered his resignation and given cogent reasons for it to be accepted, there can be no doubt that he was overjoyed to find it rejected. His obedience and loyalty to the Pope were absolute and he took his words as the words of God. He told the Irish Provincial, Father Harnett:

> It is most consoling for me to know at last from the person of Christ's vicar on earth that in spite of all my drawbacks he still thinks I should remain in charge of the mission. It gives me new courage to face once more the burden of authority. I know now that since Christ wishes me to take it or rather keep it on my shoulders, he will enable me to carry it. I am glad to be once again back at my post in Africa.[4]

* * *

The choice of his coadjutor was not an easy one. This was the man with whom he would have to work during his remaining years as Vicar and to whom he would have to entrust the continuance of the work after he had gone. On his way back to Ireland, he stopped in Paris to discuss the matter with the new Superior General. While the Pope had given him the unusual privilege of nominating whoever he wished, courtesy demanded that he consult Le Hunsec. He also had to take into consideration the recommendations of the Irish Province and the views expressed by the priests of Nigeria.

The man he finally chose for the post was the director of the seminary in Igbariam, Father Charles Heerey. It is said that his own personal preference was for Father Phil O'Connor but that he was persuaded by the Irish province to opt for Heerey instead. In any event, the ultimate responsibility for the choice was his, and it was a good choice. During his long regime of thirty-five years as Vicar Apostolic of Southern Nigeria and then as first Archbishop of Onitsha, Heerey was to continue and expand the work of his predecessor with great success. Shanahan could not have known how much personal unhappiness he himself was to suffer as a result of his choice, but even if he had it is unlikely that it would have affected his decision. The work was everything, his own feelings nothing.

Charles Heerey was just thirty-six at the time of his appointment. He was born in Castlerahan, near Ballyjamesduff, Co. Cavan, where his father had a farm. He joined the Holy Ghost Congregation after leaving school and was ordained priest in 1921. The following year he came to Nigeria, where he served for two years in Calabar before being appointed director of the new seminary. He was regarded by his contemporaries as able rather than brilliant, solid rather than imaginative. Beneath the solidity was an unexpectedly vulnerable soul. In the words of one of his priests:

> This big, rather lumbering, kindly man, on whom the achievements and honours of the passing years conferred self confidence and assurance in dealing with men and affairs, was deep down a shy and sensitive person. In a rare moment of self-revelation he once told how the shock of his appointment left him in bed for two days.[5]

He was to be spared the shock for some time yet. Even after the decision had been made, numerous channels had to be gone through in Dublin, Paris and Rome before the nomination arrived on the Pope's desk for his final seal of approval. Shanahan returned to Ireland and took up residence in Blackrock College, perhaps intending to wait until the official announcement was made.

There was plenty to occupy his time. His letters tell of some but by no means all of his activities. He travelled around the country, interviewing prospective priests and sisters for Nigeria, asking bishops to grant leave of absence to volunteer priests, visiting the families and homes of his missionaries, giving talks on the missions in churches, halls and schools. He went to Maynooth and met a number of students who were interested in volunteering after ordination. In Sion Hill Convent School he met with less success, as a priest from the Society of African Missions had been there the day before.

> He forestalled me by giving a most interesting lecture on their Missions. He asked for recruits for the Sisters. Four offered themselves. But what does it matter, so long as the

> cause of Christ is made known, what Society the missionary girls enter.[6]

The fund-raising for Killeshandra and the missions continued unabated. He tells of a concert in the hall in Blackrock which attracted two thousand people. He was happy about the resulting publicity but had his doubts about the financial side. He failed to turn up for another concert in Dublin's Theatre Royal which he had promised to attend and wrote a no-nonsense letter of apology to the Provincial. 'When I found I could not get back I should have at least written to explain my absence and ask you to excuse it. This I did not do and I was wrong in not doing it.'

By the end of September, two months after his visit to Lisieux, he was noting an improvement in his eyesight. He made no claims of a miracle and did not describe the nature of the improvement in detail. The fact remains that the threat of blindness had receded and was never to return. He suffered from trouble with his eyes for the rest of his life, but was able to read his breviary and write letters almost up to the end.

He had other health troubles to contend with. On his previous visit to Ireland, he had received injections of silver nitrate to treat arthritis in his wrists.[7] Now his regular medical adviser, Dr Jim Magennis, found that the arthritis had worsened and ordered him into Saint Vincent's Hospital for a complete series of injections. He entered the hospital on 14 January 1927. He had hoped to keep it quiet but the news went around quickly and he had a regular stream of visitors.

He was still there on 29 January when he got a telegram from Rome saying that the Pope had officially nominated Father Charles Heerey to be titular Bishop of Balanea and coadjutor to the Vicar Apostolic of Southern Nigeria. Almost simultaneously another telegram arrived from Nigeria to inform him that Heerey had suffered a breakdown in health and was about to leave the country on his way back to Ireland for a period of rest and convalescence. Officially, Heerey did not know yet of his appointment. It is possible that he had been informed confidentially and that this contributed to his illness.

This was an upset for Shanahan. The strong young man who was supposed to shoulder the burden had himself succumbed. It did not seem that his illness was serious but it was obvious he would have to spend some months in Ireland. Shanahan had

Joseph Shanahan in France between 1890 and 1894.

Father Shanahan with Bishops Allgeyer (left) and O'Gorman in 1906.

Brother Adelm with Father Shanahan.

Bishop Shanahan at Freetown in 1920. Included in the picture are Fathers Whitney, Ronayne, O'Connor, Leen and Bishop O'Gorman.

Bishop Shanahan (right) following his consecration as bishop at Maynooth in 1920. Also in the picture are (from left) Fathers Ronayne, Whitney, O'Connor and Wilson.

Bishop Shanahan (right) following Bishop Heerey's consecration as bishop at Killeshandra in 1927, with (from left) Bishops Neville, Heerey and Mulhern.

Bishop Shanahan at Blackrock College c. 1927 with Dr Edward Leen (centre) and Bishop O'Gorman.

Bishop Shanahan (centre front) flanked by Fathers Heerey (left) and John Anyogu.

Nigeria 1931. ***Front Row****: Sisters Joseph and Brigid, Mother Xavier, Sisters Catherine and Agnes.* ***Back row****: Sisters Columba, Philomena Fox, Rose and Frances Kilcoyne.*

Possibly the last photograph of Bishop Shanahan, taken in 1943 in Limuri, Kenya. He is pictured here with Fathers Giltenan and Harnett and some Loreto Sisters.

planned on holding the consecration ceremony in Onitsha. It would have been the first time a Catholic bishop had been consecrated in Southern Nigeria, a great occasion for the country in general and a particular cause for celebration among the Catholic population. All his plans had now to be thought out again.

He was not discharged from hospital until 14 February and even then was told he would have to return periodically to finish the course of injections. He lost no time in getting back into action. The day he left Saint Vincent's he made for Maynooth to meet the senior students and then went on to Belfast to give a course of lectures on the missions.

'I don't feel very much enthusiasm,' he told Mother Xavier, 'for those injections have a most dulling and depressing effect on brain and nerves.' But he seemed to have lost none of his audience appeal. One of those who were captured by his personality was Anastasia Cahill, a Belfast girl in her mid-twenties, who was nearing the end of her teacher training course. She arrived late at Saint Paul's Hall and could get in no farther than the doorway.

> Away up on the stage, in that vast crowd, Bishop Shanahan was speaking. I can still see him, tall and handsome, beard like a patriarch, but I could not catch coherently what he was saying. But it must have been interesting for the audience laughed at times and clapped with evident interest and admiration. There were persons around the doorway who knew me and I must confess I felt embarrassed and noticed that they took stock of my interest in Bishop Shanahan. I have always felt that it was on that particular evening I burned my boats and opted for Africa and the missionary life. There was some 'amazing grace' went out from that most charismatic missionary. I never spoke to him until years afterwards as a novice, when he came to visit us in Killeshandra.
>
> Later that evening, outside Saint Paul's Hall, there were many women students from the Teachers' Training College nearby. My sister Barbara was one, and she and some others of the girls were brimful of ideas about going out to Africa with Bishop Shanahan. They talked much and were so enthusiastic. I said naught. They never went.[8]

He was back in Killeshandra on 24 February for a very important event, the profession ceremony of the first group of Holy Rosary Sisters. Ten in all were to make their first vows, six of the original seven and four who came later. The missing one was Veronica Hasson, one of the Nigerian pioneers. She had been forced to return to her home in America by heart trouble and sadly had died just a month earlier. Bishop Finegan was present at the ceremony but he asked Shanahan to officiate, which he gladly did.

The ten had been making a retreat under Father Leen's direction in preparation for the profession. When the ceremony was over, Mother Xavier thought they should continue their spirit of recollection. Probably with Leen's approval, she told them not to mingle with their families and friends but to remain on retreat. Sister Philomena observed what happened:

> This doubtful serenity was unbroken for about two hours, at least until the dejeuner was over. Parents then began looking for their beloved daughters. Very soon the indignation of quite a few persons, especially those who had come a long distance, reached the ears of Bishop Finegan. He intervened. The serenity of the retreat was broken but overall peace was restored. Such was the intense care for their charges exercised by those responsible for the spiritual welfare of the sisters in those days.[9]

It was a small but revealing incident. The Dominicans belonged to an enclosed and semi-contemplative order, and they had difficulty in adapting their cloistered spirituality to the needs of a more active order. Father Ronayne had not been altogether mistaken when he made this point three years earlier.

Shanahan stayed on in Killeshandra for a fortnight, which he described as 'a period of undiluted happiness'. In addition to his talks and walks with the sisters, he had some serious matters to discuss with Mothers Xavier and Aquinas. It was now time to consider bringing some of the newly-professed out to Nigeria to begin their missionary work. They decided to send five out later in the year and to keep the other five at home, to help in the development of the order and the training of the postulants. The Dominicans themselves were due to return to Cabra in two years' time and the sisterhood would have to manage its own affairs from then on.

The official announcement was made by Bishop Finegan on the last Sunday in March, amid intense excitement. Shanahan was absent, fulfilling a lecture engagement in Rathfarnham. There was great jubilation among those chosen, deep despondency among those staying behind. The despondent ones, who included Sister Thérèse (Agnes Ryan), received little sympathy from Mother Xavier, who rebuked them for giving way to merely human emotions. Sister Dominic was to lead the group for Nigeria, accompanied by Sisters Brigid (Bessie Ryan), Patrick, Joseph and Gerard. They would celebrate Christmas in Onitsha, where the convent of the Sisters of Cluny, unoccupied for twenty years, was now being set in order for their arrival.

Father Heerey landed in Liverpool on 21 March and crossed over to Ireland a few days later. The sea-air and the restful shipboard routine seemed to have done a good deal to restore his health and spirits. As soon as he arrived, Shanahan started discussing plans for the consecration ceremony.

The fact that Heerey came from Co. Cavan suggested the convent chapel in Killeshandra as a suitable venue. Shanahan had already sounded out Finegan, who was agreeable and who insisted that Shanahan himself should be the consecrating prelate. Within a couple of days of the Bishop-elect's arrival, Shanahan brought him to Killeshandra to meet the sisters and view the chapel. It was a small convent oratory, very unlike the magnificent chapel in Maynooth where Shanahan was consecrated, and Heerey may have been disappointed by it. He delayed giving his decision for several days. But Shanahan was very persuasive, arguing that it would raise the morale of the sisters and gain valuable publicity for the cause. Heerey finally agreed and the date of the ceremony was fixed for 29 May.

A few days later, Shanahan took him to Paris. Heerey, who must have felt that he had temporarily lost control of his life, was introduced to the Superior General and other dignitaries in the Holy Ghost mother-house. Shanahan spent much of his time in Paris carrying out errands for Mother Xavier, inquiring about crosses and rosary beads for the sisters and getting catalogues of engravings suitable for the walls of the convent. Then, while Heerey returned to Ireland, he went to Switzerland to see his nephew Michael Dawson, recovering from tuberculosis in Montreux.

In nearby Leysin Mary Martin was tending her brother

Desmond, also suffering from tuberculosis. Before leaving Ireland, Shanahan had written to her, saying he would like to meet her and her brother again. The meeting took place but was not a complete success. When Mary raised the possibility of coming out to Nigeria again to do missionary work, he told her that he could no longer accept laywomen as missionaries now that a religious society had been formed for the purpose. None the less, they parted on good terms.[10]

He came back to Ireland to find preparations for the consecration at an advanced stage. He had to console Mother Xavier, who was worried about the smallness of the chapel and disappointed that Bishop Finegan could not attend because of another engagement.

> The ceremony will be all the more homely because of the fewness of those who will be present. The sisters will have a chance of witnessing the ceremony which otherwise they would not have. The Bishop will be validly consecrated and the incidental advantage of useful propaganda for the Convent secured. The rest matters little.

The consecration took place as scheduled on the last Sunday in May. Shanahan was principal consecrator and the co-consecrators were Bishop Edward Mulhern of Dromore and Bishop J. G. Neville, CSSp. The new bishop's large family were well represented. His brother, Father Patrick Heerey, acted as his chaplain and the congregation included four more brothers and two sisters.[11] Afterwards the four bishops posed for photographs in the convent grounds. They reveal that the fine beard Heerey had sported in Nigeria was now no more.

* * *

Shanahan was now anxious to return to Nigeria. He booked a passage on the *RMS Appam* from Liverpool for 13 July. He was to be accompanied by Father Bertie White, returning to Nigeria from sick leave in Ireland where he had been acting as chaplain to Killeshandra. Heerey was to remain on for a few months to restore his health fully and then come out with the sisters in November. While in England, Shanahan visited the college in Mount Pleasant to inquire about teacher training for the Holy

Rosary Sisters. 'The more I think of the idea of sending the sisters for a few months in a Training College before they sail for Nigeria, the less I like it', he told Xavier. 'I am convinced that Sister Magdalen in Nigeria knows more about school work than any sister in the English Training Colleges. Her experience in Africa is invaluable.'

His voyage to Nigeria was far more pleasant than his voyage to Ireland had been. All his worries were at an end. His health and eyesight had improved, his resignation had been definitively rejected, he was to have the assistance of an able young coadjutor, the first Holy Rosary Sisters would soon be on their way. 'I am happy with a happiness I never experienced until today', he wrote. His thoughts kept going back to what he called the House on the Hill and he wrote several letters to the convent which he posted when the ship stopped at Freetown. He assured everybody that Father White, reputedly difficult to get on with, was proving delightful company. In a long letter addressed to the sisters and novices he said:

> The voyage is very pleasant. We are few on board; only 86 instead of 350! Fr White is the most congenial of companions and one of the happiest men on earth! We have a most restful voyage. We say Mass each morning. We eat, sleep, walk, read, sleep, eat, rest, pray and idle away by way of recreation the long days spent in our floating palace. I love the sea voyage. God is good to us.
>
> Often I bless the sea over which you are soon to sail. It is Our Father's own property! We must not forget. The North Star is now on the northern horizon and the Southern Cross is to be seen in its beautiful setting in the southern skies.
>
> You all accompany me in the sacred person of Christ, of whose Mystical Body we all form part. I think of you and pray for you frequently. God bless you. And in his name I bless you.[12]

He wrote a separate and very understanding letter to Sister Agnes, still heartbroken at not having been chosen for Nigeria but now willing to accept it in the spirit of religious obedience.

> This was the only remaining obstacle. You have overcome it. God bless you! As a missioner you are called by Jesus Christ to co-operate actively as well as by personal sanctification and prayer in the salvation of souls, but your co-operation cannot be co-operation unless you do exactly what Christ tells you through obedience, and at that post alone which He assigns to you.
>
> How happy I feel now that you see this in the bright light of Divine Grace that floods your soul.
>
> You are a missioner just as well as I am; it does not matter what section of the battle line you work and fight in under Christ's orders.[13]

He was met with an enthusiastic reception when he landed in Port Harcourt. The whole Council of Priests were there to greet him, together with a huge crowd of Christians. On the journey north, he was welcomed in the various missions along the way. Arriving in Onitsha, he was met by the schoolboys with a fife and drum band at their head. A few days later all the priests of the vicariate gathered in Onitsha for a re-union in his honour. 'It was a very pleasant gathering', he told Edward Leen. 'Everyone seemed anxious to show me that they were glad to see me back.'[14] He noted with pleasure the new coat of grey and white paint and whitewash on the priests' house, the neatness of the grounds and garden, the healthy growth of the palm trees in front of the house. Trees were one of his great loves. Even on his near-fatal trek through the Cameroons, he managed to collect some rare saplings and bring them back to Nigeria.

One of his first duties was to give Father White, his genial shipmate, a new appointment. 'Father White is going to Ogoja to take Father Mellett's place and keep Father Howell company', he told Mother Xavier. 'He is very well but finds it hard to part with his old station at Aba.' This was a very kind way of describing White's reaction to the wilds of Ogoja, typical of Shanahan's charity. Only to Leen did he tell the full story.

> His whole being was in evident revolt when he heard of his appointment. He would not speak to me at my own table! It was so serious that had he not climbed down and accepted his appointment he was to sail back to Europe by the next mail! However all ended well when he found he could not choose his station.

White departed for Ogoja and Shanahan set off on a visitation of all the stations in the Vicariate. One of his first concerns was to arrange for the new sisters to receive teacher training from Sister Magdalen. He went to Calabar, visited the school and met Magdalen. Far from sinking under the burden of solitude, Magdalen was thriving and so was the school. It was now recognised as one of the finest schools in the whole of West Africa. Towards the end of 1927 it was officially classified by the Nigerian education authorities as A plus, the highest possible classification, one given to no other girl's school in Nigeria. Magdalen's presence in Calabar was a great comfort to Shanahan. Another was the absence of Father Tom Ronayne.

Ronayne's spell as Bishop's secretary in Onitsha had not lasted long and he was transferred to Calabar, where he remained during Shanahan's visit to Europe. Here he injured his shoulder in an accident and had to return to Ireland. He left Calabar just before Shanahan arrived there. From the priests' house in Calabar, Shanahan wrote nostalgically to Leen.

> I cannot but think of you while I write this note in the now famous verandah here in Calabar where you and Father Tom and Sister Mary and I sat to discuss the Rules and Regulations of our first Irish Volunteer Missionary Sisters. You are all gone and I am here alone; but the work God had assigned to us at the meeting in the verandah has been accomplished.

This letter sheds light on Shanahan's reluctance to have Mary Martin back in Nigeria. According to his account, Ronayne was not content with encouraging her to leave the Holy Rosary Sisters. He wanted to found a new and independent sisterhood with Magdalen as superior and Mary Martin as her first novice. Shanahan was happy to tell Leen that Magdalen had resisted both Ronayne's entreaties and Mary Martin's letters.

> Needless to say, Sister Magdalen refused to listen to him, even told him that if he ever attempts to speak of the subject she would there and then leave and refuse to return to see him even during his illness. And yet he would return to the subject again and again in the most insidious way, only to see her stand up and leave. He would repent, apologise,

> and all the same return to the same subject. This being the case there is even in Ireland a certain danger to be feared from this desperate man. He and Sister Mary will insist on having a Religious Family all of their own and to their own image and likeness.

Sister Magdalen declared herself very willing to receive the new sisters in Calabar and initiate them into her education methods. They would not, however, remain in Calabar but would occupy the old convent in Onitsha and start a girls's school there. As the renovation of the Onitsha convent was going slower than expected, Shanahan sent a telegram to Killeshandra: 'Let sisters sail January Convent Onitsha uninhabitable earlier.' It was a disappointment, but only a minor one.

13

The hardest year

The year 1928 should have been the year when dreams came true for Bishop Shanahan. It was the year when his new sisterhood would finally begin its work for the women of Nigeria. It was the year when his young coadjutor would come to share his work and take some of the burden off his ageing shoulders. Instead, it turned out to be a year of trial and turmoil, with the first signs of the depression that was to be a recurring feature of his later years. As it drew to its melancholy close, he was to say, 'The year that is now ending has been the hardest year of my missionary life.'[1]

It began on a note of great joy and optimism. Bishop Heerey and the five sisters took the boat from Dublin on 24 January. A large crowd of relations, friends and well-wishers were on the North Wall to see them off. The next day they boarded the *RMS Abinsi* in Liverpool for the journey to Port Harcourt.

On the voyage they tried to observe their religious life as faithfully as they could. The Bishop celebrated Mass every morning for the group and during the day they recited the hours of the Divine Office as near as possible to the appointed times. On Friday afternoons, they went to confession to the Bishop between 5.00 and 6.00 p.m. the regular time for confessions in Killeshandra.

At 5.00 p.m. on the third Friday of the voyage they were waiting in line as usual when they saw an unexpected sight. A familiar and well-loved figure was striding towards them down the narrow passageway. It was Shanahan. Unable to wait any longer, he had come out on the pilot boat which was to guide the ship up the estuary and into Port Harcourt. Confessions were forgotten in the joy of reunion, their delight at seeing him exceeded if possible by his delight at seeing them.[2]

In Port Harcourt, a big crowd of Christians was waiting to greet them and similar crowds met them all the way to Onitsha. Travelling in two battered old Fords, followed by lorries containing their boxes and baggage, they arrived at their new home to find many of the priests of the vicariate assembled there in their honour. Among them was Father Pat Whitney, now stationed at Eke, who had come with his camera to record the historic occasion. They were brought to the old convent, as good as new after its refurbishment, given a tour of all the buildings of the mission, shown the place where their new school would be built. Shanahan had delayed starting the school and other buildings until he had a chance to discuss with the sisters what exactly they required.

Gradually the sisters began to settle in. After the excitement of their arrival, they found the first few weeks difficult enough. The heat during that February was intense even by Nigerian standards and the habits they wore, topped by sun-helmets every time they went out of doors, were unsuited to the climate. They suffered from the usual ailments of any newcomer to the tropics, though not as yet to any serious degree. Their duties were for the moment ill-defined. Building work on the school was under way by the beginning of March but it would not be completed for six months. Only then would they be able to start in earnest on the work they had come to do.

From the priest's house, a short distance away across the mission compound, Shanahan kept an anxious and fatherly eye on the sisters. He did not want to interfere in any way with their community life but at the same time he was concerned for their well-being. He brought them on outings to some of the missions to help them understand the background and culture of their future pupils. He organised classes for them in the Ibo language, taking some of the classes himself and entrusting others to his senior seminarian, John Anyogu. They made good progress and he was satisfied that they would be proficient in Ibo by the time the school opened.

By the middle of April, he was becoming aware that all was not well in the little community. In a letter to Mother Xavier, he mentioned that one of the group, Sister Patrick, was finding difficulty in submitting herself to the authority of the superior, Mother Dominic. He tried to play it down as much as possible but he was clearly worried.

Later that month, he brought Dominic, Patrick and Brigid to Calabar to be 'Montessoried', as he put it, by Sister Magdalen. They were to stay for six weeks with her and study the educational methods that had made her school so successful. He described their arrival to Leen.

> Three went to Calabar and got a poor reception from Sister

> M. Mag! I was present, fortunately, and could not understand this new aspect of one whom I ever considered to be, and do still consider to be, a saint. It is just like Father T. R. There are saints made to live alone and Sr M. Mag is one such. This was a shock to the sisters. They had heard so much about this great apostle. But now they see things in a new and I think the right light. They know now that God has many ways of making his saints. And it is not for us to find fault with Him because our little ideas and faltering ideals even of sainthood are not realised.[3]

Matters improved during the six weeks and the newcomers found Magdalen helpful and instructive, though she always maintained her distance and reserve. When the time came for parting there was sadness on both sides. 'I miss them very much', Magdalen wrote to Mother Arsenius. 'They were lonely going and the Fathers teased them over their tears.'[4] But she was happy to be alone again and in spite of Shanahan's hopes had no intention of joining the new sisterhood.

The trouble between Dominic and Patrick blew up again after their return to Onitsha. Shanahan mentions it in almost every letter to Mother Xavier during this period. Patrick was not inclined to accept the authority of someone who had been her fellow-novice a short time before. Dominic lacked the experience and maturity to deal with the situation. There was a long succession of dramatic confrontations followed by equally dramatic reconciliations and the other three sisters found themselves being gradually sucked into the conflict. Reluctantly, Shanahan was forced to ask himself whether Sister Patrick would have to be sent home.

> She has the dreadful gift of a keen, critical spirit. That is the cause of the trouble. She has not succeeded in bringing it into subjection. Her influence in the community is disruptive. It little matters what other qualities she has, and she has many that are excellent, and would have made of her an excellent missionary sister; but they are of no use, since she insists on submitting all authority and those that exercise it to the judgment of her own reason, and the whim of her own will, and more frequently her own fancy.

By August he was apologising to Mother Xavier for the morbid tone of his letters and it was evident that he was sinking into a state of depression. The troubles in the convent were not the only or even the principal cause of his worries.

> For some time back I have written to you letters that left you under the impression that I was not satisfied with the sisters? No, that was not the case. The poor sisters were, on the contrary, a source of exceptional consolation to me. But for some inexplicable reason I was unable to get away from some unknown cause of mental gloom. You cannot imagine the number of sheets of paper I spoiled writing to Killeshandra, letters that never left Onitsha! Invariably I lapsed into what I knew would convey gloom instead of happiness — and the letter was torn up. I thank God that at long last this desperate state is passing away. But I am deeply grateful to God for having sent it, for it has compelled me to make a year's retreat that otherwise I would never have made and given me the grace to see how much I needed a generous application of the big stick. I'm telling you this because I know you will understand me even though I enter into no further details.

It was not until the end of September that he felt free to tell Xavier the cause of his depression. It was the controversial proposal for the setting up of a new society for missionary priests to meet the needs of Southern Nigeria. 'This it was that has been worrying me more than anything ever worried me in a life that has known not a few worries.' It had now been approved by the Cardinal Prefect of Propaganda and life was looking brighter again. He was also glad to report that the school in Onitsha was almost finished and would be ready to open shortly. For a short time the clouds parted and the sun almost shone.

The school opened on schedule on 7 October, the Feast of the Holy Rosary. After High Mass in the Church, Bishop Shanahan and a large and curious congregation walked in procession to the new building, named Immaculata school in honour of the Immaculate Conception. He read the prayers of blessing and sprinkled the building with holy water, inside and outside. The crowd were then allowed to file in awed silence through the halls of learning. They were especially impressed by the statue of Mary

Immaculate in the main classroom, surrounded by lighted candles and flowers. In the visitors' book he made an entry which was to become a kind of dedication for all subsequent Holy Rosary schools throughout the world.

The Object of the School

> The object of the school is to honour and glorify God by teaching every pupil to know, love and serve him here below, and then to share with him his happiness for ever in heaven.
>
> May every girl who enters this school reproduce in her life the virtues practised by Our Lady: faith, humility, immaculate purity, love, patience, goodness in all its forms: virtues they will continue to see exemplified in the lives of those who continue on earth to be the living models of Mary Immaculate, who was and is the greatest model of Christ, Her Divine Son.
>
> May the blessing of Jesus Christ ever come to and remain with every little girl that enters this school.
>
> May every girl who enters this school enter one day the gates of heaven.[5]

For a time all went well but by the end of November things were worse than ever. Mother Dominic and Sister Gerard were both ill, this time seriously. Sister Patrick was talking about leaving the sisterhood altogether. Only Brigid and Joseph were functioning normally. The doctor ordered the two sick sisters to go back to Ireland, but Dominic pleaded to be allowed stay a little longer. In the event it was decided that Gerard and Patrick would return in the new year, Gerard to convalesce in Killeshandra, Patrick to leave the order permanently.

It was a sad end to a year that had begun with so many hopes. Of the five sisters who had left Ireland in January, one was leaving the sisterhood, one was returning sick to Ireland, one was ill in Nigeria and would soon have to go back to Ireland also. He asked Xavier if there was any possibility of her sending out more sisters. She offered him three, Sisters Agnes, Philomena and Catherine, for early 1929. He cabled an immediate acceptance: 'Get Ag Philo Ca ready writing Shanahan.'

* * *

Concurrent with his worry over the sisters during 1928 was his worry about the founding of the new society of priests. This was the more painful of the two because it involved him in a very distressing conflict of loyalties. On the one hand was his lifelong commitment to the Holy Ghost Congregation. On the other was his duty to the people of Nigeria. It was coming to the point where the two seemed no longer compatible.

Early in 1927, while still in hospital in Dublin, he had written to the Irish Holy Ghost Provincial:

> Is there any chance of help? I see myself you can do nothing for me just now, but at the end of the year I think Nigeria would need special care if we are to keep it in the hands of the Congregation. Rome would not leave eight million souls to be evangelised by just twenty-six missioners.[6]

It seemed to him incredible and intolerable that a mission so flourishing and so full of promise should be so starved of men and resources. He had called on the secular priests to ease the situation but their coming had done little good overall. As the number of secular priests increased, the number of Holy Ghost priests diminished. He felt he was being abandoned by the Congregation. Now, a year later and back in Nigeria, the feeling had intensified. He enumerated for Leen the Holy Ghost priests who had recently left his vicariate because of age or ill-health or re-assignment.

> To replace these and add to our staff, we got one priest within the last two years — and such a man! The poor man is so shy, so little enthusiastic about work, that he can scarcely do anything else than sit down in his room from morning to night. No use delaying any longer. We have got to go elsewhere if Southern Nigeria is to get missioners and men.[7]

The problem was made worse by the fact that the secular priests had engaged to come out for a period of five years only. Many of them were now due to return, some of them overdue. Most of them did not want to return and would be willing to stay on in Nigeria, if the bishops of their home dioceses in Ireland gave their consent. They were happy in their work, and had formed close bonds with the country and the people. This had been strengthened by the death in 1926 of one of their number, young Father Mulvaney, who had served in Eke for three years and refused to return to Ireland when his fatal illness was diagnosed. His grave in Onitsha seemed to have sealed their commitment to Africa. Shanahan now had to find some structure which would enable them to remain and to be permanently attached to the vicariate of Southern Nigeria. He told Leen:

> I went to them and asked them fair and square whether if I undertake to get the proper sanction from Rome they would be ready to follow me and form a new 'Missionary Society of Secular Priests'? One and all agreed. There and then they wrote to their bishops for freedom to remain in Southern Nigeria, but they did not tell their Lordships anything about a society.

One of the Irish bishops recalled his two priests, the others gave rather grudging permission for theirs to stay. Shanahan wrote to the Prefect of Propaganda in Rome, Cardinal van Rossum, and proposed a scheme for setting up a new society of missionary priests who would help the Holy Ghost Congregation in its work in the English-speaking colonies. He emphasised that 'the new society would not supplant but supplement the Holy Ghost Society in its missionary enterprise'.

When the mother-house in Paris heard about this, they began to sit up and take notice. The charitable explanation would be that they realised Nigeria had special needs and that these would have to be met. The less charitable explanation would be that they saw a danger of their most successful African mission being taken away from them and were determined to prevent this. They told Shanahan that all the men he needed would be sent to Nigeria and that there was no reason for him to go ahead with the planned new society.

It so happened that Pius XI had recently issued an encyclical letter on the missions entitled *Rerum Ecclesiae* which warned missionary orders against being over-possessive of the territories entrusted to them and trying to exclude other orders from their own areas. Rivalry between different religious societies should never come before the pastoral needs of the people. In the spirit of the encyclical, van Rossum wrote to Shanahan giving general approval to his plan.

> I hope that the Superior General of your Institute will, as Your Excellency states, send more missionaries as quickly as possible to your Vicariate to look after its spiritual needs. However, if for any reason this should not happen, then since you have a grave obligation to evangelise the region entrusted to your care, you must know that Your Excellency is bound to use every means to see that this is done, calling if necessary on religious belonging to other Institutes in accordance with the norms of the encyclical *Rerum Ecclesiae*.[8]

Van Rossum's letter was written in early February 1928. For a long time Shanahan agonised over his reply. He was conscious as ever of the needs of Nigeria, yet he loved the Congregation which was his religious family and to which he owed his education and his priesthood. Only when he became convinced that the promises of the mother-house were not going to be fulfilled and that no new men were on their way, did he act. He wrote to Leen on 25 May.

> It has taken me four months of more hard thinking to muster up courage to write back to Rome to tell them that I am ready to face this difficult task of creating a missionary society if they simply tell me 'go ahead'. I have posted the letter today. And now my mind is at ease. No matter what happens, I won't have shirked a duty because of the hardship it entails and of the tongues it will set a-wagging ...
>
> Now you will understand how strange my letters have read. My mind was tormented. Up to the last moment I had hoped the Congregation would do something for one of its best missions. Now after twenty-five years experience, I am convinced, beyond the power of arguments to change my mind, that there's nothing to be expected from the Congregation or its Irish Province.

On 21 June van Rossum put the matter before Pius XI, who gave his full approval to the proposed new society. When Shanahan heard the news, he was jubilant. He decided to tell nobody except the secular priests and Leen, until his plans for the setting up of the society were completed. It would involve finding an Irish headquarters similar to Killeshandra. In August he spoke to Leen of his plans.

> We will have to get in the first place a Bishop that will allow us to set up in his diocese. Then a house in that diocese and then money to buy the house. That done we will need some tip-top men to take over charge and begin the training of our young missionaries. We can get any number of young fellows from the Irish colleges. All we want is the best priests in Ireland to train them and give them the missionary spirit in all its burning purifying consuming zeal for God's glory and the salvation of souls.

What happened next is not well documented. It may be that the events were too painful for him to write about. According to Bishop Moynagh, the secular priests were mostly very young men and felt the need of leadership. They told Shanahan there was no-one among themselves who had the necessary gifts and authority to lead them. He answered, 'I will be your leader! I will leave the Holy Ghost Congregation and found the new society!' When the news got out, the reaction from Paris was swift and drastic. Intense pressure was brought on him to change his mind and the damage that would be done to the Congregation if he were to leave it was strongly emphasised.

There was opposition also from Killeshandra. When planning to set up a house for the new society in an Irish diocese, he naturally thought of Bishop Finegan. He suggested to him that a house could be bought in Kilmore diocese, perhaps even built in the grounds of Killeshandra. Mother Xavier immediately became alarmed and began to worry that some of the subscriptions on which the convent depended might be diverted to the priests' society. Finegan took her side and they both urged Shanahan not to lend his name to the new society of secular priests. Because of the debt of gratitude he owed them, their opinions weighed very heavily with him.

It had cost him a great deal to make the decision to go ahead with the project. It would cost him even more to withdraw from it. He spent days in agonising thought and prayer. There were not many in whom he could confide fully. One whom he felt he could trust was Sister Joseph and on Christmas Eve he walked with her for four hours up and down the avenue of mango trees in Onitsha, arguing both sides of the question. He told her of the distressing letters he had received from Finegan and Xavier, and of a visit paid by the Holy Ghost Superior General to Killeshandra, which must have strengthened Xavier in her opposition. How could they object to anything that would bring more priests to Nigeria? Yet how could he go against those whom he respected so highly?[9]

Eventually, he made up his mind and informed the Maynooth priests that he was no longer prepared to act as leader of the new society. He ended up by pleasing nobody. The mother-house, the Irish Province, the Holy Ghost priests in Nigeria were all offended that he could even have considered leaving the Congregation. The secular priests were deeply disappointed and felt that he had deserted them in their hour of need. Everyone complained that he was indecisive and changeable. He himself found the whole experience extremely traumatic. For a time he exhibited symptoms of depression, such as difficulty in concentrating and in writing letters. As the year came to an end, he recovered much of his equilibrium and asked his friends to forgive him for not keeping in touch with them. In a Christmas letter to all the sisters in Killeshandra he wrote, 'I feel also that although I have lapsed, during the past year, into a strange and inexplicable silence, I have not lost your confidence.' To Mother Xavier he wrote:

> As regards my health, I am well. But I was unable to do any office work during the year. That was a source of great suffering. I had to do the essential. I'm better now and I feel that in time I will be able to manage to make ends meet.
>
> Don't be upset by my silence. Rather than write with a tired brain I remained silent. I have lost many friends over it. I can't help it. This is enough about me.

To his closest friend and confidant Edward Leen he revealed something more of the agony he had gone through.

> I often think of you and wish you were here. There's a fearful loneliness in my heart and soul betimes ... God has been mercifully wonderfully good to me this last year. He

> has almost knocked the devil out of me! And that's a blessing if ever there was a blessing.

The society for the secular priests was formed in due course exactly along the lines he had planned, but the honour of being its founder and leader was not to belong to him.

* * *

The decision to send three more sisters to Southern Nigeria was not made public for some time. Even the three themselves were not told until the beginning of February 1929. Sister Catherine describes how it happened.

> On February 2nd Mother Xavier tipped me on the shoulder at evening meditation and beckoned me to follow her. I saw two other figures rise and, thinking we were all needed, I tipped all sisters near me. We arrived at the back parlour door but Mother Xavier sent all back to their prayers except Sisters M. Agnes, Philomena and myself. She said very briefly, 'The sisters in Nigeria need more help and you have been assigned to go out to them. Now don't get excited about it. Those who get most excited can turn out the worst. Kneel down and say the Hail, holy Queen!'[10]

It was the middle of April when the three left Liverpool on the *Abinsi,* arriving at Port Harcourt in the afternoon of Friday 3 May. Once again, Shanahan came out on the pilot boat to be the first to welcome them to Nigeria. As the ship neared its landing place a terrific thunderstorm broke out and the sisters had to scramble through mud and rain to reach the wharf. They were conscious that their snowy white habits were soaked and spattered and their shoes oozing as they sat down to a formal dinner in the hospital attended by all the local dignitaries. The following morning the sun was shining again and they made the journey by car to Onitsha without incident.[11]

The three newcomers were well chosen and soon proved their worth. Mother Dominic was still far from well; she was suffering both from nervous exhaustion and from a heart condition. The task of running the school had fallen on Sisters Brigid and Joseph. The new arrivals got down to work at once. On Monday morning, less than three days after their landing in Nigeria, they were taking their first classes in the Immaculate girls' school. In accordance with the methods learnt from Sister Magdalen, senior girls were employed to help in the teaching so that the small group of sisters could manage a school of more than four hundred pupils without excessive strain. Even more important, the atmosphere in the community was no longer tense and prickly. 'Here in Onitsha there is perfect harmony and happiness in the Holy Rosary Convent', Shanahan told Xavier. 'After the cross the peace of heaven!'

He was once more without a secretary. Ronayne had returned from Europe but Shanahan did not recall him to Onitsha. Instead, he turned to the new sisters for help with his voluminous correspondence. Eventually one of them, the Philadelphia-born Sister Philomena Fox, was freed from most of her other duties and became his full-time secretary for the rest of his time in Nigeria.

His coadjutor, Bishop Heerey, helped to ease the burden of visiting the missions and administering confirmation and also took over much of the financial administration. In all his letters, Shanahan refers to him with approval and pays tribute to his qualities. Even when writing to Leen, he had nothing but praise for the new bishop. 'Dr Heerey is getting along very well. He will be an excellent chief whenever it pleases God to call me away. He is a man of sterling spiritual value, that's everything.' Yet all his references to Heerey suggest respect rather than warmth. There is none of the personal affection that he showed for many of the other priests and for all of the sisters.

One thing that pleased him was Heerey's own esteem for the sisters, a good augury for the future. After his consecration in Killeshandra, Heerey had visited the convent frequently and come to know the community very well. His voyage out with the first five sisters had strengthened this relationship. He, like Shanahan, was specially concerned about Mother Dominic, whose health was showing little sign of improvement. The situation was not without its comic side, as Sister Catherine relates.

> Both bishops had the greatest sympathy for her and did all they could to help. If either had to go away to a distant place, such as Lagos or Calabar, he would bring back some little thing to cheer up the invalid. Thus it happened that each

bishop, at a different time, had brought her a wrist-watch, a thing unused by us in those days. Mother then had to be very careful, if one of their Lordships was coming to see her, that she was wearing his watch. Maybe they would not have noticed, but it was a source of amusement for us.[12]

In Calabar, Sister Magdalen continued to plough her successful but solitary furrow. The school was flourishing and its reputation had spread throughout West Africa as a model of its kind. She had begun work on the founding of the native sisterhood as requested by Shanahan and had set up an informal community with five of the older girls who wished to become sisters. The problem was that she resolutely declined to join the Holy Rosary Congregation, though Shanahan had obtained the necessary permission from Rome. She even refused to take a much-needed holiday in Europe as this would mean putting the school temporarily in the care of the Holy Rosary Sisters. It was by no means clear how the work would continue in the event of her illness or death.

Her solution to the problem was to suggest that Shanahan should once again contact the Irish Sisters of Charity, of whom she was still a member, and invite them to join her in Calabar. Having been twice rebuffed, he knew that there was no point in doing this. Magdalen felt he was being unhelpful and began making her own contacts without informing him. She wrote to the Mother General of the Irish Sisters of Charity but received a decisive refusal: 'We look upon England as our Foreign Mission.' Then she started negotiations with the Holy Child Sisters, whose Mother General had been her childhood friend. It seems clear that she involved Heerey in these negotiations and that she was waiting for Shanahan to resign and make way for a more enlightened successor.[13]

This was only one symptom of a growing air of uncertainty that affected the vicariate during the course of 1929. The Bishop, who had already offered his resignation by reason of failing health, seemed to be nearing the end of his time. The division of the vicariate, proposed four years earlier, was still hanging in the air and making long-term planning difficult. Some of the Holy Ghost priests continued to be unhappy with the presence of the Maynooth men, especially when asked to work under their direction. The Maynooth priests themselves felt they were in an anomalous position and did not know whether they were staying or going.

In these circumstances, it was inevitable that the discontented should look to Heerey as their leader and hope for the future. There is no reason to suppose that he was in any way disloyal to Shanahan at this time, but his very existence helped to provide a focus for the dissidents and to make them more vocal. In July 1929 a visitator from the Holy Ghost Congregation, Father Soul, came to Southern Nigeria to make a report on the mission to the mother-house. He commented unfavourably on the fact that many of the Holy Ghost Fathers were unable to live the proper community life of religious. Some of them were living in isolation, others were living with secular priests and subject to their authority.[14]

At the same time, it was announced that an Apostolic Visitor from Rome was on his way to investigate the role of education in the Church's missionary work in British Africa. He was Bishop Arthur Hinsley, rector of the English College in Rome, later to be Cardinal Archbishop of Westminster. His report would carry great weight with the Holy See and his coming was looked forward to with considerable interest. All those who had complaints to make hoped to find in him a ready listener, and these included a few who still believed that Shanahan's whole emphasis on the schools had been a tragic mistake.

It was at this critical juncture that Mother Dominic's frail health finally collapsed. Shanahan wrote to Mother Xavier and told her that Dominic had been ordered by the doctor to return to Ireland as soon as she was able to travel.

> On Sunday the 7 July Mother got a very severe fit. She was so bad that for some hours her life was almost despaired of. She received Extreme Unction and thought the last hour had come for her. Quite willingly and lovingly she gave back her soul to God, happy that she was to die as a missionary in Africa. I was not at home but Dr Heerey was, and it was he gave the last sacraments to poor Mother Dominic.
>
> On my return, late on Sunday night, I got an awful shock when I learned from Dr Heerey the happenings of the day. And yet I could not but rejoice in the midst of this great cloud of sorrow at the first offering of the Missionary Society of Our Lady of the Holy Rosary of the greatest gift that could

> be given: the free and loving offering by Mother Dominic of her own life to Our Lord for the conversion of His poor African children.

By the beginning of August, Dominic was well enough to travel. Shanahan made the sudden and unexpected decision to travel with her. He gave various reasons for his decision, none of them entirely convincing: she could not travel alone, no other priest or sister could be spared to go with her, he needed to go to Europe for a medical check-up, he wanted to seek more missionaries, it would give Heerey a chance to get used to administering the vicariate. According to Sisters Rosarii and Philomena, his real reason was to provide moral support to Dominic on her return to Killeshandra. She was by nature of a nervous and scrupulous disposition and she felt that she was deserting her post as superior and coming back to Ireland under a cloud of failure. He wished to make her homecoming easier and to ensure that she was sympathetically received in Killeshandra.[15]

Whatever the reason, it was generally felt to be a serious error of judgement on his part. His leaving just as the Apostolic Visitor was arriving could be interpreted as a lack of respect for the Pope's representative. In addition, it left the field wide open for those who were discontented for one reason or another. They could make their complaints to Hinsley, secure in the knowledge that Shanahan was not there to give his side of the story.

The Apostolic Visitor arrived in Calabar from the Cameroons on 25 August. He was met by Shanahan and Heerey. With Shanahan, it was a case of hail and farewell. He explained the situation to Hinsley, made his apologies and left almost at once for Port Harcourt, where he and Dominic were due to embark on the *Abinsi* on the 29th. Hinsley remained for the time being in Calabar, where he was given his first detailed information on the Nigerian situation from the somewhat biased perspectives of Father Ronayne and Sister Magdalen.

The one person who should have been unreservedly grateful to Bishop Shanahan for his decision was Mother Dominic herself. On the ship as in Onitsha he was kindness itself, attentive to her every need. By a sad mischance, she misinterpreted his attentions and the signs of affection which were second nature to him. He thought nothing of putting his arms around a sister to comfort her or of letting her cry on his shoulder. He was their father, they were his daughters. What could be more natural?

Every day during the voyage, he showed his concern for Dominic's health and comfort. Every night he visited her in her cabin to make sure she was comfortable and gave her a paternal kiss on the forehead before leaving. What seemed natural to him, seemed threatening to her. Her native scrupulosity was aroused and she became a prey to feelings of guilt. It does not appear that she told him about her feelings or that he had any suspicion of their existence. But when she got back to Killeshandra she told Mother Xavier that the Bishop was in love with her, with consequences that were to be little short of tragic.[16]

14

Looking to the future

The gradual breakdown in relations between Bishop Shanahan and the order he had founded began around the time of Mother Dominic's return from Nigeria. Having heard her story, Mother Xavier felt herself confirmed in a suspicion that had been growing over the last three or four years. Greatly though she admired the Bishop, highly though she esteemed his spiritual qualities and his missionary achievements, she found herself forced to the conclusion that he was a bad influence on the sisters.

Mother Xavier was a woman of conscience and principle. The Dominican Order had completed their five-year commitment to the new sisterhood but had now agreed to continue on for a further five years. She had not sought the position she occupied, but having accepted it she was bound to carry it out to the end. Her duty was to form the young sisters in the religious life and to protect them from anything that would hinder their development. She was probably sensible enough to take Dominic's story with a grain of salt, but at the same time the incident brought home to her the attraction that the Bishop could have for young and impressionable personalities.

She knew that religious sisters must be trained in discipline and self-control. In her direction of the convent, she followed the time-honoured traditions that instilled a sense of discipline in innumerable small but significant ways. Sisters were taught to walk, not to run; to sit upright, not to slouch; to smile, not to laugh loudly. They moved in a quiet and restrained manner, they kept their hands folded and their eyes modestly downcast, they avoided unnecessary looks or gestures. They ate what was set before them at meals and avoided taking so much as a drink of water between meals. As celibates, they were particularly guarded in the presence of the opposite sex and even among themselves were careful to avoid any emotional friendships.

Shanahan's visits to Killeshandra did little to help this kind of discipline. When he spoke to the sisters in the convent oratory, he was truly spiritual and inspiring. His love of God and zeal for souls shone through everything he said. But when he met them in the parlour and especially when he took them walking through the fields, his influence was less healthy. The normal routine of Killeshandra was disrupted and the air of calm and decorum was disturbed. They came back to the convent giddy and excited, still spellbound by his magnetism, still flattered that a bishop should show them such attention and courtesy. Quite unconsciously, he could undo the work of patient weeks in a couple of hours.

Mother Xavier, like other nuns of her generation, had a keen sense of the supernatural. She saw the supernatural as something that was opposed to the natural. Human nature in itself was wounded by original sin and must be opposed and repressed. The religious life was a constant struggle against nature. Obedience to the rule was the great means of bringing nature into subjection. Even when the rule might seem arbitrary or ill-judged, submission to it was a religious act that brought its reward in grace, while opposition to it was a sign of wilfulness and pride.

Xavier had not failed to notice that Shanahan's attitude to the rule was not all it should be. She had the impression that the sisters in Onitsha were falling a little from their first fervour under his influence. This impression had been strengthened by something he had said to her in a letter regarding the illness of Dominic and Gerard.

> Had their rule permitted them to do, while in health, what they are now compelled to do by illness, we would have been spared much of the great anxiety that has affected us all — you at home no less than us out here. It does not matter now, since they are, thank God, recovering. Practical experience of missionary life and its hardships and inevitable demands where life is concerned, will enable the Sisters, little by little, to differentiate between the essentials and non-essentials in matters that concern their life and usefulness as missioners.

This was dangerous teaching. A rule which could be changed whenever it was inconvenient to observe it was no rule at all. Obeying the rule could lead to certain problems and difficulties, but disobeying it led to far greater ones. To Mother Xavier it seemed like the road to anarchy.

She said nothing of this to Shanahan, except in the most oblique and roundabout way. She confided her fears to the novice-mistress, Mother Aquinas, and to Bishop Finegan, who both agreed with her. It can be taken as certain that she spoke also to the spiritual director, Edward Leen, and that he too was in agreement. In his talks to the novices he usually emphasised the idea of *agere contra,* acting against the dictates and demands of nature, conquering what was merely human through vigilance and mortification. Many of them found his teaching harsh. 'He electrified the community with his diatribes', wrote one sister. 'His favourite words for human nature, especially feminine religious nature, were 'dwarfed' and 'thwarted' and you could have your choice of being both or either.'[1] The long-standing friendship with Shanahan was something precious to him, but the spiritual welfare of the young souls entrusted to his care was more precious still. The last thing he wanted was to hurt the Bishop's feelings, but if it came to a choice between hurting one man and stunting the spiritual growth of a whole religious order, he knew where his duty lay.

The young sisters and novices were unaware of these happenings. As time went on, however, they noticed a subtle change in attitude towards the Bishop. His name was mentioned less often. The welcomes given to him on his visits to the convent were more formal and restrained. They were reminded that it was Bishop Finegan not Bishop Shanahan who was their superior. The suggestion even began to surface that according to canon law, Finegan was not only their superior but their founder, since it was in his diocese that the order had been started. They were warned about the dangers of relaxing their observance of the rule once they had gone to Africa and they were given the impression that the sisters of Nigeria had fallen into careless ways under Shanahan's well-meant but misguided influence.

Shanahan had, in point of fact, a great respect for their rule. But he felt that it followed too closely the Dominican rule, drawn up for a semi-enclosed religious order in Ireland. The cumbersome habits, the long hours of prayer in Latin, the multiplication of bows and genuflections, even such a small thing as the ban on drinking water between meals, made less sense in Africa. He did not intervene directly, but when the sisters themselves began to make needed modifications he gave his full approval. He believed in self-control, but not in mortification for its own sake. He once told Sister Philomena, with a sweeping gesture of his hand:

> If there is a reason to run, then run. If you wish to walk, walk. If you want to enjoy eating a big fat apple, then for

> goodness sake enjoy it and thank God for it! If you find it necessary to get control over a specific appetite, then firmly set up positive mortifications to achieve control and channel these energies; but never use mortification for its own sake, and never never try to make one thing look like something else, such as running while trying to appear to be walking, half doing either and doing neither.

His attitude to material possessions was cast in the same mould. He used them gladly and generously and thanked God for them. Sister Margaret Mary's comments give a good insight into this side of his character.

> Dr Shanahan was not notable for poverty in the sense of consciously depriving himself or going without things. Rather the opposite. His princely generosity was often judged to be extravagant. When travelling, he gave generous tips to waiters and stewards. He could send long cables and telegrams of good wishes for Christmas, Easter and other feasts, at a time when telegrams were only used to announce a sudden death or some tragedy in the fewest possible words. 'I hate one of anything,' he would say, giving out pencils, pens, pictures or anything he had at hand. He could enjoy a cigar or a glass of wine or even whiskey, when the occasion called for it, but no-one would dream of thinking him intemperate. His perfect self-control was very evident. His generosity stemmed from the virtues of magnanimity and magnificence which he possessed in a high degree.
>
> All material things were our Heavenly Father's property to be used with gratitude for His glory. Once he was alone in the lodge at Killeshandra when some poor person in the neighbourhood called to ask prayers for a sick relative. He set out at once, visited the sick person, gave words of comfort, and rubbed Sloan's Liniment on the aching joints. When leaving he was offered a shilling and some coppers for the missions, which he accepted gratefully. Later he came up to the Convent and handed up the donation, with the air of one donating a handsome gift. The sister who received it knew that as a Bishop he had been accustomed to dealing in large sums. She was struck by his reverence.

> The gift of a poor person was to him a great gift, just as the mite of the poor widow was to Christ.

Among God's many gifts, Shanahan prized especially the gift of human love. He had a great love for his own family, his parents, his brothers and sisters, his nieces and nephews. His French background may be part of the reason why he was not afraid to express that love. In a letter to his nephew Michael Dawson on the occasion of his marriage, he wrote: 'Much as I loved you as a winsome boy, I love you with a new love now, the love a man has for an honest fellow man.' In a goodbye letter to his niece Josie Kelly, he wrote:

> It is hard to bid farewell to those we love. But, oh! the wretched thing life would be if we had nobody to love, nobody to return our love, nobody to share with us our joys and sorrows, our work, our very life. Now God has given us all those good things along with love and along with himself, to love and to be loved.

The love he had for his human family was extended to his spiritual family as well, especially to the sisters of the Holy Rosary Congregation, his spiritual daughters. 'Is it any wonder I love you as I know God wishes me to love you', he had written to the sisters in 1928. 'Without fail your letters come all the way from God's sanctuary on the hill, forming between Killeshandra and parched Africa a stream of divinised human affection that has been for me a source of exceptional happiness.'

Sister Margaret Mary comments, 'God permitted that in this paternal love for us, he should be suspected and misunderstood. It was considered a danger to his spiritual welfare and ours, that he should have too much social contact with us.' He himself was probably the last to realise what was happening. During his visit to Ireland from September 1929 to September 1930, he came and went at Killeshandra much as usual. He may have felt a certain sense of strain and tension, but there were many possible explanations. The idea that he could be considered a danger to the sisters and they to him was so preposterous that it never even entered his mind.[2]

* * *

In Southern Nigeria Bishop Hinsley was continuing his official visitation of the vicariate. It was obvious that the mission was in a very healthy state. He summed up his impressions in his diary. 'This is the most flourishing mission in British, if not the whole of West Africa. Many problems still unsolved, sisters, secular movement. The success of Onitsha is largely ascribed to the schools.' As he travelled from one mission station to another, his astonishment grew at the numbers who thronged the churches and schools and at the fewness of the priests and sisters who ministered to them.

He recognised two clear and immediate needs: to increase the number of sisters and to secure a steady supply of secular priests for the mission. His first informants on these two areas were Sister Magdalen and Father Ronayne respectively. Magdalen told him of her hope that the Holy Child Sisters would come to Calabar to ensure the continuation of her work there. She would be happy to hand over the school to them and to become a member of their order. He was greatly struck by her ability and dedication. He sent off a letter to Rome to Mother Amadeus, Mother General of the Holy Child Sisters, and begged her to come to Magdalen's help. 'For God's sake and for the sake of thousands of souls, secure assistance for this saint of the Nigerian mission.'

Father Tom Ronayne filled him in on the so-called secular movement, the contribution made by the Maynooth priests to the Nigerian mission. He described the efforts to start a society for these priests, so far without success because of the difficulty of finding a leader. Like most people meeting Ronayne for the first time, Hinsley was impressed, describing him in his diary as a 'zealous missionary who speaks with knowledge and interest of the working of the native minds.' Hinsley felt that a leader must be found and started to make soundings as to who would be acceptable now that Shanahan had withdrawn.[3]

The name of Father Pat Whitney began to emerge as the most likely candidate. It is probable that Ronayne was the first to suggest it. Whitney himself was in Ireland on leave at the time, but Hinsley was able to see some of the fruits of his labours when he visited Emekuku, transformed by Whitney into one of the most dynamic and progressive missions in the Vicariate. Arriving in the middle of a tropical rainstorm, the Apostolic Visitor was greeted by an immense crowd of Catholics and catechumens, and was amazed and indignant to find that there were only two priests in the mission. 'When I get back to Rome,' he said, 'I will shout at the top of my voice for more missionaries to be sent to Nigeria.'[4] He was told of the system devised by Whitney whereby the catechists from all the schools of the area came to Emekuku for a two-day retreat and reunion on the first Thursday and Friday of every month, a system being copied with great success in other missions. The more he heard about him, the more convinced he was that this was the man. He made arrangements to see him when he returned from Africa.

Unhappily, the sources Hinsley relied on for much of his information were not favourable to Shanahan. Magdalen and Ronayne both acknowledged his spirituality and saintliness but suggested that he was no longer able to keep up with the immense work-load of the vicariate. They spoke especially of the difficulty he found in making decisions and of his tendency to change them even when they had been made. There was some truth in this, in view of his back-tracking over the leadership of the society of priests, but there was also an element of over-statement and self-justification. Hinsley ended up with an exaggerated idea of Shanahan's failing powers and came to the unfortunate conclusion that the affairs of the Vicariate would have to be settled without reference to the Vicar.

Hinsley arrived back in Rome towards the end of 1929 with a fourfold plan in mind. Firstly, the Holy Child Sisters were to be persuaded to come to Nigeria and take over the schools in Calabar and its neighbourhood. Secondly, the society of secular priests was to be set up with Father Whitney as its leader. Thirdly, the division of the vicariate was to be finalised as soon as possible. Fourthly, Shanahan himself was to resign and be succeeded by Heerey.

Whitney came to Rome, was asked to lead the new society and agreed. He also agreed that the society, to be known as Saint Patrick's Missionary Society, would take responsibility for one part of the vicariate when the division was made. He did not approve of the original plan which would have divided the vicariate into an eastern and western section, one based on Onitsha and the other on Calabar. Instead, he asked that the new society be given the central part of the vicariate, the area familiar to him around the missions of Emekuku and Eke, which included two of the biggest towns in the Ibo heartland, Enugu and Owerri. This was agreed to, all unknown to Shanahan.

Gradually he began to be aware that something strange was going on behind his back. The first inkling came through the celebrated incident of the misdirected letter, which has acquired the status of a legend over the years. Whitney wrote two letters, one to Shanahan and the other to Ronayne. The one to Shanahan was polite and guarded, the one to Ronayne was brutally frank, especially in its references to Shanahan. 'We will use the old boy as long as he can help us,' he wrote, 'and ditch him when he becomes an obstacle.' He then placed the letters in the wrong envelopes and posted them off. Shanahan's feelings when he read the letter meant for Ronayne and realised that it referred to him can easily be imagined.[5]

Then Whitney wrote again to Ronayne, giving him details of the division of the vicariate. Ronayne took alarm at this, possibly because his own mission in Calabar was now excluded from the territory of the new society. He sent a telegram to Heerey in Onitsha informing him of the situation, and Heerey passed on the news in a telegram to Shanahan in Ireland.[6]

Shanahan decided to go at once to Rome. He was totally opposed to the proposed division, which meant that the Saint Patrick's Society would have the central portion of the vicariate, while all the fringe areas were left to the Holy Ghost Congregation. They would have to cross the Saint Patrick's area in order to go from one part of their territory to another. He was staying in the gate-lodge at the time, and two of the young sisters were given the task of cutting up a huge map of Nigeria so that he could fit it into his suitcase and show it to the Pope. On the way he passed through London, where he stayed the night with his friend, Archbishop Amigo of Southwark. As he entered the Archbishop's house, he met Whitney coming out, on his return journey from Rome. It was an embarrassing moment for both.[7]

He arrived in Rome at the beginning of January, 1930, and spent the whole month there. In addition to the Pope he met Hinsley, various officials of Propaganda Fide, and members of different missionary orders. The most important meeting was the one with the Pope. Pius XI with his usual brusqueness went straight to the heart of the matter. He produced his own map of the proposed division and asked Shanahan if he had been consulted about it.

When Shanahan replied that he had not, the Pope took his pen, scrawled a line through the map, and said, 'Then you divide it whatever way you think fit.'[8]

He went with Hinsley to see Mother Amadeus of the Holy Child Sisters. This too was an embarrassing meeting, since Mother Amadeus had discussed coming to his vicariate without consulting him. She felt that the meeting did not go very well and he gave her the impression that the sisters were being forced on him, understandably enough in the circumstances. A second meeting a few days later without Hinsley went much better, though she was taken aback by his reservations about Sister Magdalen, whom Hinsley had praised so highly. 'She is too individualistic and likes being alone', Shanahan told her. 'You must not go to help her; it must be your work.' Years later she was to acknowledge the wisdom of what he said.

At that meeting and in a follow-up letter he made it clear that he welcomed the Holy Child Sisters unreservedly to Calabar. 'Now at last Divine Providence comes to our assistance as a mother does when her children are in difficulty. Both Sister Magdalen and I are overjoyed at the solution. The Sisters of the Holy Child Jesus are to take over both her work and herself! I wish to make this matter very clear.' He added a generous but honest tribute to Magdalen herself. 'She is a saintly sister with some of the little failings of the saints.'[9]

He returned to Ireland for the inevitable confrontation with Whitney. It took place in Maynooth College, with the President, Monsignor McCaffrey, as mediator. Whitney had no option but to agree to Shanahan's division of the vicariate. The Society of Saint Patrick was to take charge of the Calabar and Ogoja missions. The remainder was to stay in the care of the Holy Ghost Fathers.

This was the kind of occasion which showed Whitney at his best. His unconquerable love of intrigue often landed him in awkward situations. His unconquerable resilience usually got him out of them again. Moynagh writes: 'When found *in fraudem legis* he looked so innocently guileless, so woebegone and pathetic, so patently sincere, simple and single-minded, so utterly committed to Christ's cause, that he often ended by winning a determined and convinced supporter!' Shanahan was not the man to harbour grudges and the relationship between the two men was soon restored to normal.

* * *

Shanahan decided not to return to Nigeria until the new missionaries were ready to travel. Many people noticed that he looked pale and tired, not surprisingly in view of the difficult period he had just gone through. He spent some time in Saint Vincent's Hospital in Dublin, which helped to restore his health and good humour. The depression of two years ago did not reappear. Indeed, now that the necessary decisions had at last been taken, he seemed his usual cheerful and happy self once more.

He was in Germany at the end of April, ordaining students to the priesthood and other orders in the Holy Ghost seminary at Knechtsteden.[10] He was involved at the time in negotiations to bring German missionaries to his vicariate. All the German colonies in Africa had been lost during the war, and German priests were finding difficulty in gaining entrance to British and French colonies. Eventually, the British authorities agreed to allow some into Nigeria, on condition they were properly vouched for. Shanahan's recommendation was more than sufficient. It was arranged that the first group would be sent out by the German province of the Holy Ghost Congregation before the end of the year and that they would work in the territory of the Munshi tribe, where no permanent missions had yet been set up.

There was further discontent in Killeshandra, this time over the Society of Saint Patrick and the Holy Child Sisters. Mother Xavier and Bishop Finegan, who had been largely instrumental in preventing Shanahan from taking the leadership of the priests' society, were now unhappy that Whitney had accepted the position. They still had painful memories of the way his association with the convent had ended five years earlier. They were even more disturbed to hear that a new order of sisters was coming to Calabar to take over work that in their view belonged to the Holy Rosary Sisters. It was another example of the territorial possessiveness that Pius XI was trying to weed out.

Xavier put much of the blame on Shanahan, whom she accused of weakness in giving in to Hinsley and Whitney. He did his best to explain to her that there would be no shortage of work to be done in Nigeria even after the new sisters had come. He also wrote a long letter in the same vein to Mother Brigid in Onitsha, who had been appointed superior there after Dominic left. After mentioning Xavier's unhappiness with Whitney's appointment, he went on:

> In addition to this cause of uneasiness came the news that the Sisters of the Holy Child Jesus were to go to Nigeria. Even though the Propaganda had asked me to accept them in the Vicariate yet it was thought I would have mustered courage enough to refuse in view of the fact that we had our own Sisters. But no, I weakly assented to every move.
>
> I have been praying and asking for prayers for many years past to obtain from God missionaries for Nigeria. Now God, in answer to prayer, is sending them — we need them by the thousand. Surely I am not going to refuse those whom God sends me, even though people don't agree with me.
>
> The general atmosphere over here — and maybe in Nigeria too — was slightly tinged with sadness on account of the appearance of those new and disturbing elements in S. Nigeria. Well, may God's Holy Will be done in these as in all other events on earth.
>
> The German Fathers are asked to take over the Northern Territories; the new Society will work in the Calabar and Ogoja Provinces, and the CSSp men and Holy Rosary Sisters will have as their share of the work the 4,000,000 that people the Onitsha and Owerri Provinces. I wonder how any missionary could feel any other sentiment but that of intense happiness at seeing the advent of so many new missionaries among our poor Nigerians!
>
> So long as those poor people can get to God and to heaven, it matters very little the name, the nationality, etc., of the missionary that opens the gate of heaven to them. Their salvation is what matters.[11]

He had to wait until the end of September before the new group of missionaries was ready to travel with him to Nigeria. It was well worth the wait. There were six priests and a brother from the Irish Holy Ghost Province, four of the priests coming to Nigeria for the first time. There were also three Holy Child Sisters and seven secular priests. Whitney had been working hard and successfully since his appointment. He had secured a house in Kiltegan, Co. Wicklow, as headquarters for the new society and he had persuaded seven priests from various Irish dioceses to come to Nigeria. These included five of the 1930 ordination class in Maynooth; a sixth member of the class also volunteered but was refused permission to go by his bishop, who happened to be Finegan of Kilmore. Among the newly ordained men were two future bishops, James Moynagh, first Bishop of Calabar, and Thomas McGettrick, first Bishop of Ogoja. Shanahan proudly led them on board the *RMS Appam* in Liverpool on 1 October 1930. Four days later three priests and three brothers from the German Holy Ghost province sailed from Rotterdam, also bound for Southern Nigeria.[12]

Shanahan enjoyed every moment of the voyage. McGettrick describes him as 'elated beyond words' because of the unprecedented number of new missionaries who accompanied him. Every morning from 6.00 a.m. to 7.00 a.m. one of the lounges was put at their disposal, temporary altars were set up, and each of the priests celebrated Mass. 'Never before', Shanahan told Finegan, 'was there such a number of Masses together on board any ship sailing to West Africa. Already the tropical heat is being felt. Quinine has to be taken each day, rather to get accustomed to it than to ward off fever.' The younger men, exposed for the first time to the African sun, made good use of the small shipboard swimming pool. The older men told stories about their experiences in Nigeria which were more remarkable for their colour than for their accuracy. Father Thady O'Connor claimed to have seen a whale spouting water hundreds of feet into the air, but when the others rushed to see the marvel it had disappeared. 'The whole ship', Shanahan wrote contentedly, 'has to admire this vigorous, healthy, happy group of Irish missionaries.'

In the harbour at Freetown they leaned over the side of the ship and watched men and boys diving from little canoes to catch the coins thrown by the passengers. Then they went ashore to visit Bishop O'Gorman and the other missionaries. Shanahan took the opportunity to send a letter to the Irish Provincial, Father Harnett, thanking him for sending four new priests to Southern Nigeria.

> I thank God that I have lived to see our Irish Province become definitely missionary. See how God in return is blessing it. For never did it seem so prosperous, and it is only beginning. For in years to come it will have a greater number of missioners each year than any other Province in the Congregation.[13]

They arrived in Calabar on 18 October 1930 and received an enthusiastic welcome from the local Christians, delighted to see so many priests and sisters coming among them. Shanahan proceeded to appoint the new priests to various missions in the Calabar and Ogoja areas. Though the division of the vicariate had been decided on, it would not come into effect until the newcomers had gained some familiarity with African conditions. In the meantime, the whole vicariate remained under Shanahan's direction and he arranged that some of the Holy Ghost priests would stay on for a time in Calabar and Ogoja to give the secular priests the benefit of their experience.

The Holy Child sisters were brought to the convent to meet Sister Magdalen. They found her busily engaged in the planning and building of a new convent and school. The site had been cleared and the walls of the cottages where the boarders were to live were already rising above the ground. Mother Amadeus and another nun from the Holy Child mother-house were also there, having arrived a month earlier to supervise the transition. They decided that one of the three new sisters would stay in Calabar with Magdalen while the other two would go to the school in Anua, which was also under Magdalen's care. Mother Amadeus took it for granted that Magdalen still intended to leave the Sisters of Charity and join the Holy Child Order as she had promised.[14]

As soon as he could, Shanahan went on to Onitsha where he was to fulfil a lifelong ambition by ordaining the first African priest in Southern Nigeria, John Cross Anyogu. He believed that the Church could never be really rooted in the country until it had its own Nigerian clergy and religious, but he hesitated to admit any student to the priesthood until he was convinced that he would make a good priest. He had now known John Anyogu for eighteen years and during all that time John had never wavered in his determination.

The story began on 1 January 1912, when John was fourteen years of age. He shyly handed his father a letter which read, 'My dear Father, As my new year resolution, I want to serve God all my life. I want to be a priest. John.' His father, a devout Catholic, hurried to the mission in Onitsha and asked Shanahan if a black man could be a priest. 'Why not?' said Shanahan. 'Has a black man not got a soul?' He interviewed young John and the following year sent him and his brother Luke to England, where they did their secondary studies in Castlehead. When they returned to Onitsha in 1919, Luke decided he wanted to become a teacher. John still wanted to be a priest.

He stayed at the mission house in Onitsha, helping the priests in their work and continuing his studies. In 1922 Shanahan put him to the test by asking him to go and teach in Ogoja, a two-hundred-mile trek through hostile country, the haunt of cannibals and wild beasts. He survived the journey and taught there until he was recalled to enrol in the newly founded seminary at Igbariam. As senior seminarian, he held the little group of students together by his leadership and dedication and at the same time continued to help the mission in Onitsha by giving lessons in Ibo to newly arrived missionaries. Shanahan could no longer have any doubt of his commitment.[15]

The ceremony took place in Onitsha Waterside on 8 December 1930, the Feast of the Immaculate Conception. Though plans had at last been drawn up for the new cathedral, the cathedral for which the Pope had given a donation and for which Lejeune had started making bricks nearly thirty years ago, the actual building had not yet begun. In the meantime, they continued to use the dual-purpose building erected in 1914, with the movable partitions which enabled it to serve as a school on weekdays and a church on Sundays and holidays.

The ceremony attracted an overflow congregation, many of them travelling long distances to see the ordination of the first local priest. Among them were John Anyogu's proud and happy parents, though they can scarcely have been any prouder or happier than the ordaining bishop. Shanahan had officiated at many ordinations in the past ten years but this one was unique. The most touching moment came when he imposed his hands on the head of the ordinand, followed by the other clergy present, Bishop Heerey and Bishop Broderick and fifty priests from all over Nigeria, a long line of white-robed figures welcoming the newest addition to their ranks. Afterwards they all posed for a large group photograph in the grounds of the mission. The new priest is conspicuous not only because of the colour of his skin but because he is the only one not wearing a sun-helmet.[16]

Soon afterwards, Shanahan gave him his first appointment. 'Now, Father John,' he said brusquely, 'I am appointing you to Adazi. Pack up your things and be ready to start for there as soon as possible.' John was disappointed and angry, because he felt that his status as the first African priest entitled him to a more prestigious appointment. But Shanahan spoke in a tone of voice that brooked no argument. He packed his things and went. Years later Shanahan told him that after giving him his appointment he went to his room and wept, so upset was he at the young man's obvious distress. But he felt it was essential for his priestly formation that he start with one of the humbler missions, and John agreed that he had acted wisely.[17]

In a sense Father John's ordination was Shanahan's *Nunc dimittis,* the sign that his life-work had been completed. John was to be the first of many Ibo priests, and later still the first of many Ibo bishops. Shanahan could not know this but he did know that in choosing John he had chosen well. In the new year, he intended to submit his resignation once again. This time he knew it would be accepted.

15

Magnificat

As his years in Nigeria came to a close, Bishop Shanahan drew much support from the Sisters in Onitsha, especially from his secretary, Sister Philomena Fox. Almost every day she crossed the compound from the convent to the priests' house to help him deal with his voluminous correspondence. For two years she was in a unique position to observe him and she allowed little to escape her notice. The more she saw of him, the more her respect for him increased.

She saw him under severe pressure of work and time, often interrupted, sometimes attacked. She saw some heated debates, when the Shanahan fire, if not the Shanahan temper, could still make its appearance. But when the debate was over, he never showed the slightest trace of animosity. 'Now we'll have a drink', he would say, and would soothe any ruffled feelings over a glass of beer or whiskey. He knew that others had pressures to bear that were no less heavy than his own.

> He was always on schedule and it irked him when he was held up by tardy returns from various mission stations. Gentle reminders would go out. Then a second notice, rather more peremptory, might follow. 'That should do it!' Not always. 'Well, then, send those fellows a telegram and tell them in no uncertain words that those returns are to be in here no later than tomorrow — signed Bishop.'
>
> Tomorrow came. On the dot of opening the office for the day's work came the question, 'Well, did you send those telegrams?' 'No, My Lord, I thought you wouldn't ...'. He threw back his head and laughed, relieved. 'How well you know me! Of course, I'll go out and get them. Those poor fellows have no time to be twiddling with figures. I know them, they do their best and would be hurt by such a telegram.'

He was equally sensitive to the pressures on his secretary and quick to respond. One afternoon she was filling out the five-yearly report for Rome at his dictation when he unexpectedly put down his magnifying glass and said, 'That's enough.' She said, 'There's still an hour to go. I can keep on.' He said, 'We'll take a walk.' They went out and walked up and down under the mango trees, chatting about one thing and another. Then he suddenly folded his arms and tilted his head back.

'Now,' he said, 'out with it!'

'Out with what?'

'Whatever is up to here', he said, indicating his neck.

'Everything is fine, I'm happy, I like the work, I have enough to eat, I'm in good health. There's nothing bothering me, nothing at all.' She paused. 'Unless it is this grace thing.'

'What about grace?'

'Well, I just can't live a supernatural life. I have no idea where nature ends and grace begins.' The dam was open and her words poured out in torrents. She spoke about her training in Killeshandra and the constant struggle against nature. She was forever being told not to be so human, not to be so demonstrative, not to show so much concern for others. She must always have complete control. If she was impulsive or laughed spontaneously, it was human. If she said she didn't like something or felt tired, it was human. Anything natural or human was bad.

He let her talk herself out. Then he spoke gently, almost as if he were speaking to himself. 'I had the same problem when I was a seminarian. I solved it. You can solve it the same way. You won't find the answer in spiritual books. You'll find it in the Gospels if you study them carefully. There's no such thing as the supernatural life. There's only human life lived as perfectly as possible. That's the life of God in you. You can call that the supernatural life if you want to.'

It was the way he lived his own life, intensely human yet filled with God. One day in the office she heard him gasp and turned to see him looking over her shoulder at the door, his face deathly white, his hands gripping the arms of his chair. In the doorway stood a man whom he had educated in the mission school and who had secured an important government position as a result. He had repaid him by spreading the vilest slanders about him, even writing to the Superior General asking for his dismissal. The man was involved in large-scale dishonesty and corruption and Shanahan had come to know of it. This seems to be the reason why he wanted Shanahan removed from Nigeria.

Once the initial shock was over, Shanahan received him with his usual courtesy and made no mention of past wrongs. It transpired that the man was looking for a favour. His dishonesty had been discovered and he needed the large sum of £400 immediately. Without it, he faced imprisonment and ruin. Shanahan asked Sister Philomena to give the man a cheque for the full amount, which she did with great reluctance, knowing the state of the mission's bank account and the unlikelihood of the money ever being returned. 'It is a necessary charity', he told her. 'God has never yet let me down.'

It was near the end of the month, when the bank statement would arrive on the desk of the financial administrator, Bishop Heerey. Shanahan decided it would be a good idea to set off on his motor-bike and spend a few days visiting some bush stations. 'I'm going off to parts unknown', he told her before vanishing in a cloud of dust. He was safely out of reach when Heerey discovered the shortfall.

A few days later he appeared in the office doorway as she was opening the day's mail.

'What's the weather like round here?' he asked.

'Very stormy.'

'I'll see if I can bring out the sun', he said and headed for Heerey's room.

She continued with the mail and opened a letter from Rome to find that it contained a cheque for £2,000 from the Holy Childhood Society. The two bishops came back into the office, looking reconciled but worried. She handed Shanahan the cheque. When he took it to the light to try to read it, she told him what it was. For a moment he raised his head and looked into the distance in silent prayer. 'I knew he would', he said. 'How good God is!'

His prayerfulness was something that struck her constantly. To watch him walking in the mango avenue reading his breviary was a sermon in itself. One day a weary-looking man came looking for him and asked her, 'When will the Bishop stop?' She brought him to Shanahan who put his breviary under his arm and gave him all the time he needed. Then he opened his breviary and continued his prayers. Later she asked him if he had to start the prayers from the beginning again after the interruption, as the sisters were bound to do. 'I never stopped', he said. Talking to the man was prayer.

He liked to pray late at night in the church or in the little chapel in the priests' house, often until long past midnight. One morning

Father (later Bishop) Hagan, who was stationed in Onitsha at the time, told Sister Philomena how the previous evening all the priests had said night prayer together and then gone to bed, leaving Shanahan still in the chapel. About 2.00 a.m. Hagan woke and saw a light reflected in the corridor. He got up and went to the chapel to switch it off. Shanahan was still there. 'I was going to say something to him', he told her. 'Then I saw his face. You should have seen it. It was beautiful. It had a glowing expression. I couldn't hear anything but he seemed to be talking to someone. I stayed there for about two hours and then I couldn't stay awake any longer and went back to bed. Next morning I was drooping but he was as fresh as a daisy.'

He found the long treks through the bush an ideal time for prayer. He would reflect on the Gospel stories and on the letters of Saint Paul, he would praise God for the beauty of his creation, he would pray for the people he met and greeted on the way. 'Bless everything,' he told the sisters, 'even the path you walk on. Let Christ show forth in all your actions. Be perfectly human. Perfect the human and the natural. Be fully a woman. Do not be afraid of your little heart. It is made to be used. If it becomes too exuberant, it can be cut back, pruned, and remain a healthy organ, very useful. You cannot say you love God and remain aloof from your neighbour.'

He was determined from the outset that the sisters should be firmly in control of their own affairs and not subject to the local priests. This was a break with the normal practice, which gave the priest in charge of the mission almost complete authority over the convent, especially in financial matters. It was a further cause of tension between Shanahan and some of the priests of the Vicariate, who expected the sisters to be at their service even for such tasks as cooking their meals and mending their clothes. He himself felt it was essential not only for the sisters but for the women in Nigeria that they should be seen in a position of equality with men. 'I don't know why some men can't feel they are men unless they have their foot on the neck of a woman', he told Philomena. 'The opposite is the case. A man is only truly a man when he respects a woman.'[1]

* * *

The second Holy Rosary Convent in Africa was blessed and opened at Emekuku on 11 February 1931. It was staffed by some of the sisters from Onitsha, which left both convents short of personnel, but help was on the way. Four new sisters, Rose, Felim, Francis and Columba, left for Africa on 17 March. They were accompanied on their journey by Mother Xavier in person. For some time back Shanahan had been urging her to come to Nigeria and see for herself the conditions in which the sisters had to work and live. He hoped that the experience would help to soften her views on the rule and how it should be observed.

Her visit was only partially successful. The realisation that Africa was not Ireland was borne in on her long before she reached Nigeria. On a very hot day during the voyage she asked one of the young sisters to get her a glass of water. The sister rather mischievously reminded her that Father Leen disapproved of sisters taking water between meals. Xavier made a gesture of her hand which annihilated Father Leen and drank the water.[2]

On her arrival in Nigeria, she was warmly welcomed by Shanahan and the sisters and she won their admiration by her determination to see everything and go everywhere. It was a taxing experience for a middle-aged woman who had never been outside Ireland before and who insisted on wearing her woollen Dominican habit and starched headdress everywhere she went. Sister Philomena accompanied her on some of her trips and watched her reactions.

> Hygiene, catechetical and other classes had already been organised by the sisters in outlying bush stations. They took Mother Xavier on some of these road trips to visit the stations. This was a unique experience for her which she seemed to enjoy very much and gradually began to accept the fact that the sisters' cloister was in everybody's compound. She forgot to notice that the sisters kept their heads up and their eyes on the world around them, that they swung their arms now and then, and had a word for everyone they met on the road. These changes were in![3]

Other changes were out. She felt that there had been a general relaxation of discipline and observance among the sisters and that it was her duty to call them back to their first fervour. She drew up a long list of regulations which they were to carry out. Though Shanahan was naturally disappointed, he made no protest. He could never forget the sacrifices that she had made for the infant sisterhood or cease to be grateful to her.

The Feast of Saint Dominic falls on 4 August. On that day Mother Xavier invited Shanahan and the other priests to come to tea in the convent to celebrate her founder's feastday. He sent to her across the compound a note of acceptance which turned into a moving and generous tribute to her and to the Dominicans.

> Your heart, your great big heart and great soul and great mind are all intimately united with Nigeria and all its missionaries; not alone the sisters but the priests, the catechists, the Christians, catechumens and our poor poor pagans. Your heart goes out to them all. You live in Nigeria in your heart and soul and prayers and affections and sorrows and sacrifices. You have all the happiness and peace with all the sorrows of the missioner. Happiness at seeing what God has done with the co-operation of His poor instruments, sorrow at seeing so many souls dead to the life of grace, to the love of Jesus Christ.
>
> I am so glad you are here with us for this very special feast of Saint Dominic. When many years have fled into eternity, this day shall be remembered by Nigeria, its missionary sisters and priests.[4]

She returned to Ireland and Killeshandra, bringing with her two Ibo girls who were to give the sisters instruction in the Ibo language and culture and to receive further education themselves. She brought with her also Shanahan's letter along with many memories of his achievements as a missionary and of his personal kindness to herself. But basically she had not changed her mind. She still felt in conscience that his influence on the order was not in the best interests of the sisters or of their work.

One of the Ibo girls who came to Killeshandra was Maria Anyogu, a sister of Father John Anyogu and a former pupil of Sister Magdalen. While she was there she felt called to the religious life. In the course of time she was to become the first sister and later the first Mother General of the Sisters of the Immaculate Heart of Mary, which has since spread throughout Nigeria and to other countries in East and West Africa.[5]

In Calabar and Anua the three Holy Child Sisters were settling in under Sister Magdalen's direction. She was happy that the work she had started was being taken up by the Holy Child Order and was no longer dependent on herself alone. She was now in a position to go ahead with her plans for a new African sisterhood, which would be linked to and supported by the Holy Child Order. They were to be called the Handmaids of the Holy Child Jesus. The first four members were given a retreat by Sister Magdalen in Anua in January 1931, which culminated in a Mass celebrated by Father John Anyogu. Like the Immaculate Heart Sisters, the Handmaids grew and flourished, founding convents, schools and other institutions both inside and outside Nigeria.

Neither Shanahan nor Magdalen were to have any part in the growth of the sisterhoods they had planned and worked for. Once again, Magdalen found it difficult to live and work with other sisters. Despite her previous commitment, she declined to join the Holy Child Congregation. Mother Amadeus had to admit grudgingly that Shanahan's warnings had been justified. She wrote: 'I remember old Bishop Shanahan saying to me, ''Make it quite clear that you are taking over Sister Magdalen, not Sister Magdalen you.'' He was a wise old man in many ways.'

Magdalen left Calabar and eventually returned to her native England, where she lived as a laywoman in obscurity and some poverty for twenty years. In 1955 she was received back into the Irish Sisters of Charity and was happy to return to Africa to their convent in Chikuni in Zambia. She died there in 1965, just three weeks short of her eighty-fifth birthday.[6]

* * *

Shanahan sent his resignation to Rome in March 1931. It was accepted two months later. Though he had a certain natural regret at the ending of his twenty-five-year stewardship, there was also relief at laying down the burden and happiness at what had been achieved. Some statistics printed in the Holy Ghost missionary magazine indicated the remarkable growth of the Church in the Vicariate of Southern Nigeria during his period at the helm. The number affiliated to the Church either as baptised Catholics or as catechumens preparing for baptism had increased almost a hundredfold.[7]

Year	1906	1912	1918	1924	1930
Catholics	1778	5572	13042	40768	94545
Catechumens	850	5585	37929	108233	116277
Total	2628	11157	50971	149001	210822

Everywhere he looked, there were signs of hope for the future. The Irish Holy Ghost province was at last sending men in the numbers he had hoped for. The Society of Saint Patrick was firmly established and attracting an encouraging number of vocations in Ireland. The German missionaries were breaking new ground in the north-east and the Holy Child Sisters were assuring the continuation of the work in Calabar. The Holy Rosary Congregation in Nigeria had opened its second convent, while in Killeshandra one new wing after another was being added to the old house in an effort to accommodate all the postulants. The vicariate had its first Nigerian priest and would soon have its first Nigerian sisters. In a spirit of deep thankfulness, he took out his old novitiate notebook towards the end of the year and made his last long entry.

> Since I wrote the few lines on the 25 November 1927 important events, important for me, have taken place.
>
> In March 1930 I tendered to Our Holy Father my resignation from the office of Vicar Apostolic. In May my request was granted. The letter announcing it arrived at Onitsha on 3 July. By the fact, I ceased to be Vicar Apostolic of Southern Nigeria, my co-adjutor Rt. Rev. Dr Heerey taking over de jure charge of his Vicariate.
>
> This acceptance of my resignation is another of Our Lord's exceptional favours granted to me. He is quietly detaching me from this world.
>
> I am happy as I have not been for years. No longer any responsibility beyond caring for my own soul, caring for that great day, the day of my death, when God will call me away, in His mercy, from this earth.
>
> I will not leave Nigeria until after Easter 1932. Dr Heerey is home in Ireland. He will be ready to return to Nigeria by the end of '32. I will do what I can to keep things going in such a way that the new Bishop's absence will not be felt. V. Rev. Fr Ch. O'Connor is Vicar Delegate and Principal Superior in charge during the Bishop's absence.

Thus ends my association with Nigeria as a missionary.

Once again I wish to say how full my heart is with gratitude to Our Lord and for all those who in His name and authority, with all charity and mercy, have co-operated with Him.

In bringing me into the world and into the Catholic Church:
my dear Catholic parents and the Parish Priest;
in teaching me in school:
the School Teacher;
in making my home life happy:
my brothers and sisters;
in making it possible for me to be a religious:
poor old Uncle Adelm;
in receiving me, a poor boy, for nothing into a secondary school:
Father Limbour CSSp at Beauvais;
in receiving me into the Congregation:
Father Bertsch at Cellule;
in allowing me to make my profession in the Congregation:
Rockwell 1898;
in ordaining me a priest:
Blackrock 1900;
in sending me to Africa:
1902-1932;
in appointing me Ordinary of Nigeria — Prefect Apostolic:
1905-1931;
Bishop and Vicar Apostolic:
1920-1931;
in giving me time to prepare for a good, holy, happy death:
July 1931;

For these and other countless graces, from the bottom of my heart I thank God, and all those who have been and are still His visible representatives, missionaries, and friends, for my personal welfare and sanctification.

May God grant me pardon for all the ingratitude I have shown to Him and to all his friends during these long years.

And Mary, Mother of God, Mother of Jesus Christ, Mother of Mercy, Mother of Divine Grace, Mother of Sorrows, my Mother, all my heart goes out to you with all my love —

to you, my beloved Mother, for having been such a good Mother to me.

And then you, St Joseph, my great Patron Saint — what do I not owe you?

And you, my beloved Angel Guardian, how I thank you!

I crave for mercy and pardon, for Your love and grace, my Lord Jesus, and for final perseverance at the end of my life in the Congregation of the Holy Ghost and Immaculate Heart of Mary.

✠ Jos. Shanahan C.S.Sp.
Onitsha
25 November 1931

Bishop Heerey had been forced by ill-health to go back to Ireland in July and was expected to be there for about a year. In the meantime, his administrative duties were looked after by Father O'Connor and his spiritual duties by Shanahan. On the same day that he wrote his Magnificat, he sent a letter of Christmas good wishes to Mother Xavier, now back in Killeshandra. 'The sisters are well both in Onitsha and Emekuku. So are the Fathers. The dry season is on in full and the heat is intense. My health is sufficiently good to permit me to keep on visiting some parishes and administering the sacrament of Confirmation.'

Despite the approaching departure, it was in many ways a happy time. Relieved of the burden of office work, he could do what he enjoyed most: go among the people and minister to them in their own towns and villages. He could meet his priests on a level of equality now that he no longer had any authority over them. The younger priests, who looked on him with awe as a living legend, responded eagerly to his kindness. The older priests, his companions of many years, his adversaries in more than one battle of wills, found any bitterness drained away in those last months. In February 1932 he was present at a profession ceremony in Emekuku and the letter he wrote describing it is filled with affection not only for the young sisters but for the veteran priests as well.

The profession of Sisters M. Columba and Felim was like that of Sister M. Catherine six months ago — a source of untold joy not alone for them and the sisters but for all of

> us their fellow missioners. There were twenty of them there, gathered in from the four corners of Nigeria. Father Treich was there from the wilds of Uturu. He had two new safety pins and one big new button linking up the refractory east and west boundaries of that aged venerable multi-coloured coat of his. He had the newest and most up-to-date explanation of the Apocalypse for us. The fall of the powers indicated at last the fall of the Bête. Then we had Father Walsh of Umuahia and Father Bindel on his old motor bike from Ihiala, etc. etc.
>
> The ceremony was for each and all of us a recalling as well as a renewal of that happy day long ago when we too made vows as religious and priests. It was a whole retreat, a retreat that went over all the years of our missionary life, done in one morning.

The visiting priests usually stayed the night in the priests' house, which gave a chance for a pleasant social evening to round off the day. It may have been on this occasion that a characteristic incident occurred in Emekuku involving Shanahan and eight of the younger priests. It was recalled many years later by Bishop Hagan.

> Late in the evening as they were sitting around, the Bishop said how happy he was that they had had such a good day together and such an enjoyable evening. He said how good God was to them, considering they were here in the middle of Africa with very little in the line of human comforts, and yet they were so happy, perhaps happier than anyone else in the world. Then the Bishop said that he wished them 'A very good-night.' The Fathers said, 'Good-night, My Lord', and the Bishop retired to his room.
>
> The Fathers were still in high spirits and so continued to talk in whispers at first but soon it was difficult to hear what one was saying. The Bishop returned, saying how he had been thinking of what a good day they had had, and what an enjoyable evening, and now he wanted to wish them again 'A very good-night.' They said, 'Good-night, My Lord', and the Bishop retired again to his room. The Fathers then went to their own rooms.
>
> There were four Fathers sleeping on camp beds in each

> room. Being still in high spirits, they just sat on the sides of the beds and continued to talk. Again the Bishop returned. He said that really it had been a wonderful day and he was delighted that the Fathers had enjoyed themselves and now he would be delighted if they would all go to bed.
>
> That was Bishop Shanahan, never reproachful, never unkind. He knew the Fathers did not mean to upset him, they loved him so much they would never say or do anything that would hurt him.[8]

The departure date was set for 13 April 1932. Even had he not resigned, he needed a spell in Ireland for reasons of health. He was tired after his visitation of the vicariate, during which he had confirmed five thousand adults and children. He was in need of medical attention for his arthritis and his liver condition. On 19 March, the Feast of Saint Joseph, he was back in Onitsha to celebrate his patron saint. He officiated at his last Confirmation in Nigeria on that day, after which he attended a concert in his honour organised by the sisters. It was just one of many functions and presentations that were to fill his last few weeks in Nigeria.

The formal farewell took place in Onitsha on Easter Tuesday. It came close to being ruined by a motor accident the previous day involving Sisters Rose and Catherine. Rather against Mother Xavier's wishes, Shanahan had encouraged the sisters to learn how to drive. On the road from Onitsha to Emekuku, Sister Rose took the wheel from the driver on what appeared to be a safe stretch of road, failed to negotiate a bend and crashed into a tree. Fortunately nobody was hurt, though the car was wrecked. Shanahan came in his own car to collect them, assured them it was not their fault and took them for a picnic in the Awgu Hills on the way back to Onitsha to restore their morale. He said it would be better to say nothing to Mother Xavier in case she banned the sisters from driving altogether and they were happy to follow his advice. It was not the last they were to hear of the incident.[9]

As a parting gift from the priests, Shanahan was presented with the car he normally used in Nigeria, nicknamed the *Isis*. It was brought to the ship he was sailing on, the *Appam*, and stowed on board along with the rest of his luggage. The final leave-taking was hard, but he consoled himself with the hope that he might be able to come back in a year or two, refreshed and restored, and resume work in Nigeria, this time as a simple missionary.

The ship docked at Plymouth on 1 May. A letter sent from there to Mother Xavier announcing his arrival reveals something of his feelings at that moment.

> And Nigeria! Ah, it nearly broke my heart to leave it. The sisters were wonderfully good and generous. They did all they could to make the final parting easy. The Fathers did likewise, and so did the thousands upon thousands of Catholics and catechumens — they all made me promise I would return in a couple of years — they would not consider my departure in any other light except as a temporary separation. They wired to me in Lagos to let them know — the sisters did — what month in '33 I was returning! So I am at long last separated physically at any rate from Nigeria.

16

Retirement

On his arrival in Ireland, Shanahan found himself a room in Clareville, the old house in the grounds of Blackrock College where there was accommodation for visiting priests and where he usually stayed on his visits to Ireland. He who once had an area twice the size of Ireland as his territory was now confined to a single bed-sitting-room. It was to be his home for the next six years.

It had all seemed much simpler when he was leaving Nigeria. His home in Ireland would be the gate-lodge of the convent in Killeshandra. It was the place he had founded, the place where above all others he was loved and welcomed. He had no desire to interfere in the running of the convent but would be quite content to live there quietly, saying Mass each day in the convent chapel, giving the occasional talk to the sisters, making himself available for advice and spiritual direction. With the help of the *Isis* he could travel to Dublin for medical treatment and visit his friends in various parts of Ireland. As he regained his strength he could perhaps take over the duties of chaplain to Killeshandra, saying the community Mass each day and providing Benediction and other religious services for the sisters.

He might well end his days there, usefully employed up to the last. Or he might return to Nigeria if his health improved sufficiently. There too he knew he was greatly loved and missed. Again he had no desire to interfere in what was no longer his concern. He would go to some small remote mission where he could live among his beloved Ibos and minister to them as long as God gave him strength. But all that could be decided later. First of all he would go to Killeshandra.

It is probable that he spoke of his plans to Mother Xavier before she left Onitsha. Given his sensitive nature, it is unlikely that he made a direct request. It would be more in character for him to mention the matter in a tentative and general way to avoid forcing her into giving an immediate answer. He would give her the opportunity to think it over and she could then invite him in her own good time. The invitation never came.

Instead, Xavier resolved on a pre-emptive strike. When she returned to Killeshandra, she assembled the professed sisters in the chapter room and spoke to them about Shanahan. Now that he was retired, she said, he was no longer in a position of authority over them. In Nigeria the sisters were henceforth subject to Bishop Heerey, in Killeshandra to Bishop Finegan. Nor should they refer to Shanahan as their founder. As the order had been founded in the diocese of Kilmore, their founder according to canon law was Bishop Finegan. From now on their relations with Shanahan must change. They could no longer see him or write to him freely. Any letters to him must be handed up to be read before they were sent. Any meetings with him must take place in the parlour with all due formality. No sister was to presume to invite him to come to the convent or stay in the gate-lodge. That was a matter for the Superior alone. It was for the good both of the sisters and of Bishop Shanahan himself that these regulations be observed in future.

To say that the sisters were taken aback would be an understatement. They were at a loss to imagine how contact with Bishop Shanahan could be a danger either to him or to them. Nor could they see why by ceasing to be Vicar Apostolic of Southern Nigeria he thereby also ceased to be the founder of the Holy Rosary Congregation. It was all very strange and mysterious. Yet they respected Mother Xavier for her position and experience. If they could not understand the reasons for the change in attitude to Shanahan, it must be because of their own immaturity and lack of spirituality.[1]

Shanahan visited Killeshandra as soon as possible after his arrival in Ireland. It was a strange and unnerving experience. The whole atmosphere of the convent seemed to have changed. He was received by Xavier in a correct and formal manner and no mention was made of his wish to stay at Killeshandra. The younger sisters, for some reason he could not guess, were confused and embarrassed in his presence. All the old spontaneity, all the old outpouring of joy and welcome had gone. He returned hurt and bewildered to his lonely room in Dublin.

A few days later he wrote to Xavier. Without a trace of irony, he thanked her for the warm welcome she and the sisters had given him in Killeshandra. Far from finding any fault with her, he put all the blame for the awkwardness on himself.

> I know that I was not my old self on that occasion, much as I would have liked to be, as if no change had taken place

> and the circumstances of my missionary life had remained unaltered. I have got to recognise that a complete change has taken place and that the past is gone and for ever.
>
> I know that, as a result of those changes, I am somewhat odd; aye, and maybe unreasonable too. Please God this is only a passing phase that will leave undisturbed and undiminished the sincerity of my gratitude for you, for Mother Aquinas and for all those in Cabra and elsewhere who have contributed so magnanimously towards the evangelisation of Nigeria, in bringing into existence the Missionary Congregation of the Sisters of the Holy Rosary.[2]

A week later he had to write her a second and even more apologetic letter. She had heard about the motor accident on the road to Emekuku and was upset both by the accident itself and by the fact that she had not been informed. Once again, he put all the blame on himself, admitting that it was he who had told the sisters not to write to her about it. He described the accident in detail and urged her not to forbid them to drive, as it was the kind of thing that happened to all learners. 'You will pardon me for giving my opinion — I do so as a friend and in the best interests of all concerned — for no other reason and in no other capacity have I written.' It is a sign of his growing feeling of exclusion that he could only describe himself as a friend.

A welcome distraction for him was the International Eucharistic Congress, which took place in Dublin towards the end of June. It was an occasion of great pride and joy not only for the Irish Church but for the young Irish Free State, just ten years old. The Mass in the Phoenix Park and the Benediction on O'Connell Bridge were the highlights, but there were many other events attended by dignitaries and pilgrims from all over the world. One of these was a large garden party in Shanahan's own backyard, the grounds of Blackrock College, at which the guest of honour was the Pope's representative, Cardinal Lauri. Unlike Shanahan, the sisters in Killeshandra were unable to attend any of the ceremonies but the local garage owner rigged up a wireless set in the convent parlour through which they were able to hear the final Mass with John McCormack singing *Panis Angelicus* and Saint Patrick's bell rung at the consecration.[3]

Shanahan's health appears to have improved during the

summer but as winter approached his arthritis began to trouble him. He went to his regular medical adviser, Dr Jim Magennis, and described the visit in a letter to one of his best friends in Killeshandra, Sister Thérèse, the former Agnes Ryan of Calabar.

> He gave me a warm welcome, such as he gives to all Nigerians or Africans. In addition he stuck right into my knee a most merciless needle filled with some awful stuff. Meanwhile he was lost in raptures over the Eucharistic Congress. I couldn't trouble the pious man telling me all about the men's meeting in the Park, and at the same time forcing his needle deeper and deeper into my knee. My feelings were very mixed. Violent expletives were gradually moving upwards towards my lips. An explosion seemed imminent. When he paused to ask me if I remembered the words of the great Cardinal Legate, 'For heaven's sake,' said I, 'will you remember you have a ... 12-inch needle with a pint of vitriol planted right in the centre of my being!' After about five minutes I forgave him — even though he did laugh to his heart's content at the brave warrior missioner complaining of a pin-prick.[4]

The dots are Shanahan's and presumably indicate an expletive deleted. The letter ends with a rather sad postscript. 'If you have a few Mass intentions to dispose of will you send them to me, and oblige very much — J.S.' The financial arrangements for a retired missionary bishop evidently left something to be desired, especially for one with Shanahan's impulsive generosity. A young priest living in Blackrock at this time, Father James Finucane, met him one day walking up and down at the tram stop outside the college gate.

> He walked over to me and said, 'Father, I feel ashamed to have to ask you for money but could you give me the fare in and out to the City? I brought a pound note with me, but a poor man came up to me saying he had not eaten anything since morning, so I gave it to him.'
>
> That example of humility and charity did more for my spiritual life than all the conferences I got in the scholasticate. Just imagine the most important bishop in Africa begging

> deferentially from me, a young fellow who was literally nobody. And he was so grateful when I took out two half-crowns, all I had, and gave him one. His humility just stunned me.[5]

Bishop Heerey, now fully recovered, left for Nigeria at the beginning of October 1932. He was received with great jubilation by the Catholics of the vicariate, and given elaborate welcome ceremonies in every mission he visited. One address of welcome from a small village near Emekuku has ended up by some chance in the Holy Ghost archives in Dublin. It begins:

> Welcome, Our Lord, we are today more than merry to receive you in search of your folds here in bush. We are surprised to receive you so sudden in bush as you crossed many civilised places and come to an unknown land, where the Catholic Church laid her egg unhatched.
>
> However, we must not be very much astonished for you are working with grace, and the power of Almighty God.
>
> May Your Honour allow us to ask you to give us two Rev. Fathers here. There are many Christians here, of which Rev. Fathers in Emekuku are overwhelmed with tasks.

By the end of the address, they had reduced their request to one Father. It is unlikely that they got any when Heerey made the new appointments. Priests were not yet that plentiful.

On the Feast of Saint Joseph, 20 March 1933, he blessed the site of the new cathedral in Onitsha Waterside and turned the first sod. Work went ahead rapidly under the supervision of Brother Baldomir. Among the skilled craftsmen who worked on it were Shanahan's old friends from Dekina days, Peter, Paul and Tom. It was intended to have it completed in 1935 to celebrate the fiftieth anniversary of the coming of the first Catholic missionaries to Southern Nigeria.

Shanahan devoured every scrap of news that came from Nigeria. Now that his plans to live in Killeshandra had come to nothing, his thoughts returned constantly to the country to which he had given his life and his heart. In the spring of 1933 he wrote to Sister Columba in Onitsha:

> How are you? Won't you write and tell me. You know the pleasure a letter from you gives me — not because of all the

> news but because of yourself, a fellow missioner in Nigeria. It doesn't matter what way the moon does herself up here in Ireland, it is not the same moon you and I know over the palm trees in dear old Nigeria. The charms of Spring are here and, no doubt, they are bewitching, but not for us. I look at them only to fly off to that only charming beautiful country in the world: Nigeria. A letter from you, from any of the Sisters or Fathers contains for me the voice and heart of Nigeria. Strange to say, I thought Our Lord Himself nearer to me in Nigeria. The continued miracles of the visible effects of His Divine Grace in ourselves and in all those poor children of Christ in Nigeria made His Divine Presence more like what it was when He was a missioner in Judea.[6]

There was one letter above all others that he wanted to receive from Onitsha. It was a letter from Heerey inviting him to come back and live again in Nigeria. The weeks and months passed and the letter never came.

* * *

The Dominican sisters were due to end their commitment to Killeshandra in 1934, at which time the Holy Rosary Sisters would have to take over the direction and government of their Congregation. By the beginning of 1933 the sisterhood had twenty-one novices, thirteen postulants and forty professed sisters, a total of seventy-four members in the three convents of Killeshandra, Onitsha and Emekuku. Mother Xavier was recalled in the summer of 1933 to become superior of the convent in Dun Laoghaire and her place was taken for the final year by Mother Reginald, her sister. Before leaving, Xavier gave a series of talks to the sisters designed to prepare them for self-government and to set their course for the future. The talk she gave on relations with Bishop Shanahan was the one that made the most impression on her audience. Sister Margaret Mary gave the gist of the talk in the following terms:

> You all know that Dr Shanahan is the one who started this Congregation and that he is a very saintly Bishop. It is to leave him in his sanctity and to safeguard your spiritual good

and your future welfare that I say what I am going to say.

Dr Shanahan has a very affectionate nature and a very attractive personality. He draws people to him wherever he goes. This is a great gift which helps him in his work and draws people to his missionary cause. But in regard to you, his children, it could be dangerous. You all love him as your father and founder. You enjoy being with him in the parlour, listening to him. Now all this could become too human. You are all young and immature and have little experience of life. You could become attached to him in a merely human way. You would not know your place with other bishops and priests. When the time comes for him to be taken away from you, you would have become so dependent on him that it would have become a big break and you would not be able to stand on your own feet. God is a jealous God and does not want our poor hearts to be too attached to any creature, however holy.

Long ago, Dr Finegan and Mother Colmcille pointed out all this to me and advised me not to allow too much contact with Dr Shanahan, both for your own spiritual good and his. I have had the difficult task of doing that for the last ten years. While he was away in Nigeria it was not so hard. Now that he has come to live in Ireland and would like to be with you all the time, the facts must be made clear. Although it pains me to talk like this, I feel it my duty before I leave you to advise you to be careful in this matter. In a year from now you will have your own superiors. They will have the duty of watching over this and everything else that is for your good. It is for you to co-operate with them. Don't make things awkward for them by inviting Dr Shanahan to come and stay, or by making prolonged visits in the parlour. Respect him, pray for him, show him due reverence at all times, but be careful of all that is too human and too natural.[7]

Such were the norms which were to govern relations between the sisters and their founder. The more recent arrivals, who hardly knew him, were given the impression that he was someone who should be honoured for the past but avoided in the present. The older sisters, who had known him and worked with him in happier times, could not recognise in this portrait the man they revered and loved.

Bishop Finegan continued to visit the convent regularly and to supervise its spiritual welfare conscientiously, but to these older sisters he lacked Shanahan's unique charism.

> The spiritual literature and retreats of those days leaned heavily in favour of religious observance and discipline. Dr Finegan's exhortations on the occasions of visitation always bore on this theme. He would inquire minutely if the postulants and novices broke the rule of silence, omitted spiritual exercises, saw visitors without permission.
>
> Dr Shanahan's informal talks were a complete contrast. He spoke on the fatherhood of God, His divine providence, the Holy Spirit, the indwelling of the Holy Trinity, the living love of Christ, Mary our mother and model of all virtue.[8]

Sisters returning from Nigeria to Killeshandra were saddened and disturbed by the change of atmosphere. Sisters Philomena and Catherine came back early in 1934 and were met in Liverpool by Shanahan. He travelled back with them on the boat to Dublin and then drove them to Killeshandra. He was unable to stay as he had just received the sad news of the death of his niece, May Dawson, while undergoing a tonsillectomy. It did not take the two sisters long to feel the absence of Shanahan's influence in the convent. Philomena found the change disturbing.

> To the writer at least, it seemed that the monastic and cloistered life was more emphasised than it had been in earlier days. There were long and frequent choir practices into which the returned missionaries were quickly inducted so that their spiritual life might be repaired. Certainly it was generally assumed that the missionary had lost something spiritual by a sojourn away from the mother-house. To listen to some young sisters express fear of going to the missions where they might lose part of their spirituality was a traumatic experience for this returnee.[9]

Sister Catherine's impressions were similar. Some time after her arrival, she heard that Shanahan was to visit Killeshandra and she asked for permission to see him. Mother Xavier had left at this time but Mother Aquinas was still there as novice-mistress.

She invited Catherine to walk along the back avenue with her and told her she wanted to talk about Dr Shanahan. He was a good and holy missionary and excellent in dealing with men, but he had little experience of women and did not understand sisters. It would be better for all concerned if she did not see him.

> For a long time we walked up and down that avenue and I quite failed to see why this should be so. In the end I began to cry. Mother became impatient.
>
> 'What are you crying for?' she said.
>
> I answered, 'Because the Bishop is going to be so hurt.'
>
> Her answer was the key, if I had realised it, to the matter. 'That doesn't matter, Sister Mary', she said. 'It does not matter if you are hurt or if he is hurt or who is hurt. The important thing is, what does God want? And that we must do, no matter what it costs.'[10]

In 1934 the Dominican Sisters ended their connection with Killeshandra and the Holy Rosary Congregation became self-governing. It was Bishop Finegan's duty as canonical superior to appoint the first Mother General and Council; when their term of office ended, their successors would be elected by the sisters themselves. He consulted Mothers Xavier and Aquinas about his choice. He did not consult Shanahan.

The choice of Mother General was not easy. She should obviously be one of the older sisters, ideally someone with missionary experience in Nigeria. But these were the sisters who were most devoted to Shanahan and least likely to keep him at a distance from Killeshandra. Eventually their choice fell on Sister Augustine, the former Anastasia Cahill, the teacher who had heard Shanahan in Belfast and joined the sisterhood as a result. Now in her early thirties, she was older than most of the others, experienced, capable and committed. It was a disadvantage that she had never been to Nigeria, but at least it meant she had never fallen under Shanahan's influence. Her only contacts with him were on his visits to Killeshandra, and while she admired him greatly she was, by her own account, 'very reserved and shy with the Bishop and never got to know him personally.' Unlike some other sisters, she had been greatly impressed with Mother Xavier's talk. It struck her as a wise and benevolent set of guidelines on the relations that should obtain between the sisters and those bishops and priests they came in contact with.[11]

On 15 August 1934, the Feast of the Assumption of the Blessed Virgin, the new superiors for the Congregation were appointed. The sisters assembled in the oratory at midday and sang the *Veni Creator Spiritus*. Then Bishop Finegan, standing on the altar-steps in full pontificals, addressed them on the importance of the step that was about to be taken.

> The first superior to be appointed will be the Mother General. Her responsibility will be great. She will have to answer before God for your whole Congregation and for the decisions she makes. The subjects will only have to answer for their obedience. Therefore be diligent in carrying out all commands and directions of your Mother General. Try to make her burden lighter by whole-hearted co-operation, and the same for your local superiors. Have charity for one another. May God bless you and grant you his grace to serve him perfectly.[12]

He then announced the names of the new superiors. Sister Augustine Cahill was the new Mother General. The assistant Mother General was Sister Brigid (Bessie) Ryan, and the other three Councillors were Sisters Thérèse (Agnes) Ryan, Philomena Fox and Gerard Barrett. They were formally invested with their new offices and a *Te Deum* of rejoicing and thanksgiving was sung.

Shanahan was not present on this memorable day for the Congregation he had founded. It appears that he was not invited. He came towards the end of September to congratulate the new superiors and give a talk to the sisters. The pattern established by Mother Xavier did not change with the new Mother General. He was invited for a few of the more important occasions every year but his contact with the sisters was as restricted as before.

Nowhere in his letters does he make any complaint about this or speak of the deep hurt he was feeling. One of the few references comes in a letter to Sister Margaret Mary and shows no hint of resentment.

> My visits to Killeshandra are few; and when I do go there the Sisters are so very busy I see but little of them. But I see enough to know they are perfectly happy, intent on one object only: to work, in co-operation with the Holy Ghost,

> so that their whole being may be perfectly fitted to carry out the holy will of Christ their spouse in poor old Nigeria – or maybe in some other corner of the earth where obedience may send them.[13]

His own feelings were of no importance in the ultimate scheme of things. All that mattered was that the work should go on.

* * *

In Clareville time passed slowly. As his health recovered and his vigour returned, he felt more and more frustrated at the inactivity that was thrust upon him. He was only in his early sixties and still had so much to give. Yet there seemed to be so few opportunities to use his gifts and his talents in the situation where he now found himself.

He did not fit in easily with the academic atmosphere of the place. The campus included Blackrock College, a large secondary school for boarders and day-boys, and the building known as the Castle, a senior scholasticate for students of theology. The other priests treated him with kindness and respect but they had little in common with him. Their talk was understandably about their daily work in the College or the Castle, the examination results, the triumphs or disasters of the rugby field, the latest writing in theology or metaphysics.

The students in the scholasticate observed him from a distance, too shy to approach any closer. He still had that strange power to attract people's eyes. John Jordan would stand at the window to watch him walking in the grounds and he discovered that others were doing the same. 'Just looking at that man makes me feel better', one of his friends told him. 'He's the best argument I know in favour of missionary life.'

They noticed that he did not seem wholly at ease with the other priests as they strolled in the avenue after lunch. He spoke little and laughed less. Meeting some of the theology students one day, he said, 'I've just been at recreation with your professors. I didn't understand a word they were saying.' Then he threw back his head and laughed. 'Really, God is wonderful in his saints!' Sometimes Edward Leen, now becoming widely known as a writer and lecturer, was one of the group. The two men were still on friendly terms but the old intimacy had gone for ever. The shadow of Killeshandra lay between them.

Shanahan himself was often asked to give talks and conduct retreats. He rarely turned down an invitation to speak on the missions and this brought a welcome break in the monotony. He was a little slower to undertake retreat work, conscious of his lack of theology, especially in comparison with men like Leen. He would laboriously plot out the doctrinal content of his talks, unaware of the fact that he needed only to speak from his own overflowing experience. One of his Nigerian companions, Father Phil O'Connor, told John Jordan, 'Bishop Shanahan should never be allowed to let men like Ned Leen change him to theological spirituality. He has a reservoir of faith and spirituality himself that is better than the best. He should think and speak as he feels.'

Shanahan preached a retreat for the students in Kimmage in 1934. Jordan was among those who attended and he felt that when Shanahan spoke on theological themes he was repetitive and tedious.

> It was only when he left his roughly prepared notes and let himself go about the missions that he really came to life and left us feeling thrilled and uplifted. By the end of the week we all felt renewed in spirit. The House of Theology literally became dynamised spiritually to an extent never before experienced and a deeper missionary impetus gave us new life and new hope. For although we had excellent teachers, confessors and directors, not one of them had missionary experience. With Shanahan, fresh air literally blew through the scholasticate.[14]

Another student who was profoundly moved by the retreat was Reginald Walker. Thirty-five years later Father Walker took out the notes he had made during the retreat and tried in vain to recapture the atmosphere of the occasion for Sister Brigid Ryan. The theology lay dead on the pages without the living voice.

> I have tried to reconstruct roughly, in pencil, the lines of the first two conferences. But having got that far it occurred to me that it might be ineffectual to pursue the six days to the end. As you know — and I suppose it is true of every conférencier — Bishop Shanahan's retreat was Bishop

> Shanahan himself. It was his radiant personality, the almost visible glow of his personal holiness, which affected his listeners so profoundly. He spoke — I can hear his deep booming voice still — in what are known in Irish as *rothagaí*: rushes of deeply-felt sentiments. They could be quite commonplace truths, trivialities if you like, but like the simple things said by the Curé d'Ars (and indeed by Father Kearney) they went deep into the soul. We can write down the words; the impact is irrecoverable, the magic beyond recall.[15]

For the remainder of his time in Ireland, he continued to conduct retreats from time to time, mostly to priests and students for the priesthood, sometimes to sisters. He never gave a retreat in Killeshandra.

17

Christmas in Onitsha

Some time around the middle of 1934 word came at last from Nigeria. In July of that year Shanahan wrote a long letter to the sisters in Emekuku. After speaking nostalgically of his memories of Nigeria he added, 'How good God is to allow me to see Nigeria once again! For I am going out next year: 1935.' It is the first mention of his return to Africa and he gives no details. The news is repeated in other letters from then until the end of 1934, always with great joy and anticipation but still without going into any detail.

What kind of invitation had he received and from whom? It may be that he had a letter from Heerey, expressing a wish to have him in Nigeria for the Golden Jubilee celebrations. It may be that someone else wrote, saying that Heerey would like him to be there. The vagueness of Shanahan's own references to the visit suggest that the invitation was far from being as formal and definite as he would have liked.

By March 1935 his plans had changed. In a letter to a friend, Mrs Frame, he wrote, 'I am not going to Nigeria this year. The trip is postponed indefinitely.' None of the other surviving letters even mention the cancellation of the trip, which must have been a great disappointment. Again, we can only guess at the background. Possibly the initial suggestion from Onitsha had not been followed up and he came to the conclusion that he was not after all wanted. Always sensitive to intruding on others, he would not dream of going where he was not welcome.

He was kept busy during the summer of 1935. He gave a number of retreats during May and June, including an eight-day retreat for priests. He renewed contact with a friend from the past, Mary Martin, who had been invalided by a heart ailment for several years. Now recovered, she was beginning to realise her ambition of setting up an order of medical missionaries. She visited him in Clareville and received some very useful advice based on his own experience with the Holy Rosary Congregation.[1]

In July he led a pilgrimage to Lough Derg. It was organised by a young Holy Ghost priest, Father Fullen, to pray for the missions. To prepare himself for the ordeal, Shanahan spent the previous week walking barefoot along the pebbled path of his sister's home in Maynooth. The pilgrimage island was crowded and rain fell heavily for most of the three days. Fullen remembers how the stewards invited himself and the Bishop to come to the head of the queue to walk around the first of the penitential beds. He was about to accept when he heard Shanahan say, 'Thank you very much. No, I am just a poor pilgrim here like everyone else, doing penance for his sins.' They were drenched by the end of the exercises but it did them no harm.[2]

He spent the month of August in Chevilly, making a retreat or recollection. He described it in a letter as a 'second novitiate'.

> We are a group of missionaries of all ages and nations and belonging to almost all the different African and American missions, and we are all so happy to be once again what we were oh! those long, long years ago — now God gives us the opportunity to see how we kept the vows we made the day of our Profession. What a grace that is for all of us, especially for ancients like myself!

He came back to Ireland in September and had the unusual pleasure of a stay in Killeshandra. Mother Augustine, the new Mother General, had gone to Nigeria to experience the missions at first hand and the convent was under the care of Mother Gerard, the local superior and a good friend of Shanahan's. Tired after the travels of the previous three months, he spent a happy week at the gate-lodge. It was almost like old times again and he enjoyed it, he informed Gerard, more than he could tell.

An even greater pleasure lay in store. On 30 October he wrote again to Gerard in a state of high excitement.

> I am to sail for Nigeria in a few days, a fortnight at the latest. Dr Heerey has sent me a pressing invitation, the second or third since last year — but this is final and definite — to be present at the Jubilee celebrations in Onitsha. I need not tell you how happy I am and how grateful to God — and after God, to Dr Heerey.

At last a formal and definite invitation had arrived from Bishop Heerey. There was no longer any doubt about it. The main event in the Jubilee celebration was to be the consecration of the new

Onitsha cathedral on 8 December, which left very little time for Shanahan to make all the necessary preparations. It has even been suggested that Heerey deliberately left the formal invitation until the last moment in the hope that Shanahan might decide it was too late to travel. But it could never be too late for Shanahan. He was wanted in Onitsha and wild horses would not stop him from going.

On 13 November he was steaming down the Mersey on the *RMS Adda,* en route for Nigeria. He feared he would be the only missionary travelling but he found there were four other priests on board, all from Ireland, one bound for Calabar to work with the Kiltegan priests, the others members of the Society of African Missions. 'They are all very young and very happy,' he wrote. 'We are of course all together at table and near each other in our cabins. It makes the voyage to be very pleasant indeed.'

From various stopping places along the coast of Africa he sent letters, filled with excitement at the prospect of his return to Onitsha. There is one significant omission in all of them. Nowhere does he give any hint of how long he hoped to stay. It could be for a month, it could be for the rest of his life. Though he had been invited only for the jubilee celebrations, he never makes any reference to coming back to Ireland afterwards. He clearly hoped that once he had set foot in Nigeria, he would find some way of making his stay permanent. 'For an old missionary', he wrote from the *Adda,* 'the greatest happiness in his life is to be able to see once again and, if possible, end his days among those spiritual children that he loves with an intense love, with a love granted to him by Jesus Christ, to be a very participation of Christ's own love for those self-same souls.'

* * *

Nigeria's welcome for Bishop Shanahan went far beyond anything he could have imagined. It was an explosion of love and joy that brought a lump to his throat and tears to his eyes. It began at Port Harcourt and continued all through the long drive to Onitsha. Crowds greeted him at Aba and Owerri and Onitsha and all along the road. As the car bearing him and Bishop Heerey began to approach Onitsha, the crowds grew even larger and the excitement reached fever pitch. A procession of cars from the town met them, led by the Holy Trinity Brass Band. The motorcade drove the last few miles of the journey at a snail's pace, past flags and banners and bunting, under scrolls bearing messages of welcome, through the tightly-packed mass of people, all eager to catch their first glimpse of their beloved Father and to receive his blessing as he passed.

Nearing the town, he saw the pupils of the mission schools drawn up in their hundreds, the girls resplendent in spotless white dresses and blue head-ties. He said they were like a field of bluebells that would one day spread the fragrance of their faith throughout the length and breadth of Africa. The car moved on up the mango avenue towards the mission house and he suddenly caught his first heart-stopping glimpse of the newly-built cathedral. The tall tower and spire, the rose window, the nave and aisles and transepts, the flight of steps running down to the Niger at the very spot where the first Holy Ghost missionaries had landed just fifty years previously — everything was just as he had dreamed it and planned it. 'How good God is!' he kept saying. 'How good God is!'

In the mission house many of his old friends and fellow workers were waiting to greet him. The sisters had come from convents in every part of the Vicariate, the Fathers had been arriving all day from their bush stations by car and motor-bike and bicycle. Ibo chiefs were there in their full regalia, leading citizens in their flowing and colourful robes. He had a warm greeting from the first Ibo priest, John Anyogu, whom he had ordained five years ago in the old church. He had a joyful reunion with two of his oldest and dearest friends, Peter and Paul, who had worked as mason and carpenter in so many of the churches and convents and mission houses and who had crowned a lifetime of service by their work on the magnificent new cathedral. He wept openly and unashamedly. 'How good God is!' he said again. 'How good God is!'

The next few days passed quickly in a flurry of preparations. The day appointed for the blessing of the cathedral was 8 December, the Feast of the Immaculate Conception. The building was unable to hold more than a fraction of the congregation who came to take part in the ceremony. When he came out into the brilliant sunshine to begin the blessing, he was confronted with a vast multitude, stretching far beyond the reach of his dimming and tear-filled eyes. Clothed in mitre and cope, he walked around the outside of the church, blessing the walls and sprinkling them with holy water. The crowd noticed that he had grown older and slower, his beard even whiter than before. But he was as impressive and dignified as ever, the tall mitre lending emphasis to his erect figure and stately bearing. He entered the church and walked up the centre aisle to the high altar, then turned to face the congregation. Suddenly and spontaneously, the whole church erupted in a frenzy of applause. Father Onyisi was back with his people.[3]

The two weeks that followed were a constant round of engagements. Every convent and every mission wanted the honour of a visit. The days were filled with travel and the nights with talk. He was astonished at the advances that had been made in less than four years, the churches and convents and schools that had been built or were in the process of being built. The seed that he had so laboriously tended for so many years was suddenly bursting into bloom.

On the verandah in Emekuku he had a strange conversation with Mother Augustine, the Mother General of the Holy Rosary Sisters. She had finished her visitation of the Nigerian convents and was planning to return to Ireland after Christmas. The meeting with her brought back many painful memories of events in Ireland. He surprised her by suddenly asking about the talk Mother Xavier had given to the sisters before leaving Killeshandra. He had heard about it from other sisters, who criticised it severely and said it had caused his contacts with them to be greatly restricted.

Mother Augustine was astonished at this interpretation. She told him her own memory of the talk was very different. Xavier knew that when he was gone the sisters would have no-one of experience to guide them, so she gave them her parting advice on the relations that should exist between sisters and priests. She had been at pains to inculcate respect for priests and even more so for bishops, especially Bishop Shanahan, their beloved founder. They should reverence him and pray for him and could write to him if they wished. She had pointed out to them, however, that the situation in Killeshandra was unusual. Because they were a new congregation, they were being given a great deal of attention from bishops, especially Bishop Shanahan. This could lead to young and immature sisters seeking to be noticed and made much of, and this could damage their spiritual development. They should remember that most sisters rarely spoke or wrote to a bishop.

'The Bishop thanked me', she wrote later, 'and said he would put the other accounts of the talk completely out of his head, as they were so warped and prejudiced. He thanked me greatly for my explanation and, as was usual with him, became radiantly happy and joyful.'[4]

He was back in Onitsha for Christmas, understandably exhausted and in need of rest. He sang the Midnight Mass in the cathedral and distributed communion to the large congregation, helped by some of the priests. He spent much of Christmas Day with the sisters, who thought that he looked far from well. He made light of it, saying it was an old heart condition, and went to visit one of the sisters who had been confined to bed for a long time. He gave her a blessing and the others noticed that her recovery started from his visit.

In the weeks after Christmas, he continued to visit the convent almost every day. The schools were closed for the Christmas holidays and the sisters had more free time than usual. He came in the morning to say Mass in the little oratory and stayed for his breakfast afterwards. Sister Rosarii Comer was sacristan at the time and she observed the devotion with which he said his prayers of thanksgiving after Mass, kneeling on the wooden kneeler in the sacristy. One morning the Prefect Apostolic of Jos was also there to say Mass, and Shanahan knelt on the floor so that he could have the kneeler.[5]

He came back again in the afternoons and had a cup of tea and chat with the sisters in the garden or on the verandah. He appeared to be both lonely and unwell. Sometimes he was gripped by a spasm of pain, the colour left his face and he was unable to speak for a few minutes. Then he would relax again and say it was only a touch of indigestion.[6]

He began to talk to them for the first time about going back to Ireland. They soon realised that this was not for reasons of health but because he now knew beyond a shadow of doubt he was not wanted in Nigeria. Bishop Heerey felt his authority threatened by Shanahan's presence. He could never be accepted by the people as their spiritual leader as long as Father Onyisi was living among them. Shanahan must go.

It would be easy to accuse Heerey of pettiness and jealousy. Many did accuse him and condemn him, then and since. As the priests and sisters came to realise what was happening, there was anger and resentment and distress. Shanahan had given his whole life to the Church in Southern Nigeria. Without him it would scarcely exist. To him Nigeria was the dearest place on earth, the place where he wanted to live out his days and breathe his last. He was old and ailing and no threat to anybody. All he wanted was a quiet little bush station where he could say his prayers and prepare his soul for God. How could anyone be so obtuse as to feel threatened by him? How could anyone be so heartless as to deprive him of his last wish?

Such was the opinion among many of Shanahan's friends, some of whom never forgave Heerey for what he did. But there were others who saw it differently. They thought Shanahan should have made it clear that he was going back to Ireland once the celebrations were over. By not doing so, he put Heerey in a difficult position. Father Phil O'Connor, one of Shanahan's most loyal friends, sided with Heerey in this matter. He told Sister Catherine O'Carroll, 'It was Shanahan's own impetuosity that made him think of staying on. He could not see, what we could, that it was an impossible situation. It would make things impossible for Dr Heerey. As long as Dr Shanahan, their Big Chief, was in Nigeria, no Ibo would dream of going to a young newcomer like Dr Heerey. It could split the Church in Nigeria!'[7]

For thirty years Shanahan had built up the Church in Southern Nigeria. For thirty years he had been the Church in Southern Nigeria. Every Catholic in the country knew him and revered him. He had visited their villages, founded their schools and churches, examined them in their religious knowledge, administered to them the sacrament of Confirmation. When all this was combined with the traditional reverence for elders in tribal life, it put him in a position of unique eminence. His mere presence in Nigeria must overshadow all other authority.

Heerey's worst fears must have been confirmed by the rapturous reception given to Shanahan in Onitsha. The Ibo people wanted him to stay with them and never leave again. They found a fitting spokesman in Chief Michael Onyiuke of Nimo, they boy whom Shanahan had met on his great trek twenty-five years earlier and sent to Onitsha to be educated. He was now Chief of his town and one of Nigeria's leading Catholics.

Sister Rosarii was present when the chief arrived one morning at the convent to catch Shanahan after Mass. He knelt to kiss his ring and then said to him, 'My Lord, are you going to stay with us now for the rest of your life?' Shanahan smiled and said, 'Oh, an old man like me, Michael, would be no use in the mission. You need young strong men for the work.'

The Chief answered, 'I have come in to ask you if we could have the honour of having you to come and live in our town. Our people want it and I want it. You are our father and it is fitting that a father should live amongst his children.'

Shanahan repeated that he was too old for the work of a missionary but the Chief told him it was not his work they wanted but himself. 'My Lord,' he asked, 'will you not come and leave your bones with us?'

Shanahan was deeply touched by the invitation. As he walked along the verandah with the Chief, he seemed close to tears. 'We'll see, Michael, we'll see', was all he would say.[8]

The three weeks after Christmas were spent in a kind of limbo. He did not know whether Heerey wanted him to stay or go. Heerey, for his part, could not bring himself to say what was in his mind. Though he was never very close to Shanahan, he bore him no ill-will. The last thing he wanted was to hurt him. But he was firmly convinced that it was for the good of the Church in Nigeria that Shanahan should go. He would never be able to function effectively as its leader in the shadow of the older and greater man.

It might have been more merciful if he had come out into the open and said what he felt, but he lacked the necessary ruthlessness. The strategy he adopted was that of a kinder and weaker man. He simply left him alone. He no longer involved him in any way in the day-to-day activities of the mission and he discouraged others from involving him. He allowed him to become more and more isolated, hoping he would realise he had no longer any useful contribution to make and so decide of his own accord to leave.

One thing that contributed to Shanahan's isolation was lack of transport. The mission cars that had been freely available to him before now seemed permanently busy. He came to Sister Catherine, back in Nigeria from Killeshandra, and suggested an outing in the sisters' car. 'We must have a trip to Awgu again and a picnic, as we had when you and Sister Rose were coming back from Emekuku in 1932. Remember?' Catherine had no difficulty remembering the accident on the road to Emekuku and its more pleasing aftermath and she was delighted at the suggestion. She began to plan the picnic and invited some of the other sisters to come with them.

Mother Augustine was staying in the convent at the time, preparing for her return to Ireland. A day or two later, she came to Catherine and said, 'About that trip to Awgu: Bishop Heerey doesn't want it to take place, so you had better tell Dr Shanahan that you can't go.' Catherine was very upset, not so much for herself as for Shanahan who was looking forward to the outing, but she did not want to cause any trouble between the two bishops. She just told Shanahan they were sorry but they couldn't manage to get away for the picnic. He went white and then said, 'That's all right, quite all right. I expected something like this.'[9]

He spoke with Mother Augustine. 'Do you think I should go home with you?' he asked. 'I think it would be as well', she answered. 'Your health might trouble you.' 'I think I'll come', he said.[10]

* * *

His second leaving of Nigeria was incomparably more sad than his first. This time he could see no human consolation. He was leaving a Nigeria that had rejected him for an Ireland that did not want him.

He made no complaint about the way he had been treated. He could not conceal the heart-break it caused him to leave Nigeria for ever, but he attached no blame to anyone except himself. He had let himself become too attached to the place, the work, the people. God was now gently detaching his heart from them, for his own spiritual good and growth. He wrote to the sisters in Onitsha:

> On my own side, it was quite evident from the moment I set foot in Nigeria that my visit was to be one that would bring me great supernatural happiness on one condition: the final and definite shattering of all natural attachments and affection for, and pride in, even persons and matters that I have thought purely supernatural. I did not know there was so much of my natural self in all the activities of my being!

In a sense, he was leaving of his own free will. Had he chosen to ignore the signals Heerey was sending, he could easily have stayed on in Onitsha or Nimo or elsewhere. Heerey could have ordered him to leave the vicariate but such an action would have caused a catastrophic division in which Shanahan's supporters would have far outnumbered Heerey's. But the last thing Shanahan wanted was any danger or even suggestion of a division. Even with his closest friends, he remained completely loyal to Heerey and all his references to him were marked with the same respect and esteem as before.

For his part, Heerey was equally careful to speak nothing but good of Shanahan. Father John Jordan, who later spent five years with Heerey in Onitsha, said he never heard him mention Shanahan except in praise and admiration though he sensed the absence of any close personal friendship between them. He believed that Heerey felt a sense of guilt at not letting Shanahan stay in Nigeria, even though he thought he was acting for the best.[11] Perhaps if he had been a bigger man, he could have granted an old missionary his wish and lived with the situation that resulted; but he was what he was.

Shanahan booked his passage on the *RMS Apapa,* the boat Mother Augustine was travelling on. A number of the missionaries accompanied them to Port Harcourt to see them off, among them Bishop Heerey and Sister Catherine. The Holy Rosary Sisters were starting a new convent in the town and were living temporarily in a small house that was like an oven under the tropical sun. Shanahan said Mass there on the morning of his departure, his last Mass in Southern Nigeria. He was clearly in a very emotional state but he kept control of himself almost to the end. At that time, every Mass concluded with a reading from the prologue to Saint John's Gospel. He read it as usual until he reached the touching words 'He came to his own and his own did not receive him.' Choked with feeling, he was unable to continue and left the altar. At breakfast afterwards, he seemed his usual self and made no mention of the incident.[12]

He was due to come back before the boat sailed to give Benediction and say goodbye to the sisters. He found he could not face the ordeal and asked Heerey to give the Benediction in his place. Instead he said goodbye to them on the quayside and then boarded the boat with Mother Augustine and their two travelling companions, Mother Peter and Father McAllister. As the *Apapa* pulled away from land, he stood on deck with Augustine and watched the sisters waving their last farewell. They kept waving until they felt their arms would drop off and he kept watching as they grew smaller and smaller into the distance. When he could no longer see them with his eyes, he could still see them in his mind.

The ship stopped at Lagos and he went ashore to the Bishop's house for his last day on Nigerian soil, 22 January 1936. Some of the sisters had given letters to Augustine to be handed to him after the boat sailed and he took the opportunity to answer them. In these later years of his life, the division between prayer and speech was beginning to melt away, both in his conversation and in his writing. His letter to Mother Annunciata in Enugu is addressed as much to God as to her.

> This evening we sail from Lagos. I want to send you a last farewell with my blessing before we leave this hospitable land of Nigeria, before we leave you and the whole mission in the thick of the battle. How I thank God every day more and more for the beautiful arrangement he has made for us His children to remain permanently in loving union with Him and with each other through the medium of prayer. Our Father who art in Heaven, bless Mother Annunciata and all the Sisters in Enugu, Nigeria, Killeshandra; give them, O Heavenly Father, their daily bread for body and soul; and do, Oh do, be with them in the hours of trial and sorrows. They are your own, your very own children — and mine too, in a small way, since you have asked me to represent you and act as their father. So now, using to the fullest the privilege of this spiritual fatherhood, I ask you, O Heavenly Father, to fill their hearts with peace, joy, fortitude, patience and above all your own Living Love.

He was still haunted by his last sight of the sisters on the quayside. He told Sister Matthias, 'I cannot get away from — nor indeed do I want to — from that last vision I have of the sisters standing on the Port Harcourt wharf.' He told Sister Catherine, 'While I write I can see you still as you all stood on the burning red clay of Nigeria, while we moved away over the cool waters on our way to exile in so-called comfort in Ireland — Ireland now become a place of exile for African missionaries.'

For once, the sea voyage brought him no peace or enjoyment. His return to Ireland was no home-coming. Nigeria was his home, Ireland his place of exile. Everyone noticed how pale and ill he looked. In addition to his loneliness, he seemed to be in almost constant pain. Even the ship's crew, many of whom had come to know and respect him from previous voyages, were concerned about him. One of the stewards had once told Sister Rosarii, 'He is the man most like Christ I have ever met.'[13] They did all they could for him but he seemed to be beyond human comfort.

He was back in Ireland in early February. He returned to his room in Clareville, ignoring Augustine's advice to seek medical attention. He was sick and deeply depressed. His thoughts kept going back to Nigeria, especially to the convent in Onitsha and the welcome and understanding he had found there during his last sad days. He wanted to write to them but he could not summon up the mental or physical energy. He could only pray, and even that with difficulty. One morning he came to the foot of the altar to say Mass and for a time could go no further. Finally he managed to get to the altar and proceed with the Mass. Afterwards he asked the altar-boy how long he had stood at the foot of the altar. 'About fifteen minutes', the boy said.[14]

On 15 March he at last wrote to Sister Catherine in Onitsha. It is a very long and rambling letter, shapeless and self-indulgent, a stream of consciousness that reveals even more than he intends. He speaks to her of the difficulties of her life as a missionary and tells her that prayer will give her strength in times of darkness; but in reality he is talking about himself.

> How well I know that very special sense of nothingness in presence of what looms up as an impossible and insuperable task. And yet, God is there with you all the time; just one single minute, not more, of intense pouring out of one's whole abandoned, hopeless, broken self in the presence of Jesus Christ in the little tabernacle will bring back peace, happiness, sunshine, strength, confidence, courage to take on the seemingly impossible task; because He, your spouse, the lover of your soul, the Commander-in-chief of the apostolic army tells you that all is well; stay where you are, just do what you can, and all, absolutely all, will be right, in the invisible mysterious way in which things do turn out right, in the way and in the time God wants them to turn out right.

He goes on to speak of the place of suffering in the life of the Christian. He will never pray that she will be spared suffering, but only that she will be able to bear it through an even closer union with Christ. He recalls the unforgettable day when he knelt before the Pope and asked him to bless the sisterhood he was about to found, the day when he began to carry all the sisters in his soul.

> You are for me the most powerful of all appeals to keep walking Heavenwards; to keep in and with God. So that any little thing I did for you has been repaid a million times over by God because of you, because of your prayers for this useless old man that you are humble enough to call your Father in Christ. The end of a letter I never meant to write in this shape. Since I have written it, I'll send it to you, an old man's letter to his children.
>
> You may make what use [of it] you think fit, arranging it as you know best how to convey to the Sisters in the community what few ideas may be of use to them in this long rigmarole, written to you spontaneously without any forethought or plan. They are the ideals of my life, no matter how poorly I may live up to them.
>
> You remember the heart trouble I had in Onitsha? Well, it was not the heart itself but something else that was causing the trouble. Whatever it was, it continued on till about five days from Liverpool. I was feeling it getting worse and worse. One day at last something gave way. Whether it was an abscess on the liver I don't know, but it burst at all events. For the first time in my life — often as I have been at death's door — I felt like passing away during that final crisis. It has taken me all the time since to get back to normal. I think I am very well back now. Was it not providential after all that I did not stay in Nigeria?
>
> My mind is working again today, also my will is gaining some power, for it had deteriorated badly. For all this I am grateful to God, grateful for everything, and I'd say most of all for my last journey to Nigeria with the inevitable strain.[15]

Slowly, painfully, but surely, he was coming to terms with the fact that he would never see Nigeria again. There must be some other work for him to do in whatever years of life remained for him. The God who gave the work would also give the strength to carry it out.

18

Banishment

One afternoon not long after his return from Nigeria, a knock came on Shanahan's door in Clareville. A young priest came in and introduced himself. His name was John Jordan, he had recently been ordained for the Holy Ghost Congregation and he was now finishing his studies in Kimmage. He hoped to go on the missions shortly and would love to talk to Shanahan about the missionary life.

> He was standing with his back to a small fire. I marvelled at his fine figure, his erectness of carriage, the touch of innate nobility about him, the face that was grave but not severe. He seemed rather puzzled by my request and began to shake his head in negation. Then as I drew nearer, he hesitated, peered more intently, and then:
>
> 'Oh, it's you. We have met before. I nearly said No. Thank God I didn't. Will you have a cigar?' My teeth watered. I grinned. 'If I went back to John Kearney (the Director) reeking of cigar smoke, I'd be in hotter water than if I marched back with a young lady.'
>
> He threw back his head and laughed aloud. 'You're the kind of young fellow I like to meet. Sit down and make yourself at home.' He threw a shovel of coal on the fire and stirred it to life.

So began an unexpected friendship between an old bishop and a young priest that was to touch both of them deeply. For Shanahan, the friendship brought new light and hope in a time of great darkness. For Jordan, it brought an entry into the mind and heart of the man he would later describe as the most outstanding Irish missionary since the days of Columbanus. He had long been an admirer of Shanahan and had met him briefly on a few occasions. This time he had a definite purpose. He wanted to persuade Shanahan to write the story of his life.

For years Shanahan's friends had been urging him to put into writing his experiences on the Nigerian mission. There was so much to be told. There were the strange and exciting stories with which he held an audience spellbound when he spoke from the pulpit or the platform. There were the humorous incidents that he could relate with such incomparable gusto when he had a glass in one hand and a cigar in the other. Every possible argument had been used. He had a unique knowledge of the history of the Church in Nigeria. He had a duty to commit it to writing for the sake of posterity. If his eyesight prevented him from writing, he could talk and others would do the writing. All was in vain. He adamantly refused to consider the idea. He had no gift for writing and even if he had he would not use it to describe his own experiences. It was the work that mattered, not the man.

For some time past Jordan had been on the editorial staff of the *Holy Ghost Missionary Annals,* which was published from Kimmage. He was always on the look-out for suitable material for the magazine and he knew that Shanahan was a rich gold-field waiting to be mined. Knowing how often he had refused before, he did not raise the subject with him directly. Instead, he asked questions about the early days in Nigeria and about some of the legendary French missionaries of the time.

Shanahan's response was muted. He answered the questions briefly and seemed to be abstracted and depressed. After half an hour little progress had been made. Jordan decided to change his approach. As he looked at Shanahan's patriarchal figure, the name of the founding father of the people of Israel came into his mind. 'My Lord,' he said, 'have you ever thought of yourself in terms of Abraham?'

Shanahan was startled into life by the question. 'Good gracious, no', he said. 'What has he got to do with the missions? I've often heard God's words to him quoted at professions, consecrations to the apostolate, renewal of vows and occasions like that. I've probably used them a few times myself. But something special to me that is different from other people? No, never!'

Jordan explained what he meant. Abraham was the father of the Jewish nation, the man who prepared them for the coming of Jesus Christ, the man whom Mary honoured in her *Magnificat*. In the same way, Shanahan was the father of the Ibo people and perhaps other African peoples as well, the man who had brought them the faith. He was their apostle, their prophet, their spiritual founder. He belonged to the great company of patriarchs. He had done for the people of Southern Nigeria what Patrick had done for the people of Ireland.

Shanahan listened quietly but with growing attention. The

mention of Patrick brought him to his feet. He began to speak in a rush of emotion about the way he had felt Patrick's influence in his life and how often he had drawn inspiration from his example. He had followed Patrick's lead when he left the coast and the Niger to open up the interior of the country. He had followed him again when he concentrated his resources on the schools. 'I realised', he said, 'that the keys of the Kingdom were in the tiny hands of children.'

The time had passed quickly and Jordan rose to go. Shanahan put his hand on his shoulder and said, 'You'll come again, won't you? Come as often as you can, every day if they'll let you. You have brought my soul to life.'

For the next three or four months Jordan was a regular visitor to Clareville, cycling across from Kimmage one or two afternoons every week. He sat in front of the fire, warming his hands and often drying his rain-sodden overcoat, listening to Shanahan talking about his life and times, spurring him on by an occasional well-timed interjection. Frequently Shanahan would drift into prayer, sometimes in silence, sometimes praying aloud in a rhapsody of praise and thanksgiving to God. He would move for a time into another world, surprised when he returned to this one to find that he was not alone. 'Have you been here all the time I was praying? Well, I'm glad it was you.'

He spoke about his sorrows as well as his joys. Sometimes he became very depressed about what he called the failure of his life in retirement. He felt useless and in the way in Blackrock, despite the kindness of those around him. Jordan asked him why he didn't return to some little parish in Nigeria.

'Heerey wouldn't have it', he answered. 'Now, don't get me wrong. He is doing the right thing. I would have much more influence with the people after my long years than he has. He will make his mark in time, of course. But just now my presence would be very awkward there. Nigeria is out.'

Jordan tried to cheer him by speaking of the Holy Rosary Congregation that he had founded and of the love the sisters had for him. He knew nothing of the estrangement that had occurred and was shocked when Shanahan told him about it. 'They threw me out of Killeshandra', he said. 'They wouldn't even let me talk to the novices. A few of them think I don't know how to control my affections. Of course, I love the young nuns there very much, and I don't think God will ever be displeased with me for that.'

The question of the book had not yet been raised. One day Jordan found him in a sunnier mood than usual and decided to ask a leading question. 'What was life like when you went out to Nigeria? And what kind of a man was old Lejeune?'

> That really lit a fuse. He went on almost non-stop for about two hours. At every attempt to halt, I prodded him on with relevant questions. I was wise enough to take no notes, just sat there drinking it all in. He imitated the men he described, their gestures, tone of voice, their idiosyncrasies, waving his arms and strutting about as though on a stage. Every mood and tense of the earliest missionaries came to life. Humour, pathos, irony, affection, idealisation — all were there in profusion.

Jordan left him, stopping outside the door of the room to make a few quick notes. Then he returned to Kimmage, sat down and started to write. Four or five hours later he had completed an account of Shanahan's first four years in Nigeria. He wrote it in the first person, just as he had heard it from Shanahan's lips. A few days later he brought it back to Clareville. It was the Feast of Saint Joseph, Shanahan's name-day, 19 March 1936.

'I've put together a lot of what you said the last day. Could I read it to you?' Shanahan listened intently and by the end was visibly affected. 'It's exactly what I wanted to say, but just couldn't', he said.

Jordan asked permission to publish the piece under Shanahan's name. 'Of course, of course', he answered. 'You read my soul like a book. Do what you like with anything I say. I know you'll use it for the missions. Don't even bother to ask for authorisation. You are the biggest improvement on myself I can imagine.' He put back his head and laughed. Jordan took him at his word and published the piece later on that year in the *Missionary Annals.* It was entitled 'Those Early Days' and Shanahan was named as the author.

Encouraged by this success, Jordan now raised the great question of the book. As before, Shanahan refused to entertain the idea of writing anything about himself, but he was now more open to the suggestion that somebody else might write it, if the somebody else was Jordan. He laid down conditions. The book was not to be about him but about the whole story of the coming of the Catholic Church to Southern Nigeria. All the old missionaries must be there, Lejeune, Duhazé, and their fellow-workers. He himself could be mentioned where necessary. But it would not be a book about him. Nobody would want to read a book about a missionary whose life ended in frustration and failure.

Jordan continued to visit him until the summer. Shanahan talked freely and at length about the growth of the Church of Nigeria as he had witnessed it. In the process he told a great deal about his own life, his travels on land and water, his dealings with chiefs and people, his schools policy, his mission philosophy, his spirituality, and a thousand other things. Jordan took notes discreetly for future use, and in return told Shanahan how he himself had received his missionary vocation. It had happened sixteen years earlier when he was a lad of thirteen at Rockwell College and Shanahan had come to give a talk to the boys. From that day on, his only desire was to be a missionary in Nigeria.

His last visit was in June 1936. He brought bad news. He had received his appointment from Father Murphy, the Provincial, who told him he was to remain in Ireland. Shanahan promised to intervene and have the appointment changed to Nigeria. Jordan thought he intended to approach the Provincial and told him it would be useless. 'Do you think I'm going over to Murphy and that crowd in Kimmage?' he answered. 'I'm not. I'm going right up.' And he waved his breviary in the air, his ultimate weapon.

Shortly afterwards Jordan's appointment was changed and he went to Nigeria, where he was in due course to take over the management and expansion of the network of schools built up by Shanahan. Eight years later he came home on leave and while staying in Killeshandra wrote the invaluable *Bishop Shanahan of Southern Nigeria* which preserved for posterity so much that would otherwise have been lost for ever.[1]

* * *

As the summer approached, Shanahan began to resume some of his former activities. He renewed contacts with Mary Martin and interested himself in the progress of her new sisterhood, the Medical Missionaries of Mary. She was seeking formal approval from Rome and she asked him for a letter of commendation which she could send to the Congregation of Religious, knowing the weight his name would carry. He warned her that as a retired missionary bishop he carried very little weight but gladly gave her the letter.

> God bless you and your project, along with all those who in any way helped you to carry it out. May God give you in His own way the answer you now seek from the Holy See, so that your conscience may be at rest. Should the answer be in the affirmative, then with what zeal will you not spend the remainder of your life in the building up of this work you have so much at heart![2]

He wrote regularly to Mother Augustine in Killeshandra and these letters, which she faithfully preserved, are our best source of information about his activities at this time. In July he led a pilgrimage from Belfast to Lisieux in honour of his beloved Saint Thérèse and celebrated Pontifical High Mass in the crypt of the new basilica. He had scarcely returned, when he had to lead another pilgrimage, this time to Lough Derg. It was a repetition of the previous year's pilgrimage of prayer for the missions and it was to become an annual event for him. August found him in Rockwell College, where he conducted the first three weeks of a month-long recollection for priests.

He made the occasional rather strained visit to Killeshandra. There are cryptic references in some of the letters which indicate that the tension had not gone. Once he apologises to Mother Augustine for what he calls his 'candour', which suggests he may have spoken his mind too freely on the subject.

> As for my 'candour' — Well! I hope you will forgive and forget. Please God you have listened to the last of that kind of 'candour' from me. But to finish with this matter, where my relations with you and the Congregation are concerned I have nothing to say for myself. I will leave this matter too in God's hands. I hope He will never permit me to think, say or do anything that would not be inspired by his love for those who are His consecrated spouses.

On 20 November he was ordered into Saint Vincent's Hospital by Dr Magennis. 'My circulatory and nervous systems have to a great extent got badly impaired but not beyond repair!' He was supposed to undergo treatment for fifteen days but it lengthened into five weeks and he was not discharged until 23 December. He spent Christmas in Maynooth with his sister, Mrs Mary Dawson, now in failing health. The tragic death of her daughter, May, was a shock from which she had never recovered.

Death was beginning to thin out the ranks of those he had known and worked with. After Christmas he spent some days in Killeshandra which went happily enough. He had barely returned to Dublin, when he heard that Mother Aquinas, the former Novice Mistress, was seriously ill with pneumonia. He went to see her in Sion Hill Convent, next door to Blackrock. The following day a messenger came to say she had been anointed and wanted to see him. He visited her again and it is said that she told him she was sorry for all that had happened in Killeshandra and asked him to forgive her. She died the next day, 18 January 1937. Besides Shanahan, those who knelt around her death-bed included Mothers Xavier and Augustine and Father Leen.

Bishop Patrick Finegan was unable to come to Dublin for her funeral as he was suffering from influenza. His condition rapidly worsened and he died on 25 January. He too was one of those who had tried to minimise Shanahan's influence on Killeshandra. But Shanahan never forgot that he had given the sisters their first home and watched and worried over them ever since they had come to his diocese. He paid him a generous tribute in an appreciation in the *African Rosary,* a missionary magazine which the sisters had just begun to publish. In the course of it he wrote:

> The epitaph of the late Bishop of Kilmore will remain written in the saintly lives of the spiritual children to whom he gave the bread of life and the word of life. He was for them another Christ.
>
> This was the bishop chosen by the Holy Ghost to found in his diocese a new missionary congregation for work on the missions, the Missionary Sisters of Our Lady of the Holy Rosary at Killeshandra.

These well-meant words had unexpected repercussions among the sisters, especially in Nigeria. They could not understand why Shanahan should describe Finegan rather than himself as their founder. They felt he was repudiating his own children and were deeply hurt. Afterwards he explained to Sister Rosarii that he was only trying to defuse the controversy about who was the canonical founder by yielding that honour to Finegan. He added that nothing in canon law could break the spiritual fatherhood that he had for each of the sisters since the Pope had first given him permission to set up the sisterhood.[3]

During Lent he went to Kiltegan at Father P.J. Whitney's invitation and gave a retreat to the students preparing for ordination to the priesthood. The Missionary Society of Saint Patrick was now firmly established in Kiltegan with Whitney as its first Superior General. Shanahan was a regular and welcome guest there. Kiltegan, like Killeshandra, was rapidly expanding, with new extensions being continually added on to cope with the growing number of applicants. For these young men also Shanahan could claim a spiritual fatherhood. It was now seventeen years since his appeal in Maynooth had attracted the young Father Whitney and started the secular priests' movement. A great oak was now growing from that little acorn.

He spent Easter at Killeshandra and then returned to Clareville to prepare for further retreats he was to conduct during the summer. The Feast of the Ascension prompted him to write a long and gracious letter to Mother Augustine, his first since his Easter stay at Killeshandra. In it he reflected on the meaning the Feast had for him, and how it mingled the sorrow of parting from earth with the joy of entry into heaven.

> What a wonderful welcome! The first of the sons of men to enter Heaven — and He has prepared a place there for each and all of His pre-destinated children. The Apostles are there, Our Blessed Mother is there, so is Saint Joseph with countless millions down to the latest arrivals that have left earth for Heaven since I began to write these lines. And among them how many of those we knew and continue to know and love with that love that is never to cease for it will last for eternity. There are Mother Aquinas, Dr Finegan and all those Nigerians sent to Heaven by your own good Sisters of Our Lady of the Holy Rosary. So on this anniversary of Our Lord's Ascension one cannot but think of that day when each one of us will say our final farewell with a touch of sorrow because of those we leave behind

us, but then the happiness, the joy at the thought of those we will meet at the end of this our last journey from time into eternity.

Mother Augustine wrote back almost immediately. Her letter to him has not been preserved. He destroyed almost all of his correspondence. What we do have is the letter he wrote to her in reply and from it we can make a fair guess at what she said. She must have spoken about his Easter visit to Killeshandra. She must have explained that she felt it her duty to comment on his behaviour on that occasion and to point out the harmful influence that such conduct was having on the sisters. She must have made it clear that she did not want him to have any contact with Killeshandra ever again. His reply is a lengthy document but it is so remarkably revealing that it demands to be quoted in full.

> My dear Mother General,
>
> When your big bulky letter bulging with news was handed to me a few days ago, in response as I thought to my own 'grand' Ascension Thursday letter to you, I said to myself, 'Here's a feast of some genuine Killeshandra and Nigerian news.' So off I hurried to my Clareville hermitage, not too broken hearted at having to miss the usual walk with the Ancients. Sure, the letter would make up for all I missed!
>
> Snugly ensconced in my big armchair, I sat in front of a blazing fire. The day was wet and cold. What more could the old Adam in me wish for? Old Adam was there true enough, only too soon was I to be made aware of his presence — but I must not anticipate.
>
> I started to read the letter, a grand letter sure enough. As I slowly proceeded with my lecture, bright visions of earth and heaven shone from its pages, all the more enchanting because there was I myself in the very centre of the picture. How I modestly lingered over the glowing pen-picture of a real live Saint! — silently appraising the letter writer and her beautiful thoughts, so aptly expressed to suit the masterpiece she was building up. She had me by this time in a sky of blue and white in self-admiration.
>
> All at once the letter, Part I, came to a full stop, and a truculent kind of one too, followed by a blank space beyond which one could sense something ominous about to happen.

As I glanced beyond that white space my eye caught sight of a word. At once a sudden silence seized me, while an intense blast of trumpets blared out, signalling 'Danger ahead'!

I resumed my lecture of the letter, Part no. II, and this is how the first sentence, a challenging sentence, stood up to me: 'This letter should have a festive ring about it ... but ... I would be a ... if ...'

A saint, how are you! Half way up on his way to heaven, so the stupid fellow thought, but whatever he was and wherever he was, he was brought back and up before a battery of spiritual artillery that blew the would-be saint to smithereens. A battery I said? Why, it sounded more like a spiritual volcano in violent activity. No longer air-planing now but crawling, I reached the last page. By the time I got there, I found myself standing outside the convent-lodge gates in penitential garb. Just have a good look at me!

There are people who love to have a portrait of themselves done in 'oils'. I intend to keep this little picture of myself, sculptured into my very soul by a kindly generous artist with an eye for real beauty, for the True, the Beautiful, the Good, whose heart and hand were directed by the Holy Ghost. I know that Our Blessed Mother too had a hand in it. This picture I will treasure as the priceless visit of my last visit to Killeshandra.

The fashioning of it has meant much pain and sorrow with infinite and tender care. But to me, what it will mean for the remainder of my life! Thus to see and know myself is one of God's greatest graces!

And now, Mother, I want to thank you for every line you wrote in that letter. Also I wish to express my regrets to you and to the Congregation you represent for the sorrow I caused, all unwittingly it is true, but nevertheless really. I am sorry above all for the scandal, disedification, bad example set before young religious by one who should always and ever be a model of what God expects every missionary to be.

I will do what I can to make good the harm done. Complete severance of all intercourse between Killeshandra and myself is what you have advised and what I willingly undertake to carry out to the end of my life, cost what it may.

I will continue to devote my whole life as it is, to the service of God for the Congregation of Our Lady of the Holy Rosary. Whatever free Masses I have will be offered up for you. In return I ask nothing, absolutely nothing. I want no further reference to be ever made to me by name. I want to be left alone, totally alone with God in my own Community. Therefore I expect not to be ever invited to Killeshandra. Why invite me since I will and must refuse any invitation there from this day forward? Within a very short time I will be happily forgotten except in the prayer of those who have known me. And all this for the very highest and best interests of the Congregation.

I think that at present I have handed back to God all His eternal property. There remains only the most difficult and most important of all: my own old selfish self. That too will be in God's possession before I die. I feel now the way is clear for this final purification.

Before I conclude I wish to offer you all my best wishes for a very happy Feast on Pentecost Sunday. I am celebrating Pontifical High Mass here in the College. The Mass will be offered for your intentions and for the intentions of the Congregation.

God bless you and God bless the whole Congregation. May the Holy Spirit, the Great Consoler, remain ever with you making His holy presence to be experienced ever more and more intimately by each and all of the Sisters.

Finally, may the Holy Ghost make each one of you to be a religious missionary full of love and zeal for souls and for their sanctification.

I remain,
My dear Rev. Mother General
Affectionately yours in Xsto
✠ Jos. Shanahan, C.S.Sp.

It is difficult to make any comment on this extraordinary document. His response to a letter that clearly caused him intense pain is almost beyond the understanding of ordinary mortals. There is no attempt at self-defence or self-justification. There is no sign of anger or resentment, no suggestion of counter-attack. The anguish is unmistakable but it is treated lightly, almost humorously. He does not present himself as a tragic figure but as a comic one, a faintly absurd poseur whose pretensions to sanctity have been gently and deftly deflated. His gratitude to her for opening his eyes to his faults is evidently and entirely sincere. He accepts his banishment from Killeshandra as the severing of the last attachment that binds him to earth. From now on he can live for God alone.

* * *

The summer of 1937 found him undertaking many of the same tasks as the previous year. In July he went to England to direct an eight-day retreat for priests in Castlehead and then returned to Ireland to lead the annual missions pilgrimage to Lough Derg. In August he was back again in Rockwell to conduct the month's recollection for the priests of the Irish Holy Ghost province.

That same summer the Holy Rosary Sisters rented a house in Northumberland Road in Dublin. As part of their missionary preparation, the young sisters were undergoing training in teaching and medicine. The future teachers were enrolled in the Catholic Teachers' Training College in Craiglockhart, near Edinburgh. Those studying midwifery were sent to Holles Street Hospital in Dublin and the house in Northumberland Road was intended to provide them with a residence.

Northumberland Road was only a short journey by tram from Blackrock. Banned from Killeshandra, Shanahan was able to meet some of the sisters in the new house in Dublin. He used to say Mass there on Sundays and would call in at other times during the week for a chat and a cup of tea. Sometimes when the sisters had a free day, he would take some of them on a little outing. He was now dependent on public transport, having sold the *Isis* before his visit to Nigeria.

A favourite excursion was the tram ride to the Hill of Howth. On one of these he took Sister Madeleine Sophie Cullen and another sister. As they were walking past the Dominican convent in Sutton, Madeleine Sophie said to him, 'I've just remembered. Mother Xavier is in this convent now. She'd be shocked if she saw us.' Shanahan said, 'Then let's all bend down and creep past.' They stooped down low enough to be hidden by the wall between the convent grounds and the road and crept past unobserved.[4]

By August Mother Augustine was beginning to relent. She met him in Dublin and was impressed by what she called his 'magnanimity'. She sent him an invitation to Killeshandra for a profession ceremony, but he graciously declined. 'Many thanks, but I will not be there; better than my presence will be the holy Mass which I will offer on that day for the newly professed sisters.'

He was in Cavan at the beginning of October for the consecration of Dr Patrick Lyons, Finegan's successor as Bishop of Kilmore. He paid a visit to Killeshandra and said Mass there. It was a brief visit, made out of duty. It would have caused comment if he been so close and not called in.

At Christmas he was invited again to visit the convent but he asked to be excused because of an attack of gastric flu. An invitation also came at Easter and this time he pleaded fatigue. 'I am going down to Maynooth where I hope to spend a month and at least get a good rest.' By this time the excuses must have seemed a little thin, even to himself. One part of him longed to go back, but another part dreaded what might happen, what new offence he might give, what new humiliations he might suffer. The wound of separation had been almost beyond bearing but it was beginning to heal at last. He did not want to have it opened again.

Another invitation came after Easter and this one he was unable to refuse. Bishop Heerey was home from Nigeria and staying in Dublin. He was planning a visit to Killeshandra and he asked Shanahan to accompany him. He agreed and made the journey with Heerey and Father Joe Delaney on 3 May. Apart from his brief visit in September, it was over a year since his last visit to the convent. He was a stranger to most of the young sisters and novices and postulants. Many of them had never spoken to him, some had never even seen him before. All they knew was that a shadow of disapproval hung over him. The reason for the disapproval was unknown to them. Nobody talked about such things. The very vagueness of the accusations made them all the more damaging and all the more difficult to refute. What has not been said cannot be denied.

He returned three or four times during the remainder of 1938, which was to be his last year in Ireland. They were duty visits because there was a sense in which his love for Killeshandra had died. He kept the sisters in his heart and in his prayers but he could no longer feel at home in the house on the hill. The point had come at which the sad memories outweighed the happy ones.

All during the period of estrangement, he had continued to write regular and courteous letters to Mother Augustine. Whatever differences he might have had with her, she was the Mother General of the Holy Rosary Sisters and entitled to all the respect that went with that office. The letters cannot have been easy to write, for he did not want to say anything that could be construed as interference in the affairs of the sisters, and there was little to tell about his own activities. On 5 July he had, however, some personal news of the utmost importance to report. He was going back to Africa for good.

> I know you will be pleased to hear that I am to return to Africa to reside there as a missionary again, not as a visitor or sightseer. And I am to leave Ireland in the autumn of this year. God has communicated this bit of news to me only a couple of days ago. It came most unexpectedly. Right Rev. Dr Heffernan, Vicar Apostolic of Zanzibar, on his own personal behalf and also on behalf of all the priests of his Vicariate has very earnestly and warmly invited me to accompany him on his return to Africa, to take up missionary work in his Vicariate until the end of my life.
>
> In this invitation to go to Zanzibar I hear the voice of God inviting me to follow Him once again to that land I have always loved as I love its people: Africa and the Africans. How good God is! If ever my heart and soul were full of joy it was when I heard this invitation, which had to be repeated more than once, for I could scarcely credit my hearing, could hardly believe it was in earnest. How I accepted this invitation with untold gratitude to God, to the Vicar Apostolic of Zanzibar, and to his missionary priests in that Vicariate, I can only leave you to understand from what your own heart as a missionary tells you. How great my happiness is! I feel I'm no longer on the borderland of seventy but just over twenty, with no other memory in my heart but the memory of God's ineffable goodness to me at this the end of my second novitiate of six years' duration here in exile in Clareville.

Bishop Heffernan had been Vicar Apostolic of Zanzibar in East Africa for six years. His consecration as bishop took place in the

College Chapel in Blackrock in 1932, and Shanahan was among those who attended the ceremony. Now home on leave in Ireland, he met Shanahan again and was touched by his feeling of isolation and uselessness. His offer to bring him out to Africa was an act of charity rather than of human wisdom. Shanahan's age and health suggested he might soon be a liability rather than an asset in the vicariate, at least in terms of physical work. But there are other values besides efficiency. Heffernan may have felt that the presence of a man like Shanahan would bring a blessing and a grace to the people of East Africa that could be measured only in spiritual terms.

Once the decision had been made, Shanahan was anxious to leave as soon as possible. Inevitably, there were a number of engagements that had to be fulfilled, including a retreat for the Sisters of Saint Joseph of Cluny in England at the beginning of September. When that was over, he began to make his travel plans. He heard that four Carmelite nuns from Hampton Convent in Dublin were going to East Africa to found a new convent there and he hoped to make the journey with them. However, they were due to leave on 24 October and he could not make the necessary arrangements in time. He eventually booked a passage on 1 December. He was to have as his travelling companion Archbishop James Leen of Mauritius. The Archbishop, a brother of Edward Leen, invited him to visit Mauritius as his guest before taking up his new post in East Africa and he gladly accepted.

He came to Killeshandra to say goodbye for ever to the sisters. It was an occasion of great sadness. For him and for the older sisters who had known him and worked with him and loved him it meant a final parting of the ways. There was another sadness added to the sadness of parting, which even the younger sisters could sense. It was the sadness of business unfinished, of differences unreconciled, of things said and done which could never be unsaid or undone. It was the sadness of wounds which might have healed in time but now there was no more time.

All the community gathered in one of the reception rooms to hear his final words. He spoke gently and movingly about his recent years in Ireland, with candour, without bitterness.

> I thought Nigeria could not get on without me. God brought me home and showed me it could. I thought then that Killeshandra could not get on without me. But again, God

> showed me it could. Sixteen years ago on a bleak November day I came here. What was there but a few broken-down hedges and old dilapidated buildings? And now, when I look on this beautiful building, this house on the hill, I see God's hand in it all.
>
> Those years for me when I left Africa were hard ones. My life has been a hard one. I have always found it so, but especially during that time. I have not felt a man at all. My memory, imagination, even will-power all seemed to vanish. It was God's way of purifying me. For everything I give great thanks to God. Everything that has happened to me, my faults, my failings, my shortcomings, trials, disappointments, hard sayings (and we all meet with such), God has used for the sanctifying of my soul ...
>
> My dear sisters, accept all – your weakness, imperfections, trials and difficulties — and offer all to God. Above all, do not be proud. Love God, praise God, trust God. Be true to the Mass and to Our Lady's rosary. Accept everything He deigns to send. Goodbye now, my very dear sisters, missionaries, and from my heart I bless you all.[5]

They knelt for his blessing and then he went around the entire group, taking each one by the hand, saying a few personal words of encouragement and farewell. They followed him out the main door to the driveway where his car was waiting. One of them took a photograph of the scene, the Bishop erect and cheerful, the sisters in orderly rows, hands tucked safely beneath their scapulars. As the car began to move, he raised his hat in salute. Their last glimpse of him through the window showed a look of sudden anguish on his face. Then the car gathered speed and they saw him no more.[6]

19

The last safari

The ship left Marseilles on 1 December 1938. 'One of the happiest days of my life', Shanahan wrote on a postcard. 'How good God is always, everywhere, and for all.' By the 6th it had crossed the Mediterranean and was nearing the entrance to the Suez Canal. Once again, he could feast his eyes on Africa: not West Africa, to be sure, but still Africa. He had never been to the Holy Land but he was happy to remember that Egypt too had been hallowed by the presence of the infant Christ. 'I will be passing the place where He and His Mother and Saint Joseph passed as fugitives from Herod's fury into the hospitable land of Africa. How the thought links up today with one thousand nine hundred and thirty-eight years ago!'[1]

The voyage continued down the Red Sea and then across the Indian Ocean to the tropical island of Mauritius. Shanahan landed on 31 December, and stayed there for two months. The little jewel-like island, smaller than an Irish county, had a population of almost half a million, French-speaking and with a high proportion of Catholics. A splendid welcome for the returning Archbishop Leen had been organised in the capital, Port Louis. All the bells of the town began to ring as soon as the two bishops disembarked, and a huge crowd waiting at the Custom House escorted them to the Cathedral for a liturgical reception. The Archbishop introduced his guest to the congregation and they were vastly delighted when he addressed them in perfect French. 'Clergy and laity alike', wrote an observer, 'were won by his simplicity and his distinguished bearing.'[2]

He stayed in the Holy Ghost College but he also accepted invitations to visit most of the principal mission stations on the island, social occasions which both he and his hosts enjoyed immensely. The only unpleasantness was caused by a recurrence of his eye trouble. A specialist treated him several times for what was described as an obstruction of the lacrimal duct. For some reason the treatment was given without anaesthetic and was extremely painful.

He left Mauritius on 25 February for Mombasa. Leen insisted on making him a gift of a private suite on the ship, including a balcony overlooking the sea. In spite of the unaccustomed luxury, he was sick on his arrival in Mombasa and unable to continue on to Nairobi. He spent several weeks in hospital and was given the last sacraments. It was not until the end of April that he was able to make the overland rail journey to Saint Austin's Mission, which was to be his headquarters for the rest of his life.

The mission was situated on the outskirts of the city of Nairobi, capital of the British colony of Kenya. Saint Austin's was the residence of Bishop Heffernan, from which he administered the Vicariate of Zanzibar. Heffernan had not yet returned from his visit to Europe but the other priests in the mission made Shanahan very welcome. The journal kept in the mission noted his arrival on 28 April 1939 and added:

> He has made a wonderful recovery and is definitely looking very well after those trying weeks in Mombasa. Let us hope and pray that he will now grow daily stronger in the highlands, and that the old missionary Bishop who has done such wonderful work in Nigeria may now be spared to us for many years to come.

It is doubtful if Shanahan realised how different Kenya would be from Nigeria. The land, the climate, the people, the languages, were a world removed from what he had known for thirty years in West Africa. Much of the country was highland, between five and ten thousand feet above sea-level. In place of the dense forests and swamps there were broad rolling plains, dotted with occasional trees and roamed by lions, giraffes, zebras and antelopes. Distant prospects of snow-topped mountains added to the feeling of space and openness. Because of the altitude, there were no extremes of heat or humidity and Europeans found the climate pleasant and healthy.

Southern Nigeria was one of the most densely populated parts of Africa, teeming with life and activity. In Kenya the population was sparse and included a high proportion of white settlers, attracted by the temperate climate and the fertile land. These settlers, mostly British, introduced an element of racial tension that was unknown in Nigeria. Their opulent lifestyle and their often cavalier treatment of the native population built up the resentments that led some years later to the Mau Mau rebellion. Many of the Europeans lived in a way that offended the moral sense of the Africans and added to the difficulties of the missionaries' task.

A celebrated Nairobi murder trial not long after Shanahan's arrival threw a lurid spotlight on the mores of the wealthy and aristocratic settlers who lived in the area known as Happy Valley. Sir Jock Delves Broughton was tried for the murder of his wife's lover, the Earl of Erroll. He was acquitted, though many believed him guilty. The evidence given in court told of a life of idle luxury, whose main recreations were drink, drugs, gambling and sexual promiscuity, all financed through the exploitation of ill-paid African labour.

The African population was divided into tribes, as in Nigeria. Nairobi was situated in the tribal lands of the Kikuyu, though the territory of the Kamba tribe was not far off. Each of the many tribes had its own tribal language, unknown to the others. The principal means of communication between one tribe and another and between blacks and whites was Swahili, which was widely spoken throughout East Africa. None of the tribes had the highly developed religious sense of the Ibos and conversions to Christianity were far slower than in Southern Nigeria.

It was a complex and challenging scene for a man in his late sixties with deteriorating health. On the positive side, the country was beautiful, travel was easy, law and order prevailed, and the climate was as bracing and agreeable as any in the world. Moreover, Shanahan had many friends there among the priests and sisters and even those who had never met him knew him by repute. He was assured of a welcome in any of the missions and convents of the vicariate.

On the negative side, there was the difficulty of coming to terms with a country which, though plainly Africa, was different from any Africa he had ever known. There was the problem of deciding on pastoral priorities between the Africans and the Europeans, many of the whites being more in need of conversion than the blacks. There was the problem of learning new languages in order to communicate with those who knew no English. This last was to cause him the most trouble. The tribal languages were difficult and he did not attempt to learn them. But Swahili as then spoken in Kenya was an easy language with a small vocabulary and simplified grammar. Had he been younger and fitter, he could have mastered it quickly. As it was, his failing powers of concentration betrayed him and he picked up no more than a few everyday phrases and expressions. He was never able to communicate with the African people of Kenya except through sign-language or interpreters. This was one of the greatest of the sorrows that marked these last years.

Bishop Heffernan may have foreseen this difficulty. His plan was that Shanahan would act as chaplain to the community of Irish Carmelite nuns who had come to establish a convent in Kenya. While waiting for their convent to be built, the four nuns stayed with the Irish Loreto Sisters in Limuru. Heffernan wanted them to remain in Limuru and build their convent there but they felt the place was too isolated and too cold, being twenty miles from Nairobi and two thousand feet higher. The priests in Kenya sided with them but Heffernan, still in Ireland, was slow to give his consent. Eventually he cabled a reluctant agreement and a site was chosen near Saint Austin's mission. The change of plan meant that Shanahan would continue to live at Saint Austin's, which Heffernan may have wanted to avoid.[3]

During his first few weeks in Kenya, Shanahan was brought to visit a number of the missions and religious houses. In June the four Carmelites, his special responsibility, left Limuru to supervise the building of the new convent. They stayed with the Loreto Sisters at Msongari, a short distance away. Shanahan visited them regularly and was delighted to be allowed take them on long walks through the countryside, as they were not bound by the rule of enclosure until the convent was built.

Work on the foundations of the new convent began in mid-July and the foundation stone was laid on 15 August, the Feast of the Assumption. The blessing of the stone was performed by Shanahan. The Saint Austin's journal notes: 'Great gathering of our Fathers and Brothers from different missions present for this unique occasion. The ceremony was most impressive.' The building progressed quickly and was ready for occupation at the beginning of the new year. On 5 January 1940 Shanahan performed the enclosure ceremony and ended it by dramatically closing and locking the door. He absent-mindedly put the key in his pocket and went off with it, so that the nuns could not have broken their enclosure even if they had wanted to.

From this time on, he was the regular chaplain to the convent. Every morning he said Mass for them at 6.30. He walked up the steep hill from Saint Austin's to the convent, a distance of about two miles along a rough and winding lane. He returned again in the afternoon if it was one of the days on which Benediction of the Blessed Sacrament was given. For a time he used a car belonging to the mission but gave it up after colliding with the mission gateway. The nuns were much relieved at this, as his sight made driving dangerous. Even with two pairs of spectacles and a magnifying glass, he had difficulty both in reading and in seeing distant objects. One evening Sister Bernadette drew his attention to Mount Kilimanjaro, its snowy summit bathed in the light of an unusually colourful sunset. 'You can enjoy the beauty of the sight,' he said, 'but I must live by faith.'

It did not take the nuns long to decide that he was a truly holy man. He reminded them particularly of Saint Patrick. One of them wrote later:

> We are reading about Saint Patrick in the refectory and it brings the Bishop to mind. It said that when Patrick talked about the love of God, he must have been as beautiful and compelling as any man who ever walked the face of the earth — and that description just fits our Bishop! When you met him, it was as if meeting Our Lord.

To them his most striking feature was his eyes, lively, penetrating, magnetic, in spite of his short-sightedness. At the same time, there was a withdrawn quality about his face, as if his thoughts were constantly with God. Sometimes the divine indwelling was almost visible. The Book of Exodus tells how, when Moses came down from the holy mountain, the people saw that the skin on his face was shining. The sisters noticed something similar with their chaplain. At times he looked as if his skin was made of parchment and there was a lamp burning within and shining out through his face. They called him 'our dear saint'.[4]

* * *

Bishop Heffernan returned to Nairobi on 24 January 1940 after an absence in Europe of more than eighteen months. The situation in Saint Austin's now became a little delicate. The whole of Southern Nigeria was not large enough to hold two bishops, when one of them was Shanahan. The priests' house at Saint Austin's was considerably smaller.

Heffernan had been described by those who knew him as being by nature somewhat reserved and introverted, cold in manner, with little ability to lead or inspire others. All the qualities he lacked were possessed in abundance by Shanahan. For nine months now Shanahan had been the only bishop in the vicariate and he was becoming known and loved by many. He had not the slightest intention of overshadowing Heffernan but he could not conceal his charisma. In Kenya as everywhere else he drew all eyes. People simply wanted to look at him.

It was only to be expected that Heffernan would feel a touch of resentment. If the Carmelites had stayed in Limuru as he intended, the situation would not have been so difficult. But now Shanahan was established in Saint Austin's, the nearest mission to the convent, and he could hardly be asked to move. Heffernan began to feel that he had invited a cuckoo into his nest.

On Sunday mornings, Shanahan loved to meet the people and chat with them as they left the church after Mass. This was something which Heffernan never did. One Sunday he was standing at the window of his room along with the bursar, Father O'Connor, and he saw the congregation flocking around Shanahan, greeting him and kissing his ring. 'Do you see that?' he said. 'He behaves as if he were the Bishop of Nairobi.'

In the interests of peace, O'Connor decided to have a word with Shanahan. As bursar, he had charge of the drinks and he used to bring Shanahan's sundowner, a small whiskey, to his room every evening. That evening he said to him, 'I am not pleased about one thing you are doing, My Lord, and Bishop Heffernan is not pleased either.' 'What is that?' asked Shanahan. 'You are going about among the people on Sunday mornings and giving them your ring to kiss as if you were their Bishop.' Shanahan paused and then asked, 'What do you think I should do, Father?' 'I suggest', said O'Connor, 'that you take off your ring.' Shanahan took it off immediately and never wore it again.[5]

To a man of Shanahan's sensitivity, it must have been a deeply wounding incident. Yet he could see Heffernan's point of view and he never ceased to be grateful to him for bringing him back to Africa. He never made any complaint about Heffernan and would not allow others to criticise him in his presence. Most of the priests believed that relations between the two men were always cordial. Only those who were familiar with Saint Austin's could see the underlying tension. One of these was Father J.J.

McCarthy, a frequent visitor to the house. Many years later, as Archbishop of Nairobi, he told Sister Catherine O'Carroll how saddened he had been to see the way Shanahan was treated.

> Dr Shanahan was a great man, a great Bishop, a great saint, and a great everything, but when he was invited to Kenya he was left aside, neglected by the head of the Mission. The Irish Fathers here thought the world of him but they could do little when the Bishop acted otherwise, than be kind to him individually.[6]

During this period Shanahan wrote few letters, usually a sign that he was suffering from depression. A further blow came on 19 March 1940, his name-day. News came of the death of his sister, Mrs Mary Dawson, who had been the closest to him of all his family. He was so grief-stricken that it was several days before he could tell anyone about it.

A sudden and unexpected break in the clouds came with the news that the Holy Rosary Sisters were planning a new convent in South Africa. They had been asked to start a school in the parish of Edenvale, near Johannesburg. The invitation came from the parish priest, Father Standing, with the approval of his superior, Bishop O'Leary. The sisters wanted to send out two members of the Council to visit the parish before accepting the invitation but the outbreak of the war made travel very difficult. Finally they decided that five sisters would make the journey, two councillors to decide on the viability of the project and three to remain on if the project was undertaken. They obtained a passage on a ship leaving London in early March and reached Durban in South Africa in mid-April.[7]

The two councillors were two of Shanahan's closest friends, Sister Brigid, the former Bessie Ryan of Calabar, and Sister Philomena, his secretary in Onitsha. They lost no time in writing and inviting him to pay them a visit. There was nothing he would like to do more. The prospect of meeting two of his dearest daughters in an atmosphere where both he and they could be themselves spurred him into activity. The difficulties were enormous: a journey of close on two thousand miles with a war on, no transport and no money. Somehow he managed to book and pay for a passage on a sea-plane which was leaving Mombasa for South Africa. It was the first time he had ever flown. The plane brought him to Durban and from there he took the train to Johannesburg.

On a bright morning in mid-June the sisters waiting at the station saw the familiar tall figure getting off the train. He had lost none of his old magnetism and people turned to look at him as he passed. His delight at meeting the sisters was unbounded and was surpassed only by theirs at meeting him. They noticed that he looked thinner than before and that his clothes, though as neat as ever, were old and threadbare. They asked him what happened to his ring. He told them one of the priests in Naorobi had suggested that he take it off to avoid confusing people.

They brought him to Edenvale and showed him the little house where they were staying, a gift of two brothers living in the locality, Richard and Henry Hurley. Then they installed him in the priest's house, where he was to stay. Father Standing was in hospital at the time and for a week or two Shanahan acted as parish priest. It was a time of pure joy. He was happy to be at work. He was happy with the parishioners. He was happy above all to be able to say Mass for the sisters and to chat to them about Nigeria and Ireland and to know that there was still one Holy Rosary Convent where he was welcomed as a guest and loved as a father.

One day as he was walking back to his house with Sister Philomena, the talk turned to his rift with Killeshandra. He fell silent for a while and then began to speak in a low voice, half to himself, as if he were trying to look into the future. 'For the Congregation, sometimes I am afraid, I am afraid. God has given me many graces and blessings, untold blessings, through the Holy Father. As a founder and father of the Congregation, I was cut off. I could not give them. I pray that nothing, not one of these blessings or graces, will be lost. I will spend my heaven making sure the Congregation will suffer no loss, begging Christ.' What concerned him most was not the hurt it caused him but the hurt it caused the Congregation. He saw the sisters deprived of many blessings and stunted in their growth as a result of this sad and self-inflicted wound.

In June the phoney war came to a sudden end, Italy entered the conflict, France fell, and the German U-boats made the seas unsafe for British ships. The sisters in Edenvale were now cut off from home. To add to their problems, their money was running low and the parish could not help them. In fact, the priest seemed to think that they should feed him and care for him in addition to their other work. In this difficult situation, Shanahan proved a great support. He tactfully but firmly told the priest that the sisters were educators, not housekeepers. He persuaded the wealthy Hurley brothers to build them a convent and school beside the church. He helped Brigid and Philomena, now marooned in South Africa, to set up another foundation and start teaching in the town of Vereeniging.

He himself was tempted to remain. Bishop O'Leary invited him to stay in Johannesburg. A more urgent invitation came from Bishop Klerlein of Kroonstad, whose German priests had all been interned. He went to Kroonstad but had been there only a short while when a telegram arrived from Heffernan to say that the Italian priests in Kenya had been interned and his help was needed. He wrote sadly to Vereeniging to tell Brigid of his departure.

> There is sore disappointment, and I am once again its very unwilling cause, but I have to go; I must regulate my position in Nairobi, cost what it may — and it is costing me more than I thought, in addition to the services I would render if I was near Vereeniging and Edenvale! And that meant so much. God wants me to move away once again and keep to the hard road. I thank God for showing me so clearly His Holy Will.

Brigid and Philomena came to Kroonstad to say goodbye. They found he had been seriously ill, though he dismissed it as a touch of flu. He spoke more about their problems than his own and was full of encouragement for the future. 'South Africa is a difficult mission,' he told them, 'but I am confident all will be well. Keep on.'

He came to the railway station to see them off and stood waving on the platform as the train pulled out. They found it hard to see him through their tears. They were the last Holy Rosary Sisters he ever saw.

* * *

Shanahan returned to Kenya by sea. He travelled from Durban on a Dutch ship and arrived in Mombasa on 6 October 1940. He was back in Saint Austin's in Nairobi on the 15th and at once resumed his chaplaincy to the Carmelite convent.

It was hardly a full-time job. Sometimes he administered Confirmation when Heffernan was ill or otherwise occupied, sometimes he was invited to give a retreat for priests or sisters, but on most days his only duty was to say the 6.30 Mass for the nuns, which meant that his working day was over at 7.00 a.m. There would have been plenty for him to do in South Africa if he had been allowed to stay. But obedience had called him back to Nairobi and obedience meant that it was God's will that he should fulfil this duty and no other. Still, there was little human satisfaction in the long empty days and it is not surprising that depression soon enveloped him again.

It showed itself as usual in an inability to write letters. The sisters in South Africa wrote anxiously to know if he had returned safely and got no reply. He had been back for almost two months when he finally sat down on 29 November and managed to complete a letter to Sister Brigid. He described his return to Kenya and his life in Nairobi in resolutely cheerful terms.

> It has taken me some time to get back and be all absorbed once more in this quiet little corner at my humble but highly appreciated hermitage at Saint Austin's, as chaplain to the C. Sisters. Tomorrow the eight days retreat starts. I'm directing it while doing the exercises on my account as well. I am very happy, and ask for nothing more on this earth except a peaceful end here in Africa, in peace with my Creator and my fellow-men.

He did not tell her that the letter he sent was his fourteenth attempt. Among his papers were found thirteen unfinished letters to her, all written on the same day. Some of them are a page or more in length, some only a few lines. One was abandoned after three words, another when he had got no farther than writing his own address on the top of the page. On each occasion he seems to have been overcome by the contrast between his happiness in South Africa and the bleakness of what he calls 'my quiet life as a quasi-hermit in Saint Austin's'. One of the rejected drafts reads:

> I don't find it easy to make any reference to my own thoughts during those all too short months spent in the

Transvaal, months that have come and gone as dreams come and go. Now that I am back again in my little room here in Saint Austin's I find it difficult to realise that I was absent for four months.

Each morning as I climb Mount Carmel Hill to say Mass at the monastery, I keep my eyes mentally fixed on that small cottage in the Veld beyond the barbed wire fence where I had the happiness of saying Mass each morning in Edenvale, as long ago in Killeshandra and Nigeria.

Here it stops abruptly with the mention of those well-loved names. There is no greater sorrow than to recall past happiness in time of woe.

It would be unfair to put all the blame for this on the shoulders of Bishop Heffernan. He may have thought it was a kindness to give Shanahan only light duties, as he was now obviously a sick man. He had three years of life left to him, but they would be years of sad and steady decline. There would be bouts of malaria and of 'flu', a catch-all name that he used to cover any mental or physical ailment. There would be increasing pain from arthritis, which made such simple activities as walking and dressing more and more difficult. There would be the trouble caused by an enlarged prostate gland, not yet diagnosed. He tried to hide the pain but his grey face told its own story. More than once he said he could understand how men could take their own lives to escape constant pain.

Occasionally, very occasionally, his normal good humour and self-control snapped under the pressure. One evening he came into the parlour in the Carmelite convent and smelt tobacco. When Sister Thérèse told him that two visitors, a priest and a brother, had been smoking there, he became angry. 'There should never be smoking like this in a Carmelite parlour', he said. 'It is most disrespectful and irregular. I am in charge and I will not have these irregularities.' He had no sooner returned to Saint Austin's than he realised that he had over-reacted to the situation and that his position as chaplain gave him no authority over the convent. He immediately wrote a letter of apology to the sister.

I write to tell you how sorry I am for those words I spoke to you this evening. I had no right to speak to you as I did, still less had I any right to refer to the matter I mentioned

> to you. I acted impulsively even though I meant well, but even that cannot be an excuse. So I would ask you to be good enough to forgive and forget.
>
> God permitted the mistake so that I may not again meddle with a Community so dear to God and to our Blessed Mother; a Community to which no reproach can be made even by its best friends — for our friends may err because of their affection for those who are dear to them. Tomorrow I will offer the Holy Sacrifice for your own special intentions.[8]

Needless to say, the nuns forgave him. Their kindness to him was a constant source of comfort in his last years. Many of the priests were equally kind. The younger priests often called to see him in Saint Austin's and they enjoyed his company and his conversation. He was always ready with an encouraging word when they felt despondent at the lack of progress in Kenya as compared with Nigeria. 'We're just not getting anywhere in this mission', they would say. 'It's no use going on.' 'Not at all, not at all,' he would answer, 'you're doing splendidly, everything is tip-top, splendid. Just keep on. God is with you, remember.' It was not so much his words as his faith and great-heartedness that raised their spirits and gave them new strength.

They grumbled to him about the missionary policy of their superiors. They complained that Nigeria was given everything it wanted while Kenya was starved of men and resources, an aspect which he had never considered before. They found fault with Heffernan and his choice of priorities, saying that too much attention was being paid to the Europeans and too little to the large African population. He listened sympathetically but he refused to criticise Heffernan or to compare the Kenyan mission with the Nigerian. 'It's a very different work but equally well done', was his tactful verdict. He never spoke about Nigeria unless pressed to do so. He was not going to become another Father Gaboon.[9]

The older priests, in charge of mission stations, often invited him to stay with them as a change from the regime at Saint Austin's. As he grew weaker, these visits became more prolonged. In October 1941 he spent some time in hospital and then went to Father Flavin's mission in Kalimoni. He did not return to Saint Austin's until the end of January 1942. Two months later, after performing all the Holy Week ceremonies for the Carmelites, he was very tired and went for three weeks to Limuru where he was well looked after by Father Giltenan and the Loreto sisters.

The latter part of 1942 repeated the pattern of the previous year: a spell in hospital followed by another visit to Kalimoni. This time his recovery was slower and in January 1943 he was anointed by Father Flavin. The Sisters of the Precious Blood had a school and dispensary there and under their care he rallied a little and was able to go for short walks in the grounds, though he was too weak to say Mass.

During this period he had his one and only meeting with another great Irish missionary, the Legion of Mary envoy, Edel Quinn. She came to Kalimoni to visit the Legion group which she had founded there some years earlier. Though only thirty-six years of age, she was riddled with tuberculosis and had just twelve months to live. After her Legion meeting, Father Flavin brought her to his house for a meal and they were joined at table by Shanahan. He was so silent that she was afraid she had said something that offended him. At the end of the meal, before he left, he set her fears at rest by apologising for his unsociability. He told her he was so weak that he found it impossible to carry on a conversation.[10]

In May 1943 he began to get discontented with Kalimoni. It is said that the sisters had become worried that he might collapse while walking in the grounds and lie there unattended. They asked some of the schoolboys to keep an unobtrusive eye on him while he was walking. The boys carried out their duties with more zeal than discretion, lurking in the undergrowth and peering from behind trees in the manner of a second-rate spy movie. The constant surveillance began to prey on his nerves. With an invalid's heightened sensitivity, he suddenly decided he wanted to move.

The sisters arranged a change for him to the Holy Family Convent at Mangu, where there was a community of White Sisters who would be happy to look after him. He arrived there on 3 June and was installed in the priests' house, close to the church and convent. The convent chaplain also lived there, an Alsatian priest, Father Lammer, of a rather reclusive nature. He ate his meals alone and rarely saw Shanahan, but he did not interfere with him in any way. The sisters were very attentive to him and he settled down there quickly.

He spent most of his time in the house. He rarely went to the church as he found it difficult to negotiate the steps but he was able to say Mass every morning in his room. One of the sisters had to help him into his vestments, since he found it hard to put his arm into a sleeve. Two of the schoolboys served his Mass, which he said with great devotion. Because of his failing sight he always said the Mass of Our Lady, which he knew by heart. Afterwards he would make his thanksgiving, sitting in a chair. He would go to the priests' dining room for breakfast and other meals as long as he was strong enough; when that became too much for him, his meals were brought to him in his room. During the day, he prayed a great deal, read a little, occasionally walked on the verandah saying his rosary.[11]

The Holy Ghost Fathers had a mission in Mangu and they visited him regularly. Other priest friends dropped in from time to time. Father Flavin drove him in to Nairobi to see the Carmelites, who were shocked to find how much he had failed. He was thin and stooped and during the short time he spent in the convent he was unable to speak, whether from weakness or emotion they could not say.

It was during his time in Mangu that his last surviving letters were written, or rather dictated, since he could no longer write. One of them was addressed to all the sisters, novices and postulants of the Holy Rosary Congregation and dated 19 August 1943.

> I thank you very much for all the nice letters you have sent me. I am deeply grateful for all the prayers you have said and are saying for me. You will be glad to hear that my health has improved and that I am now able to say Mass daily. Each day I pray for you all, asking God to bless you and make you efficient workers in his vineyard.
>
> I am very happy here and the Sisters, who are French, are very kind to me. The Holy Ghost Fathers from the neighbouring missions call often to see me. One of the Mangu Fathers is writing this letter for me but later on when I get stronger I hope to send a few lines personally.

The improvement in his health did not last long. On 15 November he was brought back to Nairobi, this time to the Holy

Family mission beside the cathedral in the centre of the city, as it was more convenient to doctors and hospitals. He was examined by Dr J.R. Gregory, a Protestant from Co Wicklow. Twenty-five years later the doctor described the meeting in a letter to Sister Catherine O'Carroll.

> I remember attending Bishop Shanahan as if it were yesterday.
>
> I remember being called in to the Presbytery at the Cathedral of the Holy Family and there I met the most holy man I have ever seen in my life. He had such a beautiful face and charming expression. His whole personality exuded charm.
>
> He was in great pain from arthritis but the thing that caused his death was an infection of his bladder and kidneys, which could have been prevented if he had undergone an operation for the removal of his prostate many years before.
>
> I imagine it was modesty, which was typical of this saintly man, that prevented him from seeking medical advice in time.
>
> I am sure heaven is enriched by his presence there and I can never hope to meet his like.

Gregory told him quite plainly that he had only a short time to live. To the surprise of his friends, Shanahan took the news badly. Father McCarthy decided to call on him and see if he could reconcile him to the prospect of death. He tried to comfort him by telling him that he would not go to God with empty hands, but Shanahan refused to be consoled, saying that if he could only get back to Ireland something could be done to help him. Finally McCarthy said, 'One of the great things you have done, My Lord, was to found a congregation of sisters, which will go on working for God long after you have died. These sisters must have a deep love and devotion to Our Lady. Ask them to pray for you, for the grace of resignation. And when I leave, you must say three fervent Hail Marys to her for the same grace.' As soon as he had gone, Shanahan said the three Hail Marys and at once all his fear of death vanished. To everyone who came to see him that evening he said, 'I am in perfect peace and happiness now and I owe it all to Father McCarthy.'[12]

He was taken into the Maia Carbery Hospital about 14 December. Father Tom McGennis, parish priest of Holy Family, used to bring Holy Communion to the patients in the hospital. He found Shanahan cheerful but obviously suffering greatly. 'If heaven is only the absence of pain', he said one day, 'it will be heaven.'

His friends came to visit him and saw a man who was already beginning to live in the next world. Two of the Loreto Sisters called and found him praying with his rosary beads in his hands. As they were leaving, they wished him a happy Christmas. He answered, 'I shall be with Him by then.'[13]

Father Giltenan was with him another time when he saw him raise his eyes and look at something a little to the right. His face became transfigured, glowing with beauty and love, and he seemed to be listening attentively to some unheard sound. When he came back to himself he said, 'Did you not see them? Our Holy Mother and her divine Son. They will come for me soon.'[14]

On Christmas morning, Father McGennis was due to say the 7.00 Mass in the cathedral but he managed to visit the hospital before Mass. Shanahan was dozing. The nurse touched him and he woke. 'Would you like Holy Communion, My Lord?' McGennis asked. 'Certainly, certainly, I'd love it, I'd love it', he answered. Then he asked, 'What day is it?' 'Christmas Day, My Lord.' 'Christmas', he murmured. 'Ah, a wonderful day in Onitsha.' He received Communion and they left him at his prayers.[15]

As he lay there in his hospital bed in Nairobi, his thoughts were in far-off Onitsha. All those wonderful Christmases he had spent there, all those midnight and dawn Masses he had celebrated, first in the old mud-walled chapel, then in the church-school of which he had been so proud, lastly and unforgettably in the new cathedral of his dreams. They were at Mass now in Onitsha Cathedral and the building was filled with the colour of their robes and the joy of their singing. Now they were thronging up the aisle on their way to receive Communion, now they were pressing around the crib, the children wide-eyed at the wonder of it all, now they were pouring out through the doors into the early morning sunlight, chattering, laughing, exchanging Christmas greetings with the gaiety and exuberance and vitality that he had known in Iboland and nowhere else on earth. He knew all their faces, though he could no longer see them clearly. He knew all their voices, though they were growing fainter. Their presences faded and another Presence began to take their place.

The matron of the hospital came on duty at about 7.30 and went at once to see the Bishop. She found him lying quietly, apparently asleep. There was a bright light shining on his face. She went to switch off the light over the bed in case it might waken him and found to her surprise that the light was not turned on. She looked at his face again. He was not sleeping but dead.[16]

20

Second burial

At the cathedral, Father McGennis had finished the 7.00 Mass and was unvesting in the sacristy when a boy ran in to say there was an urgent phone call for him. He hurried over to the priests' house and took up the phone. It was the nurse from the hospital. 'Bishop Shanahan has just passed away', she said.

The local regulations required that burial should take place within twenty-four hours after death. Father Wallis was given the task of making arrangements for the funeral. His task was complicated by the fact that it was Christmas Day. Many of the undertakers he approached were either absent or in no condition to do business. Eventually he found a Seychellois who was relatively sober and who tried to palm off a cheap coffin on the priest. 'No,' said Father Wallis, 'he was a Bishop and must have a good coffin.' The coffin was brought to the hospital and the Bishop's remains were taken to Saint Austin's that evening.

The next day, Saint Stephen's Day, the burial took place in the little cemetery attached to the mission. An extension of the time limit was given to allow the ceremony to be held in the evening rather than the morning. Bishop Heffernan read the prayers at the graveside. He also celebrated the Requiem Mass which took place the following morning, the 27th. Because of the Christmas season, many of Shanahan's friends did not hear of his death until the funeral was over. Father Flavin came in that day from Kalimoni to visit him in the hospital and on the way stopped at Saint Peter Claver's mission. He met a priest coming in with a surplice over his arm who told him he had been at Bishop Shanahan's Requiem Mass. Flavin was shattered at the news. 'I wouldn't have had this happen for anything', he said.[1]

Despite war conditions, the news reached Ireland quickly. On 25 January 1944 a solemn Requiem Mass was celebrated in the convent at Killeshandra by Bishop Patrick Lyons of Kilmore. 'When the history of the Irish Church comes to be written,' he said in his homily, 'the name of Dr Joseph Shanahan will shine across many of its pages, and with him will be associated this Congregation which is doing such wonderful work among the Africans.'

The next issue of the Killeshandra magazine, the *African Rosary*, was entirely devoted to his memory. An introductory note described him as 'our beloved Father and Founder, Most Rev. Dr Shanahan, C.S.Sp., one of Ireland's greatest modern missionaries', thereby ending for ever the old controversy about who was the founder of the congregation. Among the contributions was a lengthy tribute from Edward Leen, which ended with the words:

> With his great manly qualities, Dr Shanahan had the lowliness and simplicity of a child, a child of God. Habitually he wore a look of inwardness and self-control. He had a splendid physique and an attractive manner. He had personality. He was a centre of attraction wherever he appeared. He was a great apostle, a great bishop, and a great Irishman. And he looked all that he was.

In 1949 Father John Jordan published his memoir *Bishop Shanahan of Southern Nigeria,* written at the urgent invitation of the Holy Rosary Sisters, especially Sister Brigid Ryan. The book concentrated on the thirty years Shanahan spent in Nigeria, with special emphasis on his period as Prefect Apostolic from 1905 to 1920. The early years were passed over briefly as the material was simply not available. For a different reason, the sadness of the last years was hardly touched on. The events were too recent and there were too many of the people involved still living.

Within these unavoidable limitations, the book gave and still gives an unforgettable portrait of Shanahan. It relies mainly on the conversations which he had with Jordan in 1936, conversations which the young man remembered almost word for word. Even the sharpest memory is fallible and there are occasional factual errors, but there is no mistake in the overall impression it gives of a man of boundless courage and energy, inventive, innovative, charismatic, loving and lovable, deeply human and deeply spiritual. The book brought him to life for those who had never known him. Many young people were led to the missionary priesthood and sisterhood as a result of reading it.

It was in Nigeria that he was most mourned. Apart from his brief visit in December 1935, he had been absent from the country for almost twelve years before his death. But the grief for him among the people was as keen and as widespread as if he had still been living among them. The fact that he had died so far away made their grief all the more intense. It was not right that their Father Onyisi should be buried in a strange land. He always wanted his bones to rest in Nigeria among his own people. How could his spirit find rest as long as his body lay among strangers?

As time went on, a movement began to grow to have his remains returned to Nigeria. The movement was not confined to the Ibos. One of those who supported it was his old friend, Father Joe Delaney, who had soldiered with him for more than twenty years and was still active as a missionary. He said that Shanahan had appeared to him on several occasions and he took it as a sign that he wanted to be buried in Nigeria. Delaney's visions were not taken seriously by the other priests, among them Archbishop Heerey, whose approval was vital for the project. Then a strange incident occurred which changed Heerey's mind.[2]

During the mid-1950s the colonial government was making preparations for the approaching independence of Nigeria. There was strong pressure on the Catholic Church in Southern Nigeria (which had been renamed Eastern Nigeria) to hand over control of their schools to the state. Shanahan's vicariate was now an ecclesiastical province, divided into a number of dioceses and headed by Heerey as Archbishop of Onitsha. Heerey wanted to retain full control of the schools but some of the other bishops felt it would be wiser to yield on the point in the interests of Church-state relations. The debate between the bishops became very acrimonious and Heerey felt the others were conspiring against him. He described what happened next in a letter to Sister Brigid Ryan.

> Well, during that time I was going up to my room after my last visit to Our Lord about 9.30 p.m. I switched on the light at the bottom of the stairs — and there he was, as clear as ever he appeared during his life, standing looking down on me, in white soutane, purple cincture, pectoral cross and all, as he was so well known to us. He had a serene sympathetic look as if to convey to me that he understood the whole situation. I had not been thinking of him at all. His name was mentioned in passing by somebody that day. But when the vision had passed I just began to compare the situation with his experiences. His priests at times caused him bitter sufferings. It was my turn to suffer, not from the

> priests but from the bishops, my suffragans, and there is no doubt that he came to sympathise and assure me. As I said, the visit was too much of a flash, just long enough to make it real — and how sorry I was that it did not last.[3]

The situation resolved itself to Heerey's entire satisfaction. The government withdrew their proposal and the great school network which had been Shanahan's legacy was left untouched. A short time afterwards, Heerey deputed one of his priests, Father Tom Fox, to go to Nairobi and arrange the transfer of Shanahan's remains to Nigeria.

* * *

The exhumation took place at 8.30 a.m. on the morning of 20 December 1955. Father Fox supervised the operation in the presence of a number of Shanahan's priest friends. Among them were Father J. J. McCarthy, who was now Archbishop of Nairobi, and Father Ned Fitzgerald.

The gravediggers carefully removed the earth and uncovered the coffin. It seemed to be intact until they put ropes around it and tried to raise it. The lid and sides fell away and exposed the remains of the dead man, still robed in Mass vestments. The flesh had crumbled to dust and only the bones were left. Father Fitzgerald remembers noticing a fragment of his famous white beard, along with the brass crucifix from his rosary beads. The bones were taken to the city mortuary and placed in a plain teak casket, one foot in height and in width, two-and-a-half feet in length.

The Carmelites were standing by their telephone, waiting anxiously for news. They were convinced that their dear saint's body would have been preserved incorrupt in the grave, thereby proving his sanctity. When Father Fitzgerald rang to tell them that only the skeleton remained, they were greatly disappointed. The casket was brought from the mortuary to their convent and placed in the oratory between two candles, while arrangements for its transfer to Nigeria were completed.

The airlines refused at first to accept the casket. According to their regulations, a corpse had to be either embalmed or cremated before it could be transported by air. The impasse was resolved when the Chief Medical Officer of Nairobi ruled that the remains were equivalent to cremation. As there was no direct flight from

Kenya to Nigeria, Father Fox arranged to fly first to Johannesburg in South Africa and from there to Kano in Northern Nigeria.[4]

There was a two-day delay in Johannesburg, to the great joy of the Holy Rosary Sisters in Edenvale and Vereeniging, who were now forty in number. The plane landed in the afternoon of 9 January 1956 and the casket was taken at once to the convent in Edenvale, where it was greeted by sisters carrying lighted candles and borne in honour to the chapel. Here it remained all that night and the following day, while Masses were said and rosaries recited in thanksgiving for the life of the founder. The final Mass was said in the early hours of 11 January, after which the casket was taken to Jan Smuts airport to resume its journey to Nigeria.[5]

In Kano it was decided to place the remains in a full-sized coffin. None of those who remembered Shanahan — and they were literally millions — would believe that the great Bishop could be contained in such a small wooden box. The casket was placed inside a coffin and some concrete blocks were added to give the necessary weight. Then Father Fox and his precious cargo set off on their last flight, landing in Enugu airport in the heart of Iboland on 12 January.

When Shanahan left Nigeria, Enugu was a small mission station without a resident priest. Now it had become a major centre with 20,000 Catholics, four parishes, two convents, two secondary colleges, a teachers' training college and an inter-diocesan senior seminary. The growth of the Church in Enugu was typical of what had happened throughout the territory in the years since his departure.

It had originally been planned to hold the ceremonies in Onitsha on the weekend of Sunday 15 January. Then they were postponed until the following weekend because of the difficulties in Nairobi. Although these difficulties were now solved and the remains had arrived, it was too late to re-schedule the ceremonies. Someone had the happy thought of using the extra week to bring the Bishop's remains on a round of all the principal missions in the surrounding area.[6]

So began a journey that quickly became a triumphal tour. For the first two or three days, the coffin stayed in the missions around Enugu. On Monday it moved further through the hill country of Eke and Nsukka, on to Udi and Awka, then to Adazi, where it stayed the night while the people kept vigil. The next morning it moved on to Onitsha, where it was greeted by a huge crowd and where once again there was an all-night vigil of prayer. On Wednesday it came to Aguleri, where Father Joe Delaney still lived and worked. One of the most touching moments of the journey came when Father Joe, eighty-five years old, came forward and kissed the coffin which contained the remains of his old Bishop and dear friend. On Thursday it arrived in Ihiala for another vigil and on Friday it toured the new diocese of Owerri, visiting Owerri, Elele, Port Harcourt, Aba, Ahiara and Emekuku. On Saturday morning it was in Orlu and later that day returned to Onitsha for the last time.

Everywhere it went, crowds lined the roads and filled the churches and the spaces around them in such numbers that most of the ceremonies had to be held in the open air. The approach of the cortège was heralded in advance by the cloud of dust that rose in the dry January air. Then came the hearse bearing the coffin followed by a long line of cars, sometimes as many as twenty or thirty at a time, carrying priests, sisters, chiefs, government officials and other dignitaries. Then a noisy and unruly mob of young men on motor-cycles and push-bikes, followed by another mob of young men and boys on foot, running in the wake of the vehicles and caked almost white by their dust. Then the rest of the pedestrians walking more sedately, tribal elders and their wives, women carrying babies, children hanging on to their mothers' skirts, their numbers continually swelling as the spectators on the roadside fell in behind the cortège and joined the procession.

The entry into Onitsha on Saturday evening was a fitting climax to the tour. From the third milestone before the town right down to the cathedral steps, the crowds were continuous. Hundreds of cars and taxis and tens of thousands of people joined the motorcade for these last few miles. On Sunday morning an open-air Mass of thanksgiving was celebrated by the Archbishop and attended by a huge congregation. An even greater crowd took part in a torchlight procession that night. The final Requiem Mass took place on Monday morning, again in the open air, and the coffin was then brought into the cathedral and interred beneath the floor of the east transept, in front of the altar of the Blessed Virgin. Standing around the tomb were two archbishops, three bishops, a hundred and forty priests and a hundred sisters. On the slab covering the tomb was an inscription in Latin from the

Letter to the Hebrews: 'Remember your leaders, those who spoke to you the word of God; consider the outcome of their life and imitate their faith.' It was 23 January 1956.

* * *

The second burial of Bishop Shanahan in Onitsha was interpreted by many as the righting of a historic wrong. It was exactly twenty years since he had left Nigeria for the last time. He had come to his own and his own had not received him. Whatever the rights and wrongs of that rejection, there can be no doubt about the suffering that it caused him. In a life that had more than its share of disappointments and frustrations, it was the blackest moment.

He never lost his desire to return to Nigeria. If he could not return in life, he hoped that he would one day be buried there. This wish was granted in truly princely fashion. His remains were laid in the place that was dearest to him in all the world, the place where he had come ashore as a young priest to be greeted by Father Lejeune, the place where he had made bricks and preached the word and celebrated the sacred mysteries for most of thirty years, the place where he had solemnly blessed and dedicated the first cathedral of the Ibo people. The Ibo people had welcomed him back with joy and the man who was most responsible for his leaving had presided at his homecoming and second burial. Now at last his spirit could find rest.[7]

There was however one other matter still outstanding, one other item of unfinished business that had to be attended to before his second burial could be regarded as complete. This was his relationship with the congregation he had founded, the Holy Rosary Sisters. Here too he experienced suffering and rejection and the love that he gave was sadly misunderstood. Here too there were amends to be made and wounds to be healed among the living as well as the dead.

In the years following his death, the Holy Rosary Congregation had two images of their founder, a public image and a private image. The public image was of a saintly and dynamic bishop, the man who had made Southern Nigeria into one of the great success stories of modern missionary history. In support of this image, many booklets and articles were published, and two collections of his letters were carefully compiled and edited by Sister Brigid Ryan. In none of these was there any hint of the accusations that had so sadly clouded his declining years.

The private image was something that was scarcely known outside the Congregation. It was an image of a great but tragically flawed man, whose later life cast a shadow over his earlier achievements. He was a man with a dark secret, whose exact nature was never spoken of but only hinted at. Younger sisters were very conscious of this darkness without being able to understand it. When they asked about it they were given no clear information. Most of them realised that it was something not to be asked about. His character was surrounded by question marks and where answers were not available imagination filled the gaps.

It was something that Shanahan had in a way foreseen when he wondered what graces would be lost to the sisterhood as a result of their rift with him. They were children who had grown ashamed of their father. They should have had pride in their founder, studied his teachings, imitated his virtues, rejoiced in his achievements, modelled their missionary lives on his. They should have inherited all the graces that God had placed in his hands for his daughters. Instead, they had built deliberate barriers to keep his influence at bay. There was an emptiness at the heart of their community.

During the late 1960s and early 1970s, some of the sisters who had known Shanahan began to bring the whole subject into the open. A number of them wrote down their recollections of him as a priest and as a man and told what they knew of the events that led up to his exclusion from Killeshandra. Among these were Sisters Philomena Fox, Margaret Mary O'Reilly, Rosarii Comer and Catherine O'Carroll. None of these accounts was published, but the manuscripts were typed and duplicated and circulated among the sisters of the Congregation. It was only then that they began to realise how much he had been misunderstood and how greatly he had been hurt.

Shortly after his last return from Nigeria, he visited Sister Madeleine Sophie who was ill in a Dublin hospital. He said to her, 'Everybody has to suffer. I don't know why, but for some unknown reason I seem to be cut off from the sisters. Have I done anything wrong?' She told him of all the accusations that had been made against him. She didn't know whether she was right or wrong to do it, but she held nothing back. It was the first time he had heard the full story. He said, 'How wrongly construed can one's actions become!' Fifty years later she could still remember the way he looked at her, his great eyes filled with sadness.[8]

That hurt remained with him to the end of his life. It has remained with the Holy Rosary Sisters to this day. It is at their request that this book has been written. They asked to have the full story told and nothing held back. It is meant as an act of filial piety, a righting of wrongs, an exorcism of ghosts, an acknowledgement of mistakes, a plea for forgiveness. It is the final act that completes the second burial of Bishop Shanahan.

Notes

Chapter 1: Early years

1. There is some uncertainty about the date of his birth. The Borrisoleigh register gives only the date of baptism, 7 June 1871. Towards the end of his life, Shanahan told the Carmelite nuns in Nairobi that he was born on 4 June and they passed on the information to Sister Catherine O'Carroll (Holy Rosary archives, Dublin). Father John Jordan's biography, *Bishop Shanahan of Southern Nigeria,* gives the date of birth as 6 June, but cites no authority. The story about John Troy comes from M. Kenny, *Glankeen of Borrisoleigh,* Dublin 1944, p. 3.
2. Tom O'Halloran, Borrisoleigh, interview with the author.
3. Paddy Gilmartin, Templederry, letter to the author.
4. There are some problems about the names and number of the Shanahan children. A letter survives from Daniel junior stating that Joseph Shanahan was the fourth of eleven children. This conflicts with the Borrisoleigh and Templederry registers, which make him the third of ten. Also, the Templederry register names the girl born in 1878 as Margaret Catherine. There is obviously a mistake here as it is very unlikely that two girls in the same family would be given the name Margaret; moreover, family sources agree that the names of the three girls were Mary, Bridget and Margaret and that Margaret was the youngest.
5. Paddy Gilmartin, Templederry.
6. Letter to Sister Gonzaga 1963, Holy Rosary archives, Cross Avenue, Dublin.
7. R.W. Frazer, 'A Tipperary Tribute', in *The African Rosary,* April-June 1944.
8. Letter to Sister Brigid Ryan, 27 December 1937, Holy Rosary archives, Dublin.
9. The present large sanctuary lamp was presented to the church by Joe's brother Dick in 1924.
10. Seán Farragher, *Père Leman,* Dublin 1988, p. 87.
11. Most of the information given here about Shanahan's student days comes from two unpublished studies by Seán Farragher, *Shanahan in the Making: France* and *Shanahan in the Making: Rockwell.* They contain the fruits of extensive research in Holy Ghost archives in France and Ireland and were kindly made available to the author by Father Farragher.
12. Farragher, *Shanahan in the Making: France,* pp. 1-2.
13. Ibid., p. 2.
14. *The African Rosary,* April-June 1944, p. 18.

15. Farragher, *Shanahan in the Making: France,* p. 5.
16. Shanahan Papers, Holy Ghost Archives, Chevilly, Paris. This and the following letters from Shanahan's time in France were translated into English by Father Seán Farragher.
17. Farragher, *Shanahan in the Making: France,* pp. 8-10.
18. Shanahan Papers, Holy Ghost archives, Chevilly, Paris.

Chapter 2: Student and priest

1. Seán Farragher, *Shanahan in the Making: France,* pp. 14-16.
2. *Bulletin de la Congrégation,* XVIII, pp. 7-41.
3. Shanahan Papers, Holy Ghost archives, Chevilly, Paris.
4. Holy Rosary archives, Cross Avenue, Dublin.
5. Shanahan papers, Holy Ghost archives, Chevilly, Paris.
6. Farragher, *Shanahan in the Making: France,* pp. 31-32.
7. Holy Rosary archives, Cross Avenue, Dublin. Translations by the author.
8. This is incorrect. His sermon took place on 5 June, his baptism on 7 June. His long absence from home had left him vague about his early years. In a letter of 1894 he gives his birthplace as Gortnalaura, which is also incorrect.
9. John F. Hickey, *Shanahan's Country,* lecture to the Ormond Historical Society, Nenagh, 1979.
10. Farragher, *Shanahan in the Making: Rockwell,* pp. 2-5.
11. Quoted in *A Centenary Tribute to the Founder of the Holy Rosary Sisters,* p. 17.
12. Quoted in John Jordan, *Bishop Shanahan of Southern Nigeria,* p. 5.
13. Farragher, *Shanahan in the Making: Rockwell,* pp. 15-17.
14. Shanahan papers, Holy Ghost archives, Chevilly, Paris.
15. Farragher, *Shanahan in the Making: Rockwell,* pp. 18-19.
16. Quoted in Jordan, *Bishop Shanahan of Southern Nigeria,* p. 5.
17. Edward Leen, 'A Great Irish Missionary', in *Bishop Shanahan and his Missionary Family,* Killeshandra, 1967.
18. Farragher, *Shanahan in the Making: Rockwell,* pp. 27-28.

Chapter 3: Father Gaboon

1. Celestine A. Obi (ed.), *A Hundred Years of the Catholic Church in Eastern Nigeria 1885-1985,* Onitsha, 1985, chapters 1 and 2.
2. Shanahan, 'Those Early Days', in *Holy Ghost Missionary Annals,* July-August 1936. It is reprinted as chapter 3 in Jordan, *Bishop Shanahan of Southern Nigeria,* 2nd edition, Dublin 1971.
3. *Bulletin de la Congrégation,* XXIII, p. 494.
4. Shanahan, op. cit.
5. Ibid.

6. John Jordan, *Bishop Shanahan of Southern Nigeria,* pp. 95-96.
7. Traditional Ibo beliefs are described in chapter 1 of *The Advent of the Catholic Church in Nigeria,* by Rose Adaure Njoku, Owerri, 1980.
8. Shanahan, op. cit.
9. Obi, op.cit., pp. 93-94.
10. Healy papers, Holy Rosary archives, Cross Avenue, Dublin.
11. *Bulletin de la Congrégation,* XXII, p. 786.
12. Jordan, *Bishop Shanahan of Southern Nigeria,* pp. 25-27.
13. *Bulletin de la Congrégation,* XXII, p. 789.
14. Shanahan, op. cit.
15. *Bulletin de la Congrégation,* XXII, pp. 547,798.
16. Shanahan to Le Roy, September 1907, Holy Ghost archives, Chevilly, Paris.
17. Shanahan, *Those Early Days.*
18. Shanahan to Le Roy, ibid.
19. Sister Edith Dynan, *Bishop Shanahan as Remembered by Men and Women in Nigeria,* unpublished MS in Holy Rosary archives, Dublin, pp. 51-53.
20. *Bulletin de la Congrégation,* XXIII, p. 501.
21. Obi, op. cit., pp. 116-117.
22. Healy papers, Holy Rosary archives, Cross Avenue, Dublin.

Chapter 4: Schools, schools

1. Holy Ghost archives, Chevilly, Paris, Translated by Seán Farragher.
2. John Jordan, *Bishop Shanahan of Southern Nigeria,* p. 32.
3. Ibid., p. 32.
4. Ibid., p. 40.
5. Letter from Shanahan to Le Roy, 17 May 1906, Holy Ghost archives, Chevilly, Paris.
6. Seán Farragher CSSp, 'Bishop Shanahan at Blackrock' in *Blackrock Annual 1971,* p. 87.
7. The originals are lost but copies are kept in the Holy Rosary Archives, Dublin. It was actually twenty years, not twenty-one, since his arrival in Beauvais.
8. The report on the General Chapter was published as *Circulaire no. 11,* Paris, 1906.
9. Farragher, op. cit., p. 88.
10. *Bulletin de la Congrégation,* XXIV, p. 10.
11. Ibid., pp. 157-158.
12. Ibid., p. 147. The report is not signed but this section was almost certainly written by Shanahan.
13. Ibid., p. 145.
14. *Bulletin de la Congrégation,* XXV, p. 357.

Chapter 5: The Great Trek

1. John Jordan, *Bishop Shanahan of Southern Nigeria,* p. 41.
2. The account of the Great Trek given in the text is based on Jordan, op. cit., pp. 45-71, supplemented by interviews given by Father Jordan to the author.
3. The story is found on p. 35 of *Bishop Shanahan as remembered by men and women in Nigeria 1985-1987,* by Sister Edith Dynan, an unpublished collection of interviews.
4. Jordan, op. cit., p. 122.
5. Ibid. p. 197.

Chapter 6: Gods and demons

1. *Bulletin de la Congrégation,* XXV, p. 358.
2. Ibid., pp. 371-373; John Jordan, *Bishop Shanahan of Southern Nigeria,* pp. 43-44.
3. *Bulletin de la Congrégation,* XXV, pp. 386-387.
4. Jordan, op. cit., p. 154.
5. *Bulletin de la Congrégation,* XXV, p. 370.
6. Jordan, op. cit., pp. 146-149, p. 64.
7. Shanahan papers, Holy Ghost archives, Temple Park, Dublin.
8. Jordan, op. cit., pp. 78-79.
9. Healy papers, Holy Rosary archives, Cross Avenue, Dublin.
10. Jordan, op. cit., pp. 97-98.
11. Healy papers.
12. Sister Edith Dynan, *Bishop Shanahan as remembered by men and women in Nigeria 1985-1987,* pp. 76-77.
13. Ibid., pp. 67-69.
14. *Bulletin de la Congrégation,* XXVI, p. 862.
15. Jordan, op. cit., pp. 80-86.
16. *Bulletin de la Congrégation,* XXVI, pp. 878-888.
17. Jordan, op. cit., p. 108.
18. *Bulletin de la Congrégation,* XXVII, pp. 573, 657.
19. Jordan, op. cit., pp. 108-112.
20. Seán Farragher, 'Bishop Shanahan at Blackrock', in *Blackrock Annual 1971,* p. 88.
21. Colman Cooke, *Mary Charles Walker,* Dublin, 1980, chapter 3.
22. The information in this section is drawn mainly from letters from Louis Patrick and Daniel Shanahan in the Holy Rosary archives and from the Templederry registers.

Chapter 7: The thousand-mile walk

1. Healy papers, Holy Rosary archives, Dublin.
2. John Jordan, *Bishop Shanahan of Southern Nigeria,* p. 113.
3. Ibid., p. 156.
4. Healy Papers.

5. V. A. Nwosu (ed.), *The Catholic Church in Onitsha,* Onitsha 1985, p. 101.
6. *Bulletin de la Congrégation,* XXIX, p. 187.
7. Ibid., pp. 181-182.
8. Shanahan papers, Holy Ghost archives, Temple Park, Dublin.
9. Shanahan papers, ibid.
10. *Bulletin de la Congrégation,* XXIX, pp. 188-199, XXX p. 792; Jordan, op. cit., pp. 133-134.
11. Ibid., XXVIII, p. 304.
12. Healy papers.
13. The account of Shanahan's trek through Adamawa is based on three sources: 1. Shanahan's report to Rome on Adamawa, printed in the *Holy Ghost Missionary Annals,* Dublin, August 1920, pp. 7-10; 2. Jordan, op. cit., pp. 159-173; 3. Material collected by Father Bob O'Neil in Cameroun and printed in Dynan, *Bishop Shanahan as remembered by men and women in Nigeria 1985-1987.*
14. Story told to the author by Father Jordan. In his biography, Jordan tells the same story but omits the giving of the absolution, presumably out of deference to the theological sensitivities of the time of writing (1949).
15. Colman Cooke, *Mary Charles Walker,* pp. 38-41.
16. Journal kept by the scholastics in Saint Mary's, Rathmines, 20 November 1919.

Chapter 8: Bishop Shanahan

1. Colman Cooke, *Mary Charles Walker,* p. 30.
2. Michael O'Carroll, *Edward Leen, CSSp,* Dublin 1952, p. 34.
3. *Bishop Shanahan and his Missionary Family,* p. 26.
4. John Jordan, *Bishop Shanahan of Southern Nigeria,* p. 174.
5. Jordan, op. cit., pp. 179-180.
6. Pamphlet, *The Society of Saint Patrick for Foreign Missions,* Kiltegan, 1930.
7. Jordan, op. cit., pp. 175-176.
8. A biography of Marie Martin, entitled *To Africa with Love,* by Mary Purcell, was published in Dublin in 1987.
9. The correspondence between Shanahan and Marie Martin is in the Medical Missionaries of Mary archives, Drogheda.
10. Saint Patrick's Missionary Society archives, Kiltegan, Co. Wicklow.
11. *Bulletin de la Congrégation,* XXIX, p. 654.
12. Holy Rosary archives, Cross Avenue, Dublin.
13. *Bulletin de la Congrégation,* XXIX, p. 763.
14. Interview with Father Edward Fitzgerald, CSSp.
15. Seán Farragher, 'Bishop Shanahan at Blackrock', in *Blackrock Annual 1971,* p. 90.

Chapter 9: The ladies from Ireland

1. Michael O'Carroll, *Edward Leen, CSSp,* pp. 43-44.
2. Ibid., pp. 46-48.
3. *Bulletin de la Congrégation,* XXX, p. 508.
4. Ibid., XXIX, pp. 792-793.
5. Typescript in Holy Rosary archives, Dublin.
6. *Holy Ghost Missionary Annals,* August 1922.
7. Edward Leen, 'Christianity in Pagan Nigeria', *Irish Ecclesiastical Record,* January 1922, p. 21.
8. Edward Leen, 'Catechetical Instruction in Southern Nigeria', *Irish Ecclesiastical Record,* March 1922, pp. 123-137.
9. Colman Cooke, *Mary Charles Walker,* pp. 46-58. Shanahan's correspondence with the Franciscan Missionaries of Mary is preserved in their archives in Rome.
10. This section is based on letters in the Medical Missionaries of Mary archives, Drogheda, and on Mary Purcell, *To Africa with Love,* chapter 4.
11. O'Carroll, op. cit., p. 90.
12. Catherine Meagher's reminiscences are in the Holy Rosary archives, Dublin.
13. O'Carroll, op. cit., pp. 56-57. *La Grâce et la Gloire* (Grace and Glory) is the title of a well-known book on grace in the soul by the French Jesuit Jean-Baptiste Terrien, first published in 1897.

Chapter 10: The house on the hill

1. Letters from Shanahan to Mary Martin, Medical Missionaries of Mary archives, Drogheda.
2. Sister Catherine O'Carroll, *Some Personal Memories of Bishop Shanahan,* Holy Rosary archives, Dublin.
3. MMM archives.
4. MMM archives.
5. Colman Cooke, *Sister Charles Walker,* pp. 62-66.
6. *Holy Ghost Missionary Annals,* December 1922.
7. Holy Ghost archives, Dublin.
8. MMM archives.
9. *Bulletin de la Congrégation,* XXXI, p. 225.
10. Letter of 15 March 1936, Holy Rosary archives, Dublin.
11. MMM archives.
12. Cooke, op. cit., pp. 74, 86.
13. Holy Rosary archives, Dublin.
14. Reminiscences of Sister M. Vianney, Holy Rosary archives, Dublin.
15. Reminiscences of Joe Ryan, Holy Rosary archives, Dublin.
16. Sister M. Vianney, ibid.; Michael O'Carroll, *Edward Leen,* chapter 5.
17. Letter from Ronayne to Mary Martin, 3 October 1957, MMM archives.

18. Dominican Convent, Cabra, archives.

Chapter 11: Personality problems

1. Holy Rosary archives, Dublin.
2. Ibid.
3. Irish Sisters of Charity archives, Milltown, Dublin.
4. Colman Cooke, *Mary Charles Walker,* chapters 6 and 7.
5. Peter Idigo, *Our Memoirs of Father Michael Cyprian Tansi,* Onitsha 1977, pp. 40-41.
6. Celestine A. Obi, *A Hundred Years of the Catholic Church in Eastern Nigeria,* chapter 7.
7. Holy Rosary archives, Dublin.
8. Apart from the letter mentioned earlier, all Shanahan's letters to Leen are in the Holy Ghost archives, Dublin.
9. These letters of Ronayne and Leen are in the Medical Missionaries of Mary archives, Drogheda.
10. Saint Patrick's Missionary Society, Kiltegan, archives.
11. Copy in Holy Rosary archives, Dublin.
12. *Bulletin de la Congrégation,* XXXII, p. 233.
13. Holy Ghost archives, Dublin. Translation by the author.
14. MS by Mother Xavier in Kiltegan archives.
15. MMM archives, Drogheda.

Chapter 12: Choosing a successor

1. Sister Philomena Fox wrote an unpublished account of Shanahan and the Holy Rosary Sisters entitled *Lord, that I may see,* and supplemented it by an interview with the present author.
2. Seán Farragher, *Bishop Shanahan at Blackrock,* p. 92.
3. Holy Rosary archives, Dublin.
4. Holy Ghost archives, Dublin.
5. Father Roche, quoted in P.M. Idogo, *Archbishop Heerey,* Enugu, 1987, p. 66.
6. Shanahan's letters to Mother Xavier are in the Holy Rosary archives, Dublin. They are the principal source for the information in this chapter.
7. Letter to Mary Martin, Easter 1923, MMM Archives.
8. Sister Augustine, *Bishop Shanahan as I knew him,* Holy Rosary archives, Dublin.
9. Sister Philomena, op. cit.
10. Letters to Mary Martin, MMM archives, Drogheda.
11. *Bulletin de la Congrégation,* XXXIII, p. 198.
12. Holy Rosary archives, Dublin.
13. Holy Rosary archives, Dublin.
14. Holy Ghost archives, Dublin.

Chapter 13: The hardest year

1. Letter to Mother Xavier, Holy Rosary archives, Dublin. Shanahan's letters to her are the main source for the information in this section.
2. Sister Philomena Fox, *Lord, that I may see,* Holy Rosary archives, Dublin.
3. Holy Ghost archives, Dublin.
4. Sisters of Charity archives, Dublin.
5. *A Shoot that the Lord has planted,* ed. Sister Brigid Ryan, p. 81.
6. Holy Ghost archives, Dublin.
7. Letter of 24 May 1928, Holy Ghost archives, Dublin. This very long and detailed letter is the principal source for this section.
8. Copy in Holy Ghost Archives, Dublin. Translated from the Latin by the author.
9. Fox, op. cit.; Notes of conversation with Sister Joseph Byrnes, Holy Rosary archives, Dublin.
10. Sister Catherine O'Carroll, *Some Personal Memories of Bishop Shanahan,* MS in Holy Rosary archives, Dublin.
11. Fox, op. cit.
12. O'Carroll, op. cit.
13. Colman Cooke, *Mary Charles Walker,* chapter 7.
14. *Bulletin de la Congrégation,* XXIV, p. 837.
15. Fox, op. cit.; Sister Rosarii Comer, *Memories and Letters.*
16. Information provided in interviews with the author by Sisters Magdalen Brady, Edith Dynan and Madeleine Sophie Cullen.

Chapter 14: Looking to the future

1. Michael O'Carroll, *Edward Leen,* p. 207.
2. Sources for this section are the reminiscences of Sisters Margaret Mary, Catherine O'Carroll, Philomena Fox and Rosarii Comer, all in the Holy Rosary archives, Dublin.
3. Colman Cooke, *Mary Charles Walker,* chapter 7.
4. *Bulletin de la Congrégation,* XXXIV, p. 855.
5. Bishop Moynagh's memoirs, Saint Patrick's Missionary Society archives, Kiltegan.
6. Sister Philomena Fox, *Lord, that I may see,* Holy Rosary archives, Dublin.
7. Sister Rosarii Comer, *Memories and Letters,* Holy Rosary archives, Dublin.
8. Ibid.
9. Cooke, *Charles Mary Walker,* chapter 7.
10. *Bulletin de la Congrégation,* XXXIV, pp. 664-666.
11. Holy Rosary archives, Dublin.
12. *Bulletin de la Congrégation,* XXXIV, p. 883; Bishop T. McGettrick, *Memoirs,* Enugu, 1988, p. 82.
13. Holy Ghost archives, Dublin.

14. Cooke, op. cit., chapter 8.
15. Peter Idigo, *Our Memoirs of Father Cyprian Tansi,* pp. 40-41; Nwosu (ed.), *The Catholic Church in Onitsha,* pp. 144-145.
16. *Holy Ghost Missionary Annals,* April 1931, pp. 76-78.
17. Told by Bishop Anyogu to Sister Christopher, and recorded by Sister Catherine O'Carroll in her Kenya interviews.

Chapter 15: Magnificat

1. This section is based on Sister Philomena Fox, *Lord, that I may see,* Holy Rosary archives, Dublin, and on an interview given by Sister Philomena to the author.
2. Sister Rosarii Comer, *Memories and Letters,* Holy Rosary archives, Dublin.
3. Fox, op. cit.
4. Holy Rosary archives, Dublin.
5. Nwosu (ed.) *The Catholic Church in Onitsha,* chapter 4.
6. Colman Cooke, *Mary Charles Walker,* chapters 8, 9, 10 and appendix.
7. *Holy Ghost Missionary Annals,* July-August 1936.
8. Notes of talk by Bishop Hagan in Holy Rosary archives, Dublin.
9. Sister Catherine O'Carroll, *Some Personal Memories,* Holy Rosary archives, Dublin.

Chapter 16: Retirement

1. Sister Rosarii Comer, *Memories and Letters,* Holy Rosary archives, Dublin.
2. Holy Rosary archives, Dublin.
3. Sister Brigid Ryan, *A Shoot that the Lord has planted,* Holy Rosary archives, Dublin.
4. Holy Rosary archives, Dublin.
5. John Jordan, *Some Unrecorded Memories of Bishop Shanahan,* Holy Rosary archives, Dublin.
6. Holy Rosary archives, Dublin.
7. Sister Margaret Mary, *Our Relations with Doctor Shanahan,* Holy Rosary archives, Dublin.
8. Ibid.
9. Sister Philomena Fox, *Lord, that I may see,* Holy Rosary archives, Dublin.
10. Sister Catherine O'Carroll, *Personal Memories of Bishop Shanahan,* Holy Rosary archives, Dublin.
11. Sister Augustine Cahill, *Bishop Shanahan as I knew him,* Holy Rosary archives, Dublin.
12. Ryan, op. cit.
13. Letter of 22 November 1933, Holy Rosary archives, Dublin.

14. Jordan, *Some Unrecorded Memories of Bishop Shanahan,* and *Some Reminiscences of Bishop Shanahan,* both in Holy Rosary archives, Dublin.
15. Letter and notebook in the Holy Rosary archives, Dublin.

Chapter 17: Christmas in Onitsha

1. Mary Purcell, *To Africa with Love,* pp. 65-68.
2. F. Fullen, *Recollections of Bishop Shanahan,* Holy Rosary archives, Dublin.
3. Sister Rosarii Comer, *Memories and Letters,* Holy Rosary archives, Dublin.
4. Sister Augustine Cahill, *Bishop Shanahan as I knew him,* Holy Rosary archives, Dublin, and interview with the present author.
5. Comer, op. cit.
6. Sister Catherine O'Carroll, *Personal Memories,* Holy Rosary archives, Dublin.
7. Ibid.
8. Comer, op. cit.
9. O'Carroll, op. cit.
10. Interview with Sister Augustine.
11. John Jordan, *Unrecorded Memories,* Holy Rosary archives, Dublin.
12. Sister Philomena Fox, *Lord, that I may see,* Holy Rosary archives, Dublin.
13. Comer, op. cit.
14. Sister Philomena Fox, interview with the author.
15. Letters quoted in this chapter are all from the Holy Rosary archives, Dublin.

Chapter 18: Banishment

Except where otherwise stated, material for this chapter is drawn from Shanahan's letters in the Holy Rosary archives, Dublin, mainly to Mother Augustine.

1. This section is based on Father Jordan's MS, *Some unrecorded Memories of Bishop Shanahan* and *Some Reminiscences of Bishop Shanahan,* both in the Holy Rosary archives, Dublin, and interviews given by Father Jordan to the author.
2. Medical Missionaries of Mary archives, Drogheda.
3. Sister Rosarii Comer, *Memories and Letters,* Holy Rosary archives, Dublin.
4. Sister Madeleine Sophie Cullen, interview with the author.
5. Sister Philomena Fox, *Lord that I may see,* Holy Rosary archives, Dublin.
6. Comer, op. cit.

Chapter 19: The last safari

1. Letter to M. Augustine. All sources quoted in this chapter are from the Holy Rosary archives, Dublin, unless otherwise stated.
2. Monsignor J. Maunet, *Séjour de Mgr Shanahan à Maurice.*
3. Martin Reidy, CSSp, interviewed by Sister Catherine O'Carroll. Sister Catherine visited Kenya in 1969 and spoke with many of those who knew Shanahan there. Her transcriptions are preserved in the Holy Rosary archives, Dublin, and are the basis for most of this chapter. They are referred to in these notes by the abbreviation C.O'C.
4. Carmelites, Nairobi (C.O'C.). Cf. Exodus 34:29-35.
5. Father M. C. O'Connor, CSSp (C.O'C.).
6. Archbishop J. J. McCarthy, CSSp (C.O'C.).
7. The account of Shanahan's visit to South Africa is drawn from Sister Philomena Fox, *Lord, that I may see.*
8. Carmelites, Nairobi (C.O'C.).
9. Father M. Reidy (C.O'C.).
10. Carmelites, Nairobi (C.O'C.).
11. White Sisters, Mangu (C.O'C.).
12. Archbishop McCarthy (C.O'C.).
13. Mother Consiglio (C.O'C.).
14. Sister Philomena Fox, *Lord, that I may see.*
15. Tom McGennis, CSSp (C.O'C.).
16. Sister Rosarii Comer, *Memories and Letters.*

Chapter 20: Second burial

1. Interviews with Fathers McGennis, Wallis and Flavin (C.O'C).
2. John Jordan, *Unrecorded Memories,* Holy Rosary archives, Dublin.
3. Copy in Holy Rosary archives, Dublin.
4. Father T. Fox, MS in Holy Rosary archives, Dublin; Father Ned Fitzgerald, interview with the author.
5. Edenvale MS in Holy Rosary archives, Dublin.
6. The return of Shanahan's remains to Nigeria is described in a special edition of *Catholic Life,* Onitsha, March 1956.
7. Traditional Ibo beliefs about second burial are described in Jordan, *Bishop Shanahan of Southern Nigeria,* pp. 123-130.
8. Sister M.S. Cullen, interview with the author.

Index